Introduction to Management Accounting

Introduction to Management Accounting

Chloe Hill

STATES ACADEMIC PRESS
www.statesacademicpress.com

Introduction to Management Accounting
Chloe Hill
ISBN: 978-1-63989-306-5 (Hardback)

STATES
ACADEMIC PRESS

Published by States Academic Press,
109 South 5th Street,
Brooklyn, NY 11249, USA

Cataloging-in-Publication Data

Introduction to management accounting / Chloe Hill.
p. cm.
Includes bibliographical references and index.
ISBN 978-1-63989-306-5
1. Managerial accounting. 2. Accounting. I. Hill, Chloe.
HF5657.4 .I58 2022
658.151 1--dc23

Table of Contents

Preface

The process of identifying, analyzing and communicating information to managers which would help in achieving business goals is termed as management accounting. Also known as cost accounting, it encompasses information regarding all financial and non-financial decisions. The discipline of management accounting can be broadly classified into strategic management, risk management and performance management. Strategic management studies the role of management accountants in organizations. Risk management focuses on decision making techniques and management of performance within organizations. Risk management contributes to frameworks and practices which are used for the identification and management of risks. Some prominent methodologies studied under this discipline are activity based costing, lean accounting, throughput accounting, resource consumption accounting and transfer pricing methods. The book studies, analyzes and upholds the pillars of management accounting and its utmost significance in modern times. While understanding the long-term perspectives of the topics, it makes an effort in highlighting their impact as a modern tool for the growth of the discipline. This book is a complete source of knowledge on the present status of this important field.

A short introduction to every chapter is written below to provide an overview of the content of the book:

Chapter 1 - The process of preparing reports regarding business operations which assist the managers in making long-term and short-term decisions is referred to as management accounting. It can comprise of financial and non-financial information. This chapter provides a brief introduction to the different concepts related to management accounting such as responsibility accounting and transfer pricing; **Chapter 2** - The financial plan for a certain period of time is called budgeting. Some of the different types of budgets are operating budget, financial budget, master budget, and fixed and flexible budget. The topics elaborated in this chapter will help in gaining a better perspective about budgeting and these types of budgets; **Chapter 3** - The practice which is associated with the estimation of a production process is termed as standard costing. It involves variance analysis which compares actual and budgeted costs of raw materials and labor during production. This chapter discusses in detail the different types of variance which are studied in relation to standard costing; **Chapter 4** - The change in cost which occurs when the quantity produced of a particular product increases, is known as marginal cost. Some of the major concepts which are studied under marginal costing are break even analysis and decision regarding sales mix. The diverse aspects of marginal costing have been thoroughly discussed in this chapter; **Chapter 5** - The process which is involved in the analysis of the financial statements of a company for the purpose of decision making is known as statement analysis. It comprises ratio analysis, horizontal and vertical analysis, and cash flow analysis. This chapter has been carefully written to provide an easy understanding of these facets of statement analysis.

Finally, I would like to thank my fellow scholars who gave constructive feedback and my family members who supported me at every step.

Chloe Hill

1

Management Accounting: An Introduction

The process of preparing reports regarding business operations which assist the managers in making long-term and short-term decisions is referred to as management accounting. It can comprise of financial and non-financial information. This chapter provides a brief introduction to the different concepts related to management accounting such as responsibility accounting and transfer pricing.

Managerial accounting may be regarded as a body of knowledge that is concerned with concepts and decision-making tools that enable management to make better decisions and to evaluate results. As a body of technical knowledge, management accounting primarily consists of certain decisionmaking techniques or tools drawn from financial and management theory and practice. A basic premise is that the primary task of management is to make decisions and that this task is greatly improved by the knowledge and skills of the management accountant. A corollary premise is that the management accountant's ability to serve management is greatly enhanced by knowledge of management and, in particular, a sound knowledge of the fundamentals of marketing, production, and finance.

The accountant in the role of advisor to management must understand basic management concepts, particularly those concepts embedded in the function of decisionmaking. Only if the accountant has a proper understanding of management's needs will he or she be able to furnish the data and special analyzes that will enable management to make consistently good decisions. Management must understand accounting and the type of information that the accountant can provide. Without an understanding of some accounting, the manager or decision-maker may fail to request information or seek help at a critical time.

What is accounting? A very old but frequently used definition states: "Accounting is the art of recording, classifying, and summarizing in a significant manner and in terms of money, transactions, and events, which are, in part at least of a financial character, and interpreting the results thereof." A more recent definition states: "Accounting is a service activity. Its function is to provide quantitative information, primarily financial in nature, about economic entities that is intended to be useful in making economic decisions in making reasoned choices among alternative courses of action." This latter definition is more appropriate to managerial accounting because of its emphasis on decision-making.

Management accounting may be simply defined as a body of accounting knowledge primarily consisting of concepts and techniques (tools) useful to management in making better decisions and evaluating performance. Most managerial accounting theorists and writers agree that the following concepts and tools represent the foundation of management accounting:

Decision-making Tools	Concepts
Cost–volume–profit analysis.	Fixed and variable costs.
Comprehensive budgeting.	Escapable and inescapable costs.
Flexible budgeting.	Relevant costs.
Incremental analysis.	Incremental costs.
Return on investment.	Sunk costs.
Direct costing.	Opportunity costs.
Capital budgeting.	Common costs.
Inventory models.	Direct and indirect cost.
Cost analysis for marketing, production, and finance.	Contribution margin.
Segmental income statements.	Planning.
Financial statement ratio analysis.	Control.
	Standards.
	Organization.

It is apparent that the subject matter of management accounting has little to do with transactions analysis and the preparation of statements from historical data. However, management accounting is not independent of financial accounting. Financial accounting is a foundation requirement for management accounting and a study of financial accounting must precede the study of management accounting. The basic carryover from the study of financial accounting is a solid understanding of financial statements. An understanding of how to analyze and record the effects of individual transactions of assets, liabilities, capital, and revenue is helpful but not essential.

Management: The Focal Point of Management Accounting

The term management accounting obviously consists of two words each of which represents highly developed areas of study. The term management accounting suggests an important relationship between management and accounting. Furthermore, there is implied an area of common interests. Management accounting is not merely the application of accounting to management; rather it is a study of analytical techniques that result from the combining of accounting fundamentals with the fundamental concepts of management.

The student that is planning a professional career in accounting must develop an appreciation and understanding of management. It is management that guides the business and makes the decisions which determine the success or failure of a business. The accountant serves in a staff or advisory function under management. On the other hand, those students planning a professional career as managers need to understand and appreciate that knowledge of accounting is critically important. Although accountants use technical accounting expertise to prepare financial statements, it is management that receives and uses financial statements. Management, not accountants, has the need and responsibility to read and understand financial statements. Financial statements, in one sense, are summary reports of how well management has performed (made decisions) for a given period of time. For management to have a negative attitude towards accounting is tantamount to being negative towards their own responsibilities and accomplishments.

Accounting as an Organizational Function

Management accounting techniques are useful in all types of businesses. Managers of service, merchandising, manufacturing, banks, insurance companies, etc. all can benefit from the use of management accounting. Management accounting is frequently associated with fairly large corporate businesses; however, it is equally useful to small businesses.

When a business reaches a certain size, then the accounting activity is of such a volume that the accounting activity must be organized and managed. Consequently, accounting in larger businesses can be thought of as a departmentalized function appearing on the organization chart as a staff function. While the term management accounting implies to individuals possessing specialized knowledge of management and accounting, the term can also be applied to the accounting department as a whole. A simple model of the accounting function is shown in figure. The management techniques would primarily be used in the budgeting and revenue and cost analysis section of the accounting department.

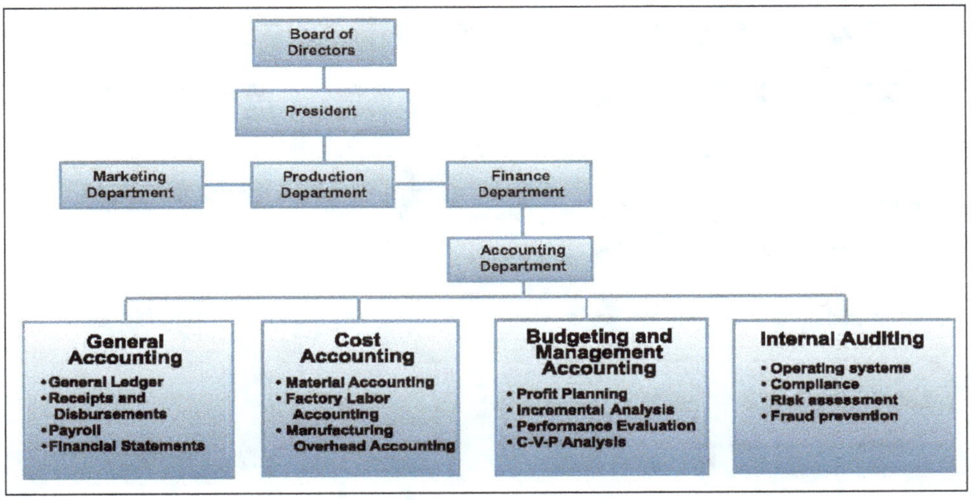

Diagram of the Accounting Function.

From a departmental viewpoint, all accounting activities are management in nature. The accounting department exists to serve the financial data needs of management. The controller or head of the accounting department in many companies is considered to be a part of the decisionmaking team. Therefore, from an organizational viewpoint, the distinction between financial accounting and managerial accounting is somewhat artificial. The controller, the chief executive officer of the accounting department, is always serving as an management accountant, regardless of what type of accounting is being done. However, the majority of accounting activities he or she supervises would from an academic viewpoint be classified as financial accounting as opposed to management accounting.

Relationship of Financial and Managerial Accounting

The study of accounting is normally divided into two broad categories: financial and managerial. This division is somewhat arbitrary in that the study of managerial accounting requires a strong foundation in financial accounting. However, there is a definite difference in orientation and methodology which needs to be understood. Accounting exists in a network of complex business relationships both internal and external. In management accounting, the focal point is the role of management within the organizational structure. Both the financial accountant and the managerial accountant need knowledge of external factors and relationships as well as a conceptual knowledge of accounting principles and procedures. Accounting as a function within a business organization is service oriented. Accounting serves the financial information needs of many different types of groups including investors, governments, customers, employees, unions, and bankers. Most importantly, it serves the internal information needs of management. Figure illustrates the environment in which management and the management accountant operate.

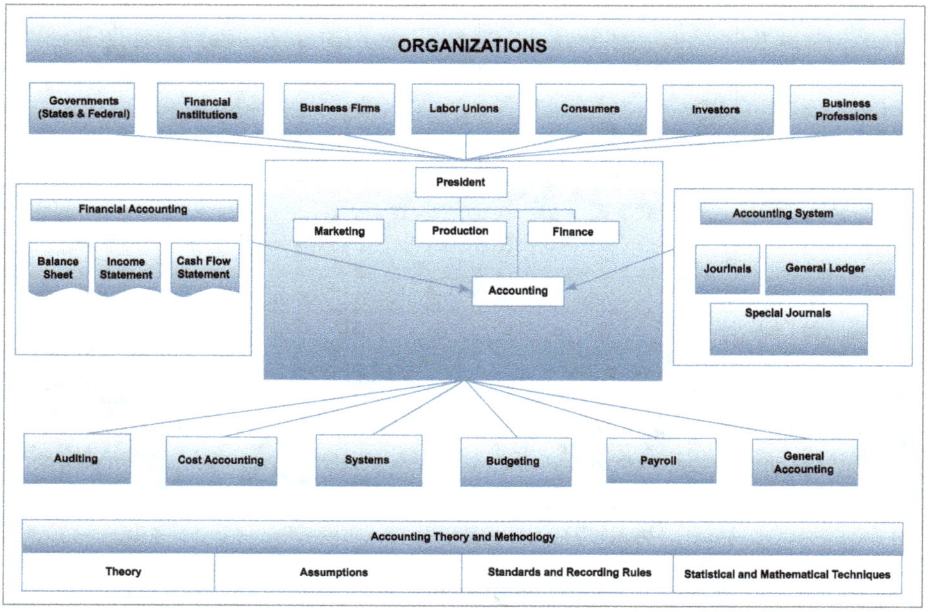

Accounting Environment.

In a broad sense, financial accounting, as a branch of accounting in general, serves all types of users. Management accounting, on the other hand, is intended to serve primarily management's internal information needs; therefore, managerial accounting is not governed by strictly defined and publicly promulgated principles and standards.

Financial accounting is concerned with the reporting of operations to external parties; whereas, management accounting is internal in direction and is primarily concerned with serving the decisionmaking needs of management.

Management accounting as a body of technical knowledge is, in fact, a synthesis of various disciplines. Many of the techniques such as capital budgeting models and EOQ models have been borrowed from other disciplines. The conceptual framework of management accounting, then, has building blocks in its foundation from:

- Management theory (planning, control, organization).
- Financial accounting (financial statements).
- Finance theory (capital budgeting, working capital).
- Economic theory (pricing, forecasting, supply, demand, cost behavior).
- Marketing theory (order getting, order processing, order delivery).
- Mathematics (algebra, calculus).

Therefore, an understanding of management accounting is greatly enhanced, if preceded by knowledge of the fundamentals of management, finance, production, marketing, economics, and mathematics.

Environmental Structure of Accounting

Accounting is a complex body of knowledge and procedures that has evolved over the last few hundred years. The complexity of accounting in the last fifty years has greatly accelerated as more complex financial transactions have been developed and regulatory agencies, both private and non-private, have come into existence. Voluminous rules and regulations, (for example, Financial Accounting Standards) have been written and put into practice. Also, the rapid development of personal computers and very powerful accounting and systems software has had its impact in accelerating the complexity of accounting. Within accounting, there are highly developed specialized areas such as the following:

Tax accounting	Accounting Information Systems
Financial auditing	Internal auditing
Management accounting	Financial accounting
Not-for-profit accounting	Governmental accounting

Accounting as a profession employs hundreds of thousands of individuals who serve both in public accounting and private accounting. As of 2006, there were approximately 650,000 CPAs in the USA. Accounting is needed in every type of business and organizations including state and federal governments, banks, not-for-profit businesses, manufacturing and retail businesses of all types, and labor unions. The professional accountant needs to have an awareness and knowledge of how the financial and economic environment has an impact on business. Also, an acute awareness of the many different types of organizations that a business interacts with is crucial to being a successful management accountant.

Comparison to Financial Accounting

The differences between financial and managerial accounting can be effectively illustrated by using:

- An input and output approach.
- A financial statement approach.

Input/Output Approach

Although narrower in scope of users, management accounting, nevertheless, is broader in scope in the type of data used in the models through which data is processed and analyzed. The input and output diagrams illustrated in figures reveal the differences in the nature of inputs and the mode of processing between financial and management accounting.

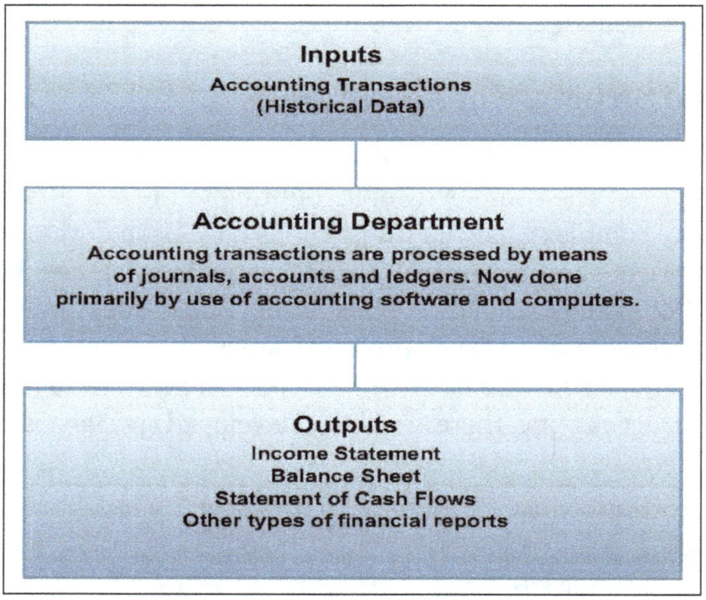

Financial Accounting.

The input/output diagram shown in figure reveal that management accounting deals with a wider range of inputs and outputs. Also, the methodology of processing data involves numerous types of mathematical model. The inputting, processing, and outputting of data in management accounting is not limited to a prescribed set of rules dealing only with historical data as is the case in financial accounting.

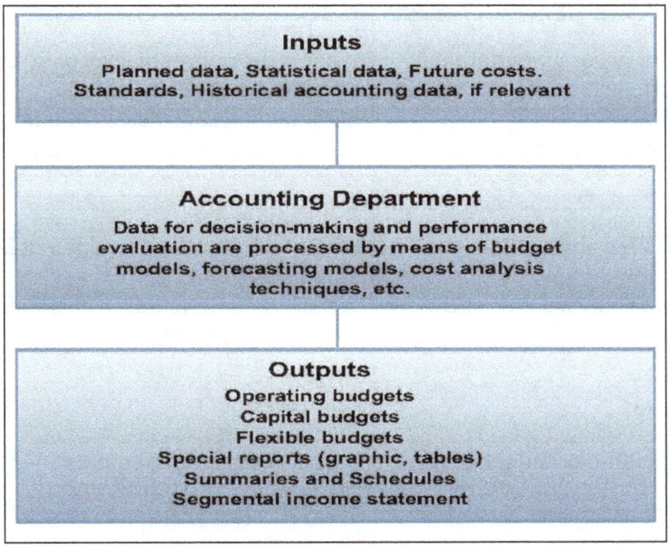

Managerial Accounting.

Financial Statement Approach

Both financial accounting and management accounting are concerned with financial statements. The financial accountant is concerned with analyzing and recording the historical transactions (past decisions) of the business. A primary objective of the financial accountant is to fairly present financial statements based on past events. The management accountant is primarily concerned with desired future events. Future events will be the results of decisions to be made by management. The management accountant, then, is also concerned with financial statements (e.g. budgeted financial statements) that reflect the anticipated consequences of planned decisions (planned transactions). For example, the financial accountant is concerned with questions such as: What is the amount of cash on hand? What is the cost of inventory on hand? The management accountant, however, is concerned with questions such as: What amount of cash should be on hand? What is the desired level of inventory? Table summarizes the differences in viewpoint for each item on the balance sheet and income statement.

Summary of Financial And Managerial Accounting Points of View	
Financial Accounting Viewpoint	Managerial Accounting Viewpoint
• Cash What is the balance? Emphasis is on: General journal entries, bank reconciliations, petty cash.	• Cash How much cash should be on hand? Emphasis is on: Cash budgeting, cash flow, alternative uses of cash.
• Accounts Receivable What is the amount that is collectible? Emphasis is on: Estimation of bad debts, factoring, recording of collections.	• Accounts Receivable What should the credit terms be? Emphasis is on: Effect of different credit terms, bad debt factors, analysis of credit revenue and expenses.

• Inventory What is the historical dollar amount that should be assigned to inventory? Emphasis is on: Inventory cost methods, methods of estimating inventory.	• Inventory What is the optimum level of inventory? Emphasis is on: EOQ models, safety stock, quantity discounts.
• Fixed Assets What is the unamortized amount? Emphasis is on: Depreciation methods, journal entries or trades and retirements.	• Fixed Assets How much plant and equipment is needed? Emphasis is on: Capacity requirements, capital budgeting, replacement of equipment.
• Short-Term Debt What amount is owed? Emphasis is on? Recording accrued liabilities and interest expense.	• Short-Term Debt How much short-term debt is needed? Emphasis is on: Cost of capital, debt/equity ratios, cash budgeting, and risk.
• Long-Term Debt What amount is owed? Emphasis is on: Amortization of bond premium and discount, accrued interest, and bond refunding.	• Long-Term Debt How much long-term debt should be issued? Emphasis is on: Cost of capital, debt/equity ratio, cash budgeting, issuance of different types of securities
• Stockholders' Equity What is the amount of stock issued? How should different types of stock transactions be recorded? Emphasis is on: Recording different types of stock transactions, recording of different types of dividends.	• Stockholders' Equity How much stock should be issued? What kind of stock security should be issued? Emphasis is on: Cost of capital, debt/equity ratio, cash flow, and amount of dividends.
• Sales How much were sales? Emphasis is on: Recording of sales and purchases transactions.	• Sales What will the amount of sales be? Emphasis is on: Sales forecasting, pricing, cash budgeting, methods of increasing sales.
• Expenses How much were expenses? Emphasis is on: Journal entries, accrued expenses, depreciation, bad debts.	• Expenses What should the amount expenses be? Emphasis is on: Budgeting, flexible budgeting cost-volume-profit analysis.

Management Accountant

The management accountant is a professional accountant just like the CPA. He or she is likely to possess a degree in accounting. However, unlike the CPA, the management accountant is more likely to work for an industrial firm rather than an accounting firm. In a manner similar to the CPA, he or she may even be certified. The Institute of Management Accountants which is the professional organization of management accountants has over 70,000 members. The IMA gives twice a year a comprehensive three day exam over the knowledge expected of the management accountant. Individuals passing all parts of the exam are awarded a Certificate in Management Accounting (CMA). CMA's are governed by a set of ethical rules and are also required to accumulate a certain number of CPE hours each year. The exam is a difficult test with less than 20% of those taking the exam passing in one setting. The exam is given in five parts covering the following subject areas:

- Managerial economics and business finance.
- Organization and behavior.
- Public reporting standards, auditing and taxes.
- Periodic reporting for internal and external purposes.
- Decision analysis, including modeling and information systems.

Responsibility Accounting

Responsibility accounting may be defined as an accounting system that collects, summarizes, and reports accounting data relating to the responsibilities of individual managers. Responsibility accounting is a management control system based on the principles of delegating and locating responsibility. Responsibility accounting is a system where managers are given decisions making authority and responsibility for every activity occurring within a specific area of the company. Under this system, managers are made responsible for the activities of segments, which are known as responsibility centres. These segments are called as departments, branches or a division etc., one of the uses of management accounting is to exercise managerial control. Among all the control techniques "responsibility accounting" has achieved considerable significance. While the other control devices are applicable to the organization as a whole, responsibility accounting represents a method of measuring the performance of various divisions of an organization. The word 'division' with reference to responsibility accounting is practiced in general sense to include any logical segment, component, sub-component of an organization. Defined in this way, it includes a decision, a branch office, a service centre, a product line, a channel of distribution, a department.

Significance of Responsibility Accounting

The significance of responsibility accounting for management is as follows:

- Easy Identification: It allows the identification of individual managers accountable for satisfactory or unsatisfactory performance.
- Motivational Benefits: If a system of responsibility accounting is implemented, substantial motivational benefits are guaranteed.

- Data Availability: A device for presenting performance data is provided. A structure of managerial performance appraisal system can be established on that base, besides motivating managers to act in the best welfare of the enterprise.
- Ready-hand Information: Significant and up to the minutes information is made available which can be used to estimate future costs and or revenues and to set up standards for departmental budgets.
- Planning and Decision Making: Responsibility accounting is useful in control as well as in planning and decision making also.
- Delegation and Control: The double objectives of management are delegating responsibility while retaining control is achieved by adoption of responsibility accounting system.

Objectives of Responsibility Accounting

Responsibility accounting is a technique of dividing the organizational structure into a number of responsibility centers to measure their performance. In other words responsibility accounting is a device to determine divisional performance measurement that may be stated as follows:

- To determine the contribution that a division as a sub-unit makes to the total organization.
- To provide a basis for evaluating the quality of the divisional managers performance. Responsibility accounting is applied to calculate the performance of managers and it therefore, influence the manner in which the managers behave.
- To inspire the divisional manager to operate his division in a manner consistent with the basic goals of the organization as a whole.

Process and basic requirement for implementing responsibility accounting:

- To implement a responsibility accounting system, the business must be organized so that responsibility is assignable to individual managers.
- The various managers and their lines of responsibility should be completely defined.
- The organization chart is generally used as a basis for responsibility reporting.
- If clear definition of responsibility cannot be determined, it is very uncertain that responsibility accounting can be implemented effectively.
- Though decision-making power may be delegated for many items, like decisions related to particular revenues, expenses, costs or actions, it may remain exclusively under the charge of top management.

- A number of items will be directly traceable to a particular manager's area of responsibility but not in reality be controllable by that manager.

Responsibility Accounting and Controllability

Controllability

The concept of controllability is important in a system of responsibility accounting. A responsibility centre is accountable for controllable factors only. It is but natural also, since how can one are held responsible for factors beyond one's control. Therefore, it is vital to identify which costs are controllable and which costs are not controllable. For example, a cost is treated as controllable only when the person responsible for incurring it can exercise his influence over it. Costs which cannot be so influenced are termed as uncontrollable costs.

Concept of Control

- Absolute Control:
    - In theory, a manager should have absolute control over an item to be held responsible for it.
    - Absolute control is rare practically.
    - Often, external or internal factors that are exceeding a manager's control may affect revenues or expenses under that manager's responsibility.
    - The theoretical condition about absolute control must often be compromised, since some degree of non-controllability usually exists.
    - The manager is therefore usually held responsible for items over which that manager has comparative control.
- Relative Control:
    - Relative control denotes that the manager has control over the majority of the factors that influence a given budget item.
    - Application of relative control as a basis for evaluation may result in some motivational problems, as managers may be judged upon the results that may not reflect the manager's efforts or decisions.
    - Most budget plans assign control on a relative basis in order to develop and use segmental budgets.

To sum up, we have to understand that, manager's control of the variables in question is immaterial. But the manager's control (or influence) on the variable in question, conditioned on whatever other information is present, is the key notion. That is, information content is a precisely defined controllability notion that accounts for other sources of information. With the traditional controllability notion, we need to analyze whether the manager can control the variable in question, but with conditional or information content notion, we must first state what other information is being used in the evaluation process. Once this source of information is accounted for, we study whether any new information is produced by the variable in the question. This proves the manger's conditional control of the variable in question.

It is important to set responsibility for different managers. But the question is how to set responsibility for managers. Should a manager be evaluated as the head of a cost center or profit center? One of the familiar and intuitive analysis of this question focuses on whether the manager controls cost or revenue or both. If the manager controls only costs, a cost center evaluation is appropriate. If the manager only control revenues, a revenue center evaluation is appropriate. If the manager controls both costs and revenue, a profit center evaluation is appropriate. So, it is clear that it is manager who is responsible for the variables on which he/she can exercise control. It means responsibility and controllability go hand in hand.

Responsibility Reports

- Basic Features: A characteristic of a responsibility accounting system is the varying amount of detail is included in the reports issued to different managerial levels of the firm. Although the amount of detail differs, reports issued under a responsibility accounting system are interrelated. Totals from the report on one level of management are carried forward in the report to the management level immediately above. Data is appropriately abstracted, filtered, and/or condensed as information flows from lower to higher levels of management. It encourages "management by exception" in the organisation Two fundamental methods are applied to present revenue and expense data:
    - Items upon which a manager has direct control are included in the responsibility report for that management level. Any revenue or expenses on which the manager cannot directly exercise his control are not included.
    - All revenue and expense items that can be traced directly or allocated indirectly to a particular manager, whether or not they are controllable, are included. In this approach, due care must taken to divide controllable from non-controllable items in order to differentiate those items for which a manager can and should be held responsible.
- Desired Features:
    - Results should be stated in physical terms where appropriate, since such figures may be more familiar and understandable to managers.

- To help out management in rapidly spotting budget variances, both budgeted and actual amounts should be reported. Budget variance is the difference between the budgeted and actual amounts of an item. As variances draw attention to areas which require investigation, they are useful in applying the management by exception principle.
- Reports often include both current and year-to-date analyses.
- Issued Regularly and Timely.
- Format should be comparatively simple and easy to read.
- Confusing terminology should be avoided.

Responsibility Centres

Below are the types of responsibility centers.

- Cost Center: These are the center in which individual persons are responsible only for cost control. They are not responsible for any other functions. In this center, it is essential to differentiate the controllable costs and uncontrollable costs. A person responsible for a particular cost center will be held accountable only for controllable costs. The performance of each center is evaluated by comparing the actual cost vs. targeted cost.
- Revenue Center: The revenue center takes care of revenue with no other responsibility. Mainly sales teams of the company are responsible for these centers.
- Profit Center: These are the center whose performance is measured in terms of cost and revenue. Generally, the Factory of the company is treated as a profit center where consumption of raw material is a cost and finished product sell to its other department is revenue.
- Investment Center: A manager responsible for these centers is responsible for utilizing the assets of the company in the best manner so that the company can earn a good return on capital employed.

Examples of Responsibility Accounting

Example: Cost Center - Below is the responsibility report on the cost of production. ABC Pharma Inc is engaged in the manufacturing of medicine company has decided to produce 10000 medicine in the year 2018 for which the company has defined the budget of $90000 at the beginning of the year. Still, at the end of the year, it has noticed the actual cost incurred for the production is $95000. There is an excess expenditure of $5000 over-budgeted expenditure, which the responsibility manager has to explain why this has increased. It may be possible that Govt. has increased the rate of electricity charges and water charges because of which overhead has increased. Manger has used the superior quality of the material. Therefore, the cost of material has increased, but at the same time, it takes less no. of manpower hour due to which labor cost has decreased.

ABC Pharma Inc			
Responsibility Report of Cost of Production			
For the year ended 31sr December 2018			
Controllable Cost	Budget	Actual	Favourable/Unfavourable
Units in Production(No.s)	10,000	10,000	
Direct Material(in $)	50,000	52,000	-2000
Direct Labour(in $)	20,000	18,000	2000
Overhead(in $)	20,000	25,000	-5000
Total Cost(in $)	90,000	95,000	-5000

Example: Revenue Center - Below is the responsibility report of the revenue center of Samsung Inc. Samsung Inc. had targeted revenue of $95000 from their electronic segment for the year ended 2018. But at the end of the year, they achieved revenue of $93000. There is a decrease of $2000 in their revenue. It has been seen that company has achieved its target in Television and washing machine division. In contrast, they have outperformed in Microwave and Mobile division. But their Refrigerator and Air conditioner division have not achieved the targeted revenue due to which their electronic division target falls short by $2000 for which Manager of a Revenue center will be responsible, and he has to explain about the underperformance of these two divisions.

SAMSUNG Inc			
Responsibility Report of Revenue Centre			
For the year ended 31sr December 2018			
Revenue	Budget (in $)	Actual (in $)	Favourable/Unfavourable (in $)
Television	10,000	10,000	0
Refrigerator	20,000	16,000	-4000
Washing Machine	15,000	15,000	0
Air Conditioner	25,000	22,000	-3000
Microwave	10,000	11,000	1000
Mobile	15,000	19,000	4000
Total Cost (in $)	95,000	93,000	-2000

Components of Responsibility Accounting

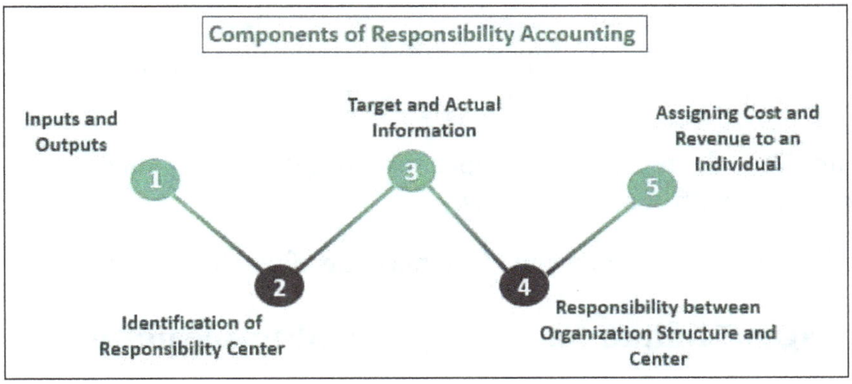

Below are the components of responsibility accounting:

- Inputs and Outputs: The implementation of responsibility accounting based upon information relating to inputs and outputs. The resource utilized in an organization like qty of raw material consumed, Labor hours consumed are termed as Inputs, and finished product generated is termed as outputs.
- Identification of Responsibility Center: The whole concept of responsibility accounting depends upon identification of responsibility center. The responsibility center defines the decision point in the organization. In small organizations generally, one person who is probably owners of the firm can manage the entire organization.
- Target and Actual Information: Responsibility accounting requires target or budget data and Actual data for performance evaluation of the responsible manager of each responsibility center.
- Responsibility between Organization Structure and Responsibility Center: An organization structure with clear authority and responsibility is required for a successful responsibility accounting system. Similarly, the responsibility accounting system must be designed as per the organization structure.
- Assigning Cost and Revenue to an Individual: After defining the authority: responsibility relationship, cost, and revenue which are controllable should be assigned to individuals for evaluating their performance.

Advantages of Responsibility Accounting

Following are some benefits of Responsibility Accounting:

- It establishes a system of control.
- It is designed according to the organization structure.

- It encouraged to budget for comparison of actual achievements with the budgeted data.
- It encourages the interest and awareness of in-office staff as they have to explain about the deviation of their assigned responsibility center.
- It simplifies the performance report because it excludes those items which are beyond the control of individuals.
- It is helpful for top management to make an effective decision.

Disadvantages/Limitations of Responsibility Accounting

- Generally, a prerequisite for establishing a successful responsibility accounting system like proper identification of responsibility center, an adequate delegation of work, proper reporting is missing that makes it difficult for establishing a responsibility accounting system.
- It requires skilled manpower in each department, which increases the cost of the company.
- The responsibility accounting system applies only to controllable costs.
- If the responsibility and objective are not properly explained to the person, then the responsibility accounting system will not give proper results.

Transfer Pricing

Transfer pricing is a profit allocation method used to assign an MNE's net profit (or loss) before tax to the countries where its business activity is conducted. Transfer pricing involves the setting of prices among divisions within an enterprise. Transfer prices are charges for goods and services between controlled (or related) legal entities within an enterprise. The branches and companies that are wholly or majority owned ultimately by the parent corporation are considered as legal entities under the control of a single corporation. Transfer pricing is a unique methodology to transfer the goods from one company division or department to another which entails minimal postings on the accounts receivable and accounts payable books. It is a process that greatly simplifies the process.

Normally, there is a simple form that accompanies the physical transfer of the goods, and it is used by both the sender and the recipient to make appropriate posts in company accounting records. This process eliminates the necessity for invoices, tariffs, internal bills of lading, and other documents that would normally apply to a new purchase using an outside vendor.

While the main purpose of transfer pricing is to enhance the overall value of the corporate family of companies, there are instances when this type of transaction can be abused. This is especially true when transfers to international locations are conducted. Today, many countries have regulations to help prevent the use of this pricing method as a means of evading taxes or similar unethical and illegal activities.

Concept of Transfer Pricing

Transfer pricing is a profit allocation method used to attribute a multinational corporation's net profit (or loss) before tax to countries where it does business. Transfer pricing results in the setting of prices among divisions within an enterprise. Transfer prices are charges for goods and services between controlled (or related) legal entities within an enterprise. Legal entities considered under the control of a single corporation include branches and companies that are wholly or majority owned ultimately by the parent corporation.

A transfer pricing is the notional value at which goods and services are transferred from one division or department to another within a decentralized organization. Transfer prices are normally set for intermediate products which are goods and services that are supplied by the selling division to the buying division. The goods that are produced by the buying division and sold to the outside world are known as final products. The price charged to the interdivisional transfer of goods and services is revenue to the selling division and cost to the buying division.

Therefore, the price charged is bound to affect the profits of both the divisions; benefit (revenue) to one division will be created at the expense of the other division. For example, the selling division will benefit from charging prices for such transfers of goods and services. However, for the buying division, this will result into higher costs. The transfer prices, thus, can have impact on the evaluation of each division's performance and measures applied for such measurement of performance.

Objectives of a Sound Transfer Pricing System

- Transfer pricing should help in the accurate measurement of divisional performance (profitability) measurement.
- Transfer pricing should motivate the divisional managers into maximizing the profitability of their divisions and making decisions that are in the best interests of the organizations as a whole.
- Transfer prices should ensure that the divisional autonomy and authority remains well intact.
- Transfer prices should allow goal congruence to take place, which in effect means that the objectives of divisional managers are compatible with the objectives of overall company.

- A transfer pricing system, if duly established, can keep a vigil on the multinational companies and international groups which may try to falsify the transfer prices between countries in order to curtail the overall tax burden and take the required action, as may be required.
- To ensure that the information provided (e.g., division Profit & Loss Accounts) is useful for evaluating the economic performance of divisions and the managerial performance of division managers.
- Transfer prices should be such that actions which will have the effect of increasing a division's reported profit will also have the effect of increasing the company's reported profit.
- MNEs use various market-based and cost-based transfer pricing mechanisms to accomplish the objective of goal congruence. Transfer-pricing system must, however, have in-built mechanisms to ensure smooth negotiation and conflict resolution.

Different Methods of Transfer Pricing

Different methods of transfer pricing are: Market Prices, Cost-Based Prices, Negotiated Prices and Dual Price.

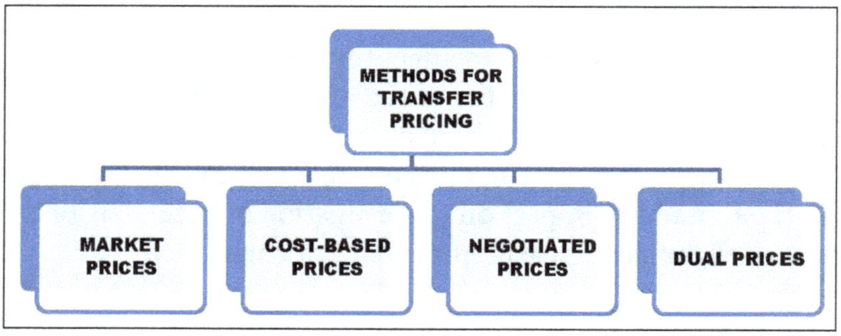

Market Prices

- Market prices refer to a price in an intermediate market between independent buyers and seller.
- In competitive external market for the transferred product, market prices work well as transfer prices.
- In market price, divisional performance is more likely to represent the real economics contribution of the division to total company profit.
- Market-prices are based on opportunity costs concept.
- In market price, no division can be benefit at the expense of another division.

- Managers of both buying and selling divisions are indifferent between trading with each other or with outsiders.
- In market transfer pricing, minimum transfer price for the selling division is the market price and maximum transfer price for the buying division is also the market price.
- The market price can resolve conflicts among the buying and selling divisions.
- Market price is the optimal so long as the selling division is operating at full capacity.
- Finding a competitive market price may be difficult if such a market does not exist.
- Market price may change often that why it is very cumbersome used as a transfer price.
- Problem with market prices can occur when a selling division is not operating at full capacity and cannot sell all its products.

Cost-Based Prices

- When external market do not exist or are not available to the company or when information about external market prices is not readily available, companies may decide to use some form of cost-based transfer pricing system.
- Variable cost-based pricing approach is useful when selling division is operating below capacity.
- The manager of selling division will generally not like this transfer price because it yields no profit to that division.
- In actual full cost approach, transfer price is based on the total product cost per unit which will include direct material, direct labour and factory overhead.
- A full cost transfer price would have shut down the chances of any negotiation between divisions about selling at transfer prices.
- Standard cost-based pricing approach is useful & reduces risk to the buyer.
- Transfer pricing based on opportunity cost identifies the minimum price that a selling division would to accept and the maximum price that the buying division will be willing to pay.
- The opportunity cost approach is used in situation where the market is imperfect.
- A transfer is in the best economic interest of the company if the opportunity cost for the selling division is less than the opportunity cost for the buying division.

Negotiated Prices

- Negotiated prices are generally preferred as a middle solution between market prices and cost-based prices.
- Under negotiated prices, the managers involved act much the same as the manager of independent companies.
- Negotiation strategies may be similar to those employed when trading with outside markets.
- Negotiated prices avoid mistrust, bad feeling and undesirable bargaining interests among divisional managers.
- It provides an opportunity to achieve the objectives of goal congruence autonomy and accurate performance evaluation.
- The overall company is beneficial if selling and buying divisions can agree upon some mutually transfer prices.
- The agreed prices also can be used for performance measurement without creating any friction.
- The use of negotiated prices is consistent with the concept of decentralized decision-making in the divisionalised firms.
- In negotiated transfer price, a great deal of management effort, time and resources can be consumed in the negotiating process.
- In negotiated transfer price, one divisional manger having some private information may take advantage of another divisional manager.

Dual Price

- Dual prices of transfer pricing, selling division sells the transferred goods at a profit using full cost plus profit margin.
- Transfer price for the buying division is the market price.
- The difference in transfer prices for the two divisions could be accounted for by special centralized account.
- Dual pricing system has the function of motivating both the selling division and buying division to make decisions that are consistent with the overall goals of decentralization goal congruence, accurate performance measurement, autonomy, adequate motivation to divisional manager.
- Dual prices provide incentive to selling divisions in the form of the profit or mark up at which the goods are transferred.

Example: A company has two divisions, A and B. the division A is currently operating at full capacity. It has been asked to supply its product to division B. division A sells its product to its regular customers for $30 each. Division B (currently operating at 50% capacity) is willing to pay $20 each for the component produced by division A (this represents the full absorption cost per component at division A). The components will be used by division B in supplementing its main product to conform to the need of special order. As per the contract terms of sales, the buyer calls for reimbursement of full cost to division B plus 10% Division A has a variable cost of $17 per component. The cost per unit of division B subsequent to the buying part from division A is estimated as follow:

Purchased parts- outside vendors	$90
Purchase part – division A	$20
Other variable costs	$50
Fixed overheads and administration	$40 -------
	$200

The company uses return on investment in the measurement of division and division manager's performance. Required:

1. As manager of division A, would you recommend sales of your output to division B at the stipulated price of $20?

2. Would it be in the over-all interest of the company for division A to sell its output to division B?

3. Suggests an alternative transfer price and show how could it lead to goal congrenuence?

Solution:

1. As manager of division A, sales at $20 per unit to division B, should not be recommended. The division is already operating at its full capacity and the market is presumably absorbing all its output at $30 per unit.

2. Decision analysis (whether to transfer part from division A to division B of $20 per unit or not). It will be in the over-all interest of the company that the transfer takes place as it would increase the firm's profit by $50 per unit.

Particulars	Sold externally ($)	Transferred to division B ($)
Sale price (division A)	30	
Sale price (division B) ($200+10%)		220
Less: relevant incremental cost		
For part of division A	(17)	(17)

Purchased parts from outside	------	(90)
Other valuable costs	------	(50)
Profit per unit	13	63

3. Dual price basis of effecting transfer is the most appropriate. In this case, the relevant transfer price will be $30 (sale) so far as division A concerned and $20 (purchase) so far as division B is concerned. It will keep the profits of division A unaffected and will facilitate the utilization of idle capacity of division B, as also increase its profit:

Sale price ($210+10%)	$231
Less: costs ($90 + 50)	($140)
Profit	$91

Rules for Successful Pricing

- It should be simple to understand and easy to operate.
- It should enable fixation of fair transfer prices for the output transferred or service rendered.
- Ideally the business unit/divisional manager must be given autonomy and freedom to sell in open market.
- The business unit/divisions should have free access to various sources of market information.
- There should be a negotiation for transfer prices between the business unit/ divisional managers of the selling business unit/division and the buying unit/ division.
- Negotiated transfer prices are far more motivating than the prices imposed by the top management or determined by the finance department.
- Sound transfer pricing ground rules must be framed to guide negotiations between business unit/divisional manager.
- It must promote consistency in transfer pricing decisions, but also minimize interdivisional conflicts.
- A system of arbitration with ground rules must also be established.
- Top management should discourage prolonged arguments between business unit/divisional manager.
- Transfer prices can be reviewed annually or as dictated by the demand and supply conditions in the market.

- Transfer pricing guidelines must state the circumstances under which a revision of transfer prices can be made during the year.
- When transfer prices are based on market price, long-run competitive/normal prices must be considered.
- Transfer pricing and arbitration rules can be reviewed once in four years or earlier if there is a major change in business conditions.

Various Problems Associated with Transfer Pricing

- "Transfer pricing" as shorthand for multinational corporations shifting profits to tax havens to avoid tax in developed countries.
- If a division is transferring goods to another division located in a high tariff country, a low transfer price reduce the tariff.
- A company can shift income from a division (foreign country) to itself (home country) by charging a management fee.
- In transfer pricing, the reported performance of the local managers is influenced by corporate policies.

Responsibility Centres - Objectives and Determinants

A responsibility center is a part of a company for which a manager has ability and responsibility. The company's complete organization chart is a logical source for formative responsibility centers. The most frequent responsibility centers are the departments within a company. When the manager of a responsibility center can control only costs, the responsibility center is referred to as a cost center. If a manager can control both costs and revenues, the responsibility center is known as a profit center. If a manager has power and responsibility for costs, revenues, and investments the responsibility center is referred to as an investment center.

Responsibility centres are identifiable segment within a company for which individual managers have an established authority and accountability. Responsibility centres define accurately what assets and activities each manager is responsible for. How to classify any given responsibility depends on which aspects of the business the department has authority over. Managers prepare a responsibility report to evaluate the performance of each responsibility centre. This report compares the responsibility centre's budgeted performance with its actual performance, measuring and interpreting individual variances. Responsibility reports include only controllable costs so that managers are not responsible for activities they have no control over. Using a flexible budget is helpful for preparing a responsibility report.

Objectives of Responsibility Center

The responsibility centre is a difficult structure which can settle its own multiple objectives, according to the strategy of the business it is part of, as follows:

- Devise its own planned activities (satisfying the needs of the clients, respecting the delivery deadlines, promoting creativity etc.).
- Optimizing the method of using the source as for the enhancement of the entity's global presentation and that of the responsibility centre.
- Establishing the systems of evaluation and control of performance (financial, operational, personnel, management, marketing etc.).
- Establishing valid procedures of devising the expense budgets corresponding to the responsibility centre with the possibility of integrating and emphasizing within the general budget of the entity, unravelling and allotting expenses for fix and variable costs.
- Simplifying the system of emphasize the procedures for communication, reporting and collaboration, amplifying the operating speed by installing information procedures.
- Introducing and perfect procedures for financial - accountancy balance.
- Increasing the capacity to regulate production to the requirements of the clients in terms of quality.
- Changing the employees' mentality in the sense of increasing awareness of the need for them to be active, participatory, and efficient.

Measures of Divisional Performance

The responsibility centre is a difficult structure which can settle its own multiple objectives, according to the strategy of the business it is part of, as follows:

- Devise its own planned activities (satisfying the needs of the clients, respecting the delivery deadlines, promoting creativity etc.).
- Optimizing the method of using the source as for the enhancement of the entity's global presentation and that of the responsibility centre.
- Establishing the systems of evaluation and control of performance (financial, operational, personnel, management, marketing etc.).

- Establishing valid procedures of devising the expense budgets corresponding to the responsibility centre with the possibility of integrating and emphasizing within the general budget of the entity, unravelling and allotting expenses for fix and variable costs.
- Effectiveness implies contribution to the achievement of ultimate goals of the responsibility centre, division or department.
- Performance measures should be competent enough to evaluate both short-term and long-term performance of a division.
- Multiple measures enhance goal congruence and reduce sub-optimization.
- Multiple measures or goals include productivity, profitability, human resources development, employee attitudes, market share, customer relations, and contribution to social responsibility.
- It is argued that too many goals sometimes may confuse the divisional managers.
- Adequate as well as manageable measures, say four to five, can be preferably used.

Various Determinants and Technique of Measurement

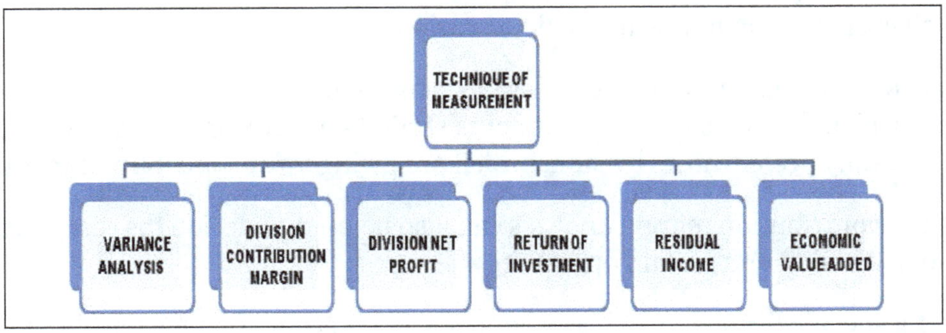

Variance Analysis

- Variance analysis may be cost variance and revenue variance analysis.
- Presentation of a cost centre can be evaluated using cost variance analysis, i.e., by comparing the actual costs with the standard costs.
- Any variance between the actual costs and standard costs require corrective action by the management.
- On the measure of performance (in term of incurrence of costs) attempt are made to reduce the costs of cost centre.

- Measuring the presentation of cost centre only in terms of cost incur without relating to benefits achieve by the centre is not measured fair by many companies.
- Revenue variance study can be used in evaluate the presentation of revenue centre.
- If Revenues (Actual Sale) are different from budgeted sales, they become the primary focus of management attention.
- While evaluating the performance of a revenue centre, costs incurred are not used as a measure.

Division Contribution Margin

- Division contribution margin is defined as the total division revenue less the direct costs of the division.
- Measures of performance emphasizes the contribution of each division to overall company profit.
- In this measure, all revenues and costs traceable to the division are included and all common, indirect costs of the company are excluded.
- The direct contribution margin is the most useful profit measure for comparing divisional performance, for making resources allocation decisions and for overall corporate planning and policy decisions.
- Top management of the business often us the direct payment margin to decide in which divisions other investments should be made and in this decision will certainly prefer those divisions which are giving most contribution margin.
- The contribution margin analysis can also be used to decide the discontinuance of a division or a certain operation.
- If a specific division provides a contribution margin, the division should not be eliminate but retained, although the allotment of indirect costs results in a net loss for that allotment.

Division Net Profit

- The division net profit is the most proper profit determine for evaluation of a division's performance.
- This analysis can be used to judge the presentation of a profit centre as both cost and revenue data measured in financial terms are available.
- Division net profit is obtained after considering related revenues, direct costs and a part of indirect costs incurred for the benefit of the division.

- The division net profit standard is useful in understanding that a division manager becomes aware of the full costs incurred for the entire company and allocated full costs to the specific division.
- Measuring the presentation of a profit division, it is better to use a measure of divisional revenue less divisional costs and divisional revenue less divisional controllable costs should be used to measure the performance of division manager.
- If the presentation of the manger is being assessed, then it would seem sensible to base that assessment that is controllable by him.

Return on Investment

- It expresses divisional profit as a percentage of the firm's investment in the division and is similar to widely accepted 'return on capital employed' measure used in the external analysis and interpretation of accounts.
- ROI = divisional profit/divisional investment.
- ROI = net profit/sales *sales/investment.
- ROI = net profit margin * asset turnover.
- The ROI ratio can be divided into other ratio such as net profit margin and the asset turnover.
- The net profit margin is the result of firm's pricing policy and its cost control.
- It is a measure of the relationship among sales, expenses, volume and profit.
- The assets turnover shows the amount of sales generated by the assets available and whether a division has over- or- under-utilized its assets.
- ROI can be increased by any of the following actions, all other factors being held constant:
    - An increase in sales price or sales volume.
    - A decrease in operating costs (fixed or variable).
    - A reduction in divisional investment.

Residual Income

- Residual income can be defined as the net income of a division, less the 'imputed' capital charge on the asset used by the division.

- The capital charge is the minimum acceptable rate of return and is calculated by applying this required (or target) rate of return to the division's investment base.
- RI = divisional profit – (percent capital charge * divisional investment).
- It avoids suboptimal decision as investment is not rejected merely because they lower the divisional manager's ROI.
- It maximizes growth of the company and increase shareholders' wealth by accepting opportunities which earn a rate of return in excess of the cost of capital.
- The cost of capital charge on divisional investment ensures that divisional managers are aware of the opportunity cost of funds.
- Charging each division with the company's cost of capital ensures that decisions taken by different divisions are compatible with the interests of the organization as a whole.

Economic Value Added (Eva)

- 'Economic value added' can be used for evaluating the performance of a division or segment.
- Economic value added is generated only if after – tax operating income exceeds the cost of investing the capital.
- EVA = after- tax operating income – (weighted average cost of capital * total capital employed).
- To improve EVA, managers must earn more after-tax operating income with the same capital, use less capital to earn the same after-tax operating income, or invest capital in high-return projects.
- If EVA is positive, the company is creating wealth.
- If EVA is negative, the company destroying wealth.

Evaluate Measurement Technique

- A distinction is (or should be) made while measuring the presentation of a division and that of evaluate a division manager's presentation while using ROI and RI tools.
- It is advisable to discriminate between the measure of a division's performance and that of a division's manager.
- Return on Investment and RI give clues to where an organization might be wise

to raise, maintain investment and other things being equal, higher ROI and RI are desirable.

- Thus, the evaluation of a manager is not identical to the evaluation of the cost, revenue, profit or investment division.
- Budgets and targets are useful tools for assessing the performance of division managers when managers participate and commit themselves to meeting budgeted goals or targets.
- Comparing among different division within a business enterprise can be made and subsequently divisions can be ranked in terms of relative profitability.
- Comparing current performances of a division with the historical performances of the same division is a preferable tool.
- Comparing divisional consequences with averages can be useful because differences among divisions resulting from differences in industry do not influences the comparison.

References

- Foundations-of-Management-Accounting: microbuspub.com, Retrieved 29, June 2020
- Responsibility-accounting: wallstreetmojo.com, Retrieved 02, April 2020

2

Financial Budgeting

The financial plan for a certain period of time is called budgeting. Some of the different types of budgets are operating budget, financial budget, master budget, and fixed and flexible budget. The topics elaborated in this chapter will help in gaining a better perspective about budgeting and these types of budgets.

We are all well-familiar with the term budget. Budgeting is a powerful tool that helps the management in performing its functions such as planning, coordinating, and controlling the operations efficiently. The definition of budget is, "A plan quantified in monetary terms prepared and approved prior to a define period of time usually showing planned income to be generated and/or expenditure to be incurred during the period and the capital to be employed to attain a given objective."

Budget, Budgeting and Budgetary Control

Let us go through the terms sequentially:

- Budget: Budget represents the objectives of any organization that is based on the implication of forecast and related to planned activities. Budget is neither an estimate nor a forecast because estimation is a predetermination of future events, may be based on simple guess or any scientific principles. Similarly, a forecast may be an anticipation of events during a specified period of time. A forecast may be for a specific activity of the company. We normally forecast likely events such as sales, production, or any other activity of the organization. On the other hand, budget relates to planned policy and program of the organization under planed conditions. It represents the action according to a situation which may or may not take place.
- Budgeting: Budgeting represents the formation of the budget with the help and coordination of all or the various departments of the firm.
- Budgetary Control: Budgetary control is a tool for the management to allocate responsibility and authority in planning for future and to develop a basis of measurement to evaluate the efficiency of operations. A budget is a plan of the policy to be pursued during a defined time period. All the actions are based on planning of budget because budget is prepared after studying all the related activities of the company. Budget gives a communication ground to the top management with the staff of the firm who are implementing the policies of the

top management. Budgetary control helps in coordinating the economic trends, financial position, policies, plans, and actions of an organization. Budgetary control also helps the management to ensure and control the plan and activities of the organization. Budgetary control makes it possible by continuous comparison of actual performance with that of the budgets. Budgets are the individual objectives of a department whereas budgeting may be said to be the act of building budgets. Budgetary Control embraces all this and in addition, includes the science of planning the budgets themselves and utilization of such budget to effect an overall management tool f or the business planning and control.

Types of Budgets

Functional Budgets

It relates to any function of the firm such as sales, production, cash, etc. Following budgets are prepared in functional budgets:

- Sales Budget.
- Production Budget.
- Material Budget.
- Manufacturing Budget.
- Administrative Cost Budget.
- Plant Utilization Budget.
- Capital Expenditure Budget.
- Research and Development Cost Budget.
- Cash Budget.

Master Budget or Summarized Budget or Finalized Profit Plan

This budget is very useful for the top management of the company because it covers all the information in a summarized manner.

- Fixed Budget: It is a rigid budget and is drawn on the assumption that there will be no change in the budget level.
- Flexible Budget: It is also called a sliding scale budget. It is useful in: the new organizations where it is difficult to foresee, the firms where activity level changes due to seasonal nature or change in demand, the industries based on change of fashion, the units which keep on introducing new products, and the firms which are engaged in ship-building business.

- Zero Base Budgeting: Zero base budgeting is not based on the incremental approach; previous year figures are not adopted as base. CIMA has defined it as: As a method of budgeting, where all activities are revaluated each time a budget is set, discrete levels of each activity are valued and combination is chosen to match the funds available.

Control Ratios

Following ratios are used to evaluate the deviations of the actual performance from the budgeted performance. If the ratio is 100% or more, it represents favorable results and vice-a-versa.

Capacity Ratio = Actual hours worked / Budgeted hours

Activity Ratio = Standard hours for actual production / Budgeted hours × 100

Efficiency Ratio = Standard hours for actual production / Actual hours worked × 100

Calendar Ratio = Number of actual working days in a period / Number of working days in the budgeted period × 100

Cash Budget

Cash budget comes under the category of financial budget. It is prepared to calculate budgeted cash flows inflows and outflows during a specific period of time. Cash budget is useful in determining the optimum level of cash to avoid excessive cash or shortage of cash, which may arise in future. With the help of cash budget, we can arrange cash through borrowing funds in case of shortage, and we may invest cash if it is present in excess. It is necessary for every business to keep a safe level of cash. Being a part of master budget, the following tasks are included in a cash budget:

- Collection of Cash.
- Cash Payments.
- Selling Expenses and administrative expensive budget.

Format

If a firm wants to maintain cash balance of $50,000 and in case of shortage the firm borrows funds from Bank, following cash budget is prepared:

Particulars	Q-1	Q-2	Q-3	Q-4	Total
					Yearly
Opening Cash Balance	40,000	50,000	50,000	50,500	40,000

Add; Cash receipts	80,000	1,00,000	90,000	1,25,000	3,95,000
Total available Cash A	1,20,000	1,50,000	1,40,000	1,75,500	4,35,000
Less: Cash Payments:					
Direct Material	30,000	40,000	38,000	42,000	1,50,000
Direct Labour	12,000	15,000	14,000	16,000	57,000
Factory Overheads	18,000	19,000	17,000	20,000	74,000
Administrative Expenses	16,000	16,000	16,000	16,000	64,000
Selling & Distribution Exp.	9,000	10,000	11,000	12,000	42,000
Purchase of Fixed Assets	-	-	40,000	-	40,000
Total Cash Payments B	85,000	1,00,000	1,36,000	1,06,000	4,27,000
Cash in hand C A – B	35,000	50,000	4,000	69,500	8,000
Financing Activities:	15,000	-	50,000	-	65,000
Borrowings		-	-3,000	-18,000	-21,000
Repayments of Borrowings		-	- 500	-1,500	-2,000
Interest paid					
Net Cash Flows from financing	23,000	0	46,500	-19,500	50,000
Activities D					
Closing Cash Balance E C + D	58,000	50,000	50,500	50,000	50,000

Operating Budgets

The budgets related to the physical activities or operations of a business are called operating budgets. The various operating budgets are:

- Sales budget.
- Production budget.
- Production cost budget.
- Ending inventory budget.
- Cost of goods sold budget.
- Selling expenses budget.
- Administrative expense budget.
- Budgeted income statement budget.

The sales estimate is the foundation for other operating budgets, so the budgeting process begins with the determination of Sales Budget.

Sales Budget

The sales budget is a forecast of total sales to achieve in a budget period expressed in monetary or quantitative terms. It is prepared by the sales manager. This budget acts as a foundation for all the other functional budgets like production budget, cash budget, cost of goods sold budget etc., which depend on budgeted sales volume. It is the most challenging budget because estimating future sales is difficult due to continuous changes in the conditions of the economy and the company itself. Therefore, both internal and external factors are taken into account before making a sales forecast. The important factors that should be considered while making sales forecasts are as follows:

- Past trend in sales: This is the most authentic and easily accessible source of information which companies use in predicting future sales. Analyzing past sales product wise, area wise and customer wise can prove very useful in devising appropriate marketing and pricing policies.
- Estimates by sales force: Since salesmen are in direct contact with the customers and know their behavior better, they are in a position to estimate the potential demand more accurately.
- Company specific factors: The plant capacity, the availability of raw materials and supplies, the size of workforce and procurement of labor with required skills, the arrangement of finance are some of the critical factors to be considered in making projections about sales.
- Changes in firm's price policies: The firm should assess its pricing policies to see how the customer demand would react to the change in the prices of its commodities. Generally sales can be increased by reducing the prices and vice versa.
- Changes in the product mix: The firm should also study the effect of changes in the product mix on the sales level as well as contribution margin. Then efforts should be made to increase the sales of the most promising products.
- Marketing research: Surveys and market research should be conducted to collect information about customer tastes, preferences, purchasing patterns, disposable incomes etc. Such information leads to better product mix decisions and sales forecast.
- Advertising and sales promotion plans: The impact of advertising campaign and sales promotion techniques should be assessed and incorporated in the sales forecast. If the company is proposing to undertake some major expansion or discontinuation plan, it will affect the sales volume.
- Competitors actions: The strategies and actions of competitors such as changes in their prices, product quality, promotion policies or new features in their

products can greatly affect the sales of the organization and therefore must be considered.

- General economic conditions: The sales forecast should be made in the light of general economic conditions prevailing in the economy like composition and purchasing power of population, growth in the national income and disposable income, seasonal and cyclical factors, international developments like petroleum prices and gold prices, labor market conditions, presence of substitutes etc.
- Government policies: The government policies on exports -imports, taxes, interest, inflation, FDI, foreign exchange etc. have bearing on the operations of the business and should also be analyzed before making sales forecast. The forecasters should take note of government published predictions/forecasts for many economic indicators such as GDP, national income, production indexes, inflation etc. while making sales forecasts.

Having made sales forecast the sales budget is prepared according to products, territories, customers and period:

- Product wise Sales Budget: Incase a company manufactures several products or variations of products, sales budget is prepared product wise. This will apprise management about the popularity of its various products.
- Territory wise Sales Budget: When a company sells its products in different geographical territories, then sales budget should be prepared for each territory. This will help management in fixing separate sales targets for each territory, distribution of costs among them, devising incentive schemes based on their performance etc.
- Customer wise Sales Budget: If a company sells its products to different customers such as wholesalers, retailers, public, government agencies, and foreign businesses and like, then it should prepare the budget customer wise. This will help in revealing the contribution of each type of customer to the total sales of the business firm and help in drawing proper marketing policies.
- Period wise Sales Budget: The sales budget in terms of quantity and value should be broken down further into quarterly sales figures or monthly sales figures. This would ensure coordination between production, purchasing and sales department and would also help in fixing quotas for salesmen. The specimen of a Sales Budget is given below:

Table: Specimen Sales Budget.

ALPHA COMPANY LIMITED
SALES BUDGET FOR THE PERIODENDING --------------------

Division	Product	Budgeted Sales Units	Budgeted Sales Price	Budgeted Sales Value
North Division Total	A B			
South Division Total	A B			
North + South	A			
North+ South	B			
Total				

Production Budget

A production budget is a plan that shows the quantity of units of each product to be manufactured to cater to the sales forecast and to keep the desired level of inventories. It is prepared by the production manager. It is generally expressed in physical units. The production budget is based on sales budget but in those cases where sales cannot be precisely forecasted due to frequent change in fashion and style, it is based on past experience.

Units to be produced = budgeted sales + desired level of closing inventory of finished goods – opening inventory of finished goods

The objectives of production budget are:

- To plan what to produce, how much to produce, when to produce and where to produce.
- To lay down the production program that helps in maintaining optimum balance between sales, inventories and production at the minimal cost.
- To serve as the foundation for the preparation of production cost budget, cash budget, material requirement budget, direct labor budget and factory cost budget.
- To maintain the desired level of inventory so that there is neither shortage of goods during the peak season nor surplus stock during the slack season.
- To make optimum utilization of plant capacity.
- To make proper arrangements for material, labor, power etc. so that production can take place smoothly.
- To highlight the weaknesses and source of potential trouble which could be averted by taking timely actions.

In the production budget, the annual budget figures could be further broken down into monthly or quarterly estimates. The key factors i.e. factors which can limit the volume of production, should be identified. The following measures should be taken to insulate the production from the adverse effects of key factors:

Key factor	Preventive measures
Plant Capacity	• Adoption of latest modern techniques. • Timely repair and maintenance. • Improving the plant lay out. • Multiple shifts, night shifts.
Raw Material	• Scouting for alternative raw materials. • Re designing the product. • Product modification. • To reduce intake of scarce raw material.
Labor	• Overtime working. • Proper incentive schemes. • Training of labor to improve efficiency. • Replacing labor intensive technology with capital intensive technology.
Power	• Installing captive power unit. • Diesel generator for power supply. • Low power consumption devices.

Factors to be considered while preparing Production Budget are as follows:

- Inventory policy of the firm: The inventory standard should be laid down so that there is neither surplus nor shortage of goods.
- Sales requirements: The quantity of goods to be produced depends largely on the quantity of goods to be sold. Hence, preparation of sales budget precedes production budget.
- Production stability: In order to have stability in employment, better use of plant facility and reduction of costs, the production should be evenly spread throughout the budget period.
- Key factors: Key factors should be identified and proper preventive measures should be taken to minimize their adverse impact.
- Time taken in production process: The production should commence depending upon the time it takes the factory to translate raw material into finished goods.

Production Cost Budget

Production budget is the key to the Production Cost Budget. After determining the volume of production, it is desired to determine the cost of producing this output. Just as cost of production comprises of material, labor and overhead, similarly production cost budget comprises of materials cost budget, direct labor cost budget and factory overhead budget.

Material Budget

A material budget specifies the expected quantities of each raw material required for the budgeted production. Materials used in the production process could be direct or indirect. The material budget includes only direct material and the indirect materials are considered in the factory overhead budget. The material budget can be divided into two parts:

- Material Usage Budget which tells us the total raw material required to be used in the production process in terms of quantity/value.
- Material Purchase Budget which tells us the raw material required to be purchased for producing the required output in terms of quantity/value.

The material budget could be expressed in physical terms but when prices of materials are also considered then we can ascertain the cost also. The material budget helps purchasing department to prepare purchase schedule to enable uninterrupted delivery of materials for production. It helps finance managers to determine finances required to meet the production targets. Factors to be considered while preparing materials budget are as follows:

- Production Budget: The budgeted production will determine how much materials will be required for producing required output.
- Prices of raw material: To determine the cost of raw material, quantity of raw material is multiplied by its price.
- Standard usage: In case, raw material requirements can be standardized, the budget can be prepared precisely. Standard usage refers to input- output ratio i.e. how many units of material is used in producing one unit of output. If it is not possible to work out standardized raw material requirements, then percentage of raw material to total cost of product should be calculated on the basis of historical data and this ratio can be used as a basis for ascertaining material cost.
- Normal loss/wastage in the production process: The material budget should also consider what percentage of raw material normally gets wasted in the production process. Efforts should be taken to keep normal loss to minimum.
- Inventory Policy: The re order level, Economic Order Quantity, the desired level of minimum stock and maximum inventory, operating inventory, closing inventory – all have bearing on material cost budget.

Direct Labor Budget

This budget gives the estimates of direct labor requirements essential for carrying out the budgeted output. This budget is devised to ensure that the required number of employees of relevant grades and suitable skills are available at the right time. This budget considers only the direct labor while the indirect labor is included in the factory overhead budget. Direct labor budget may be expressed in physical terms (labor hours) but when wage rates are also available then we can ascertain the cost also. The Direct Labor Budget may be divided into two parts:

- Direct Labor Requirement Budget which specifies the total direct labor required for carrying the estimated production in terms of quantity or value.
- Direct Labor Procurement Budget which specifies the additional workers required to be recruited for carrying out the required production.

Direct Labor Budget enables the Personnel Department to recruit the required number of workers of suitable skills and provide them necessary training. It is also used for preparing the Cost of Sales Budget and Cash Budget. Factors to be considered while preparing Labor Budget are as follows:

- Production Budget: The budgeted production will determine how much of labor hours are required.
- Wage rate: To determine the cost of labor, the labor hours are multiplied by the average wage rate per labor hour. Also overtime wage rate should be considered if workers work more than normal hours.
- Standard labor usage: When labor usage can be standardized, the budget can be prepared precisely. Standard usage refers to input- output ratio i.e. how many labor hours are required to produce one unit of output. If it is not possible to standardize labor requirements, then percentage of labor cost to total cost of production should be calculated on the basis of historical data and this ratio can be used as a basis for ascertaining labor cost.

  Labor cost = Labor cost per unit × No. of budgeted production.

  Labor cost per unit = Number of labor hours required per unit of output × wage rate per labor hour.

Factory Overhead Budget

This Budget sets out the estimated cost of indirect material, indirect labor and indirect factory expenses during the budget period. Steps to be taken to prepare Factory Overhead Budget are as follows:

- Classification of overheads into fixed, variable and semi variable expenses: Fixed overheads are those which remain constant irrespective of level of activity e.g. property tax, supervisory salary, depreciation etc. Variable overheads are those which vary with the level of activity. E.g. supplies, repairs etc. Semi variable overheads are those which are partly variable and partly fixed. Fixed overheads can be estimated with a fair degree of accuracy on the basis of past experience. Variable overheads are estimated on the basis of scheduled production and operating conditions in the budget period.

- Departmentalization of expenses: The expenses should be classified department wise. This would help in determining how much expenses are incurred by various departments and the departmental heads can be held accountable.
- Determining the level of activity: The level of activity will be determined on the basis of production schedule. Once the level of activity is determined, per unit overhead rate will be computed and applied on goods to find their cost of production.

Ending Inventory Budget

Ending Inventory Budget shows the quantity as well as value of the closing inventory of the direct materials as well as finished goods of the company. These figures are used in the preparation of budgeted balance sheet of the organization. If varieties of direct materials are used, then category wise break up should be shown. Similarly, if numbers of products are manufactured then product wise break up should be shown. The quantities must be multiplied by the applicable rate to determine the cost of material in the inventory and cost of finished goods in inventory. The specimen of Ending Inventory Budget is given below:

Table: Specimen Cost of Ending Inventory Budget.

ALPHA COMPANY LIMITED		
ENDING INVENTORY BUDGET FOR THE PERIOD ________________		
	Applicable Rate	Cost (Rest.)
Direct Material Inventories Material X Material Y		
Finished Goods Inventory Product A Product B		
Total cost of ending inventory		

Cost of Goods Sold Budget

Cost of Goods Sold Budget shows the budgeted manufacturing cost (direct material, direct labor and factory overhead) adjusted for beginning and ending inventory of finished goods. This budget can be prepared only after material cost budget, labor cost budget, and factory overhead budget and ending inventory budget have been prepared.

This budget uses the estimates produced by the above said budgets to determine the budgeted cost of goods sold. Specimen of cost of goods sold budget is given below:

Table: Specimen Cost of Goods Sold Budget.

ALPHA COMPANY LIMITED	
Cost of Goods Sold Budget for the year ending ________	
Particulars	Amount ($)
a) Cost of direct material used (from material budget)	
b) Cost of direct labor used (from labor budget)	
c) Cost of factory overheads (from factory overheads budget)	
Budgeted total manufacturing costs (a) + (b) + (c)	
+ Beginning finished goods (from production budget)	
- Ending finished goods (from ending inventory budget)	
Budgeted cost of goods sold	

Selling Expenses Budget

This budget includes all expenses relating to selling, advertising, distribution and delivery of goods to the customers. Selling expenses includes salesmen salaries, sales office establishment expenses, travelling expenses, commissions etc. Advertising expenses include expenses relating to publicity, samples, advertisement expenses in journals, press, radio and television etc. Distribution expenses include transportation, freight charges, packaging charges, warehousing charges, insurance etc. This budget is based on sales budget and is prepared on the basis of past experience, advertising policies, research programs, market analysis etc. It is generally prepared territory wise by the sales manager of each territory. The costs are segregated into fixed and variable cost. Specimen of selling expenses budget is as under:

Table: Specimen Selling Expenses Budget.

ALPHA COMPANY LIMITED		
SELLING EXPENES BUDGET FOR THE PERIOD ENDING ________		
Items	Cost	Total Cost
Variable Selling Expenses • Sales Commission • Salary & Wages • Advertising • Travelling • Package Charges		
Fixed Selling Expenses • Ware housing charges • Advertising • Marketing managers salary • Depreciation		
Total Selling Expenses		

Administrative Expenses Budget

This budget covers the expenditure related to management, legal, financial, accounting and administrative activities of the organization. Formulation of this budget poses problems such as:

- Some expenses such as engineering cost, purchasing cost are such as they can be classified under both production as well as administrative costs. So, difficulty arises in deciding their correct classification.
- It is difficult to identify the persons responsible for the incurrence and control of these costs.

Administrative expenses could be directors' remuneration, legal charges, audit fees, office expenses, rent, interest, taxes, postage etc. Generally these expenses are fixed and are shown in the budget under different catagories. Specimen of Administrative Expenses Budget is given as under:

Table: Specimen Administrative Expenses Budget.

ALPHA COMPANY LIMITED		
ADMINISTRATIVE EXPENES BUDGET FOR THE PERIOD ENDING ___________		
Items	Cost	Total Cost
Variable Administrative Expenses Supplies		
Fixed Administrative Expenses Directors' fees Legal charges Salaries Rent Insurance		
Total Administrative Expenses		

Budgeted Income Statement Budget

A Budgeted Income Statement is prepared by using estimates provided by individuals operating budgets such as sales budget, cost of goods sold budget, selling expenses budget and administrative expenses budget. This budget shows the expected income that would be generated in the organization in the budgeted period. If tax rates are known income before and after taxes can also be ascertained. Specimen of Budgeted Income Statement is given below:

Table: Specimen Budgeted Income Statement.

ALPHA COMPANY LIMITED	
BUDGETED INCOME STATEMENT FOR THE PERIOD ENDING ___________	
Sales	Amount

Less: Cost of Goods Sold	
Gross Margin	
Less: Selling Expenses Admn. Expenses	
Income before taxes	
Less: Taxes on income	
Income after taxes	

Financial Budget

Capital Expenditure

Capital expenditures refer to funds that are used by a company for the purchase, improvement, or maintenance of long-term assets to improve the efficiency or capacity of the company. Long-term assets are usually physical, fixed and non-consumable assets such as property, equipment, or infrastructure, and that have a useful life of more than one accounting period. Also known as CapEx or capital expenses, capital expenditures include the purchase of items such as new equipment, machinery, land, plant, buildings or warehouses, furniture and fixtures, business vehicles, software, or intangible assets such as a patent or license.

The expenditure amounts for an accounting period are disclosed in the cash flow statement. Capital expenditures normally have a substantial effect on the short-term and long-term financial standing of an organization. Therefore, making wise CapEx decisions is of critical importance to the financial health of a company. Many companies usually try to maintain the levels of their historical capital expenditure to show investors that the managers of the company are continuing to invest in the growth of the business.

Types of Capital Expenditures

There are normally two forms of capital expenditures: Expenses to maintain levels of operation present within the company and expenses that will enable an increase in future growth. A capital expense can either be tangible, such as a machine, or intangible, such as a patent. Both intangible and tangible capital expenditures are usually considered assets since they can be sold when there is a need. It is important to note that funds spent on repair or in conducting continuing, normal maintenance on assets is not considered capital expenditure and should be expensed on the income statement whenever it is incurred as repair and maintenance expense.

Importance of Capital Expenditures

Decisions on how much to invest in capital expenditures can often be extremely vital decisions made by an organization. They are important because of the following reasons:

- Long-term Effects: The effect of capital expenditure decisions usually extends into the future. The range of current production or manufacturing activities is mainly a result of past capital expenditures. Similarly, the current decisions on capital expenditure will have a major influence on the future activities of the company. Capital investment decisions are a driver of the direction of the organization. The long-term strategic goals, as well as the budgeting process of a company, need to be in place before authorization of capital expenditures.

- Irreversibility: Capital expenditures are often difficult to reverse without the company incurring losses. Most forms of capital equipment are customized to meet specific company requirements and needs. The market for used capital equipment is generally very poor.

- High Initial Costs: Capital expenditures are characteristically very expensive, especially for companies in industries such as production, manufacturing, telecom, utilities, and oil exploration. Capital investments in physical assets like buildings, equipment, or property offer the potential of providing benefits in the long run but will need a huge monetary outlay initially, and much greater than regular operating outlays. Capital costs also tend to rise with advancing technology.

- Depreciation: Capital expenditures have an initial increase in the asset accounts of an organization. However, once capital assets start being put in service, depreciation begins, and they decrease in value throughout their useful lives.

Challenges with Capital Expenditures

Even though capital expenditure decisions are very critical, they create more complexity:

- Measurement Problems: The accounting process of identifying, measuring, and estimating the costs relating to capital expenditures may be quite complicated.
- Unpredictability: Organizations making large investments in capital assets hope to generate predictable outcomes. However, such outcomes are not guaranteed, and losses may be incurred. The costs and benefits of capital expenditure decisions are usually characterized by a lot of uncertainty. Even the best forecasters sometimes make mistakes. During financial planning, organizations need to account for risk to mitigate potential losses, even though it is not possible to eliminate them.
- Temporal Spread: The costs, as well as benefits related to the capital expenditure, are usually stretched over a relatively long period of time for both industrial projects and infrastructure projects. Such a temporal spread leads to problems in discount rate estimation and the establishment of equivalence.

Efficient Capital Expenditure Budgeting Practices

Major capital projects involving huge amounts of money, as well as capital expenditures, can get out of control quite easily if mishandled and end up costing an organization a lot of money. However, with effective planning, the right tools, and good project management, that doesn't have to be the case. Here are some tips that will ensure that the budgeting of capital expenditure is efficient.

- Structure before You Start: Capital expenditure budgets need adequate preparations before commencement. Otherwise, they might get out of control. Before starting a project, you need to find the scope of the project, work out realistic deadlines, and ensure that the whole plan is reviewed and approved. It is at this stage that you should think about how many internal resources will be required by the project, including manpower, materials, finances, and services. To have a more accurate budget, you should have more detail going into the project.

- Think Long-Term: At the start of your capital expenditure project, you need to decide whether you will purchase the capital asset with debt or set aside existing funds for the purchase. Saving money for the purchase usually implies that you will have to wait for a while before getting the asset you need. However, borrowing money leads to increased debt and may also create problems for your borrowing ability in the future. Both choices can be good for your company, and different choices might be needed for different projects.
- Use Good Budgeting Software: From the beginning of the project, you should choose a reliable, practical program to manage the budgeting. The type of budgeting software you choose will depend on such things as the scale of the project, speed of the program, and risk of error.
- Capture Accurate Data: Accurate data is very crucial if you want to manage capital projects efficiently. To create a realistic budget and generate valuable reports, you need to gather reliable information.
- Levels of Detail Should Be Optimal: Trying to put in too much detail will result in too much time being spent in gathering information to make the budget, which may be outdated by the time the budget is finished. However, too little detail will make the budget vague and, therefore, less useful. The right optimal balance needs to be found.
- Form Clear Policies: Since the management of capital expenditure in a large organization may involve numerous employees, departments, or even regions, clear policies for everyone to follow should be put in place to put the budget on track.

Example of Capital Expenditures

Below is an accounting example of Amazon's capital expenditures in 2015, 2016, and 2017.

AMAZON.COM, INC. CONSOLIDATED STATEMENTS OF CASH FLOWS (in millions)						
	Year Ended December 31,					
	2015		2016		2017	
CASH AND CASH EQUIVALENTS, BEGINNING OF PERIOD	$	4557	$	15,890	$	19,334

OPERATING ACTIVITIES:						
Net income		596		2,371		3,033
Adjustments to reconcile net income to net cash from operating activities:						
Depreciation of property and equipment, including internal-use software and website development, and other amortization, including capitalized content costs		6,281		8,116		11,478
Stock-based compensation		2,119		2,975		4215
Other operating expense, net		155		160		202
Other expense (income), net		250		(20)		(292)
Deferred income taxes		81		(246)		(29)
Changes in operating assets and liabilities:						
Inventories		(2,187)		(1.426)		(3,583)
Accounts receivable, net and other		(1,755)		(3,367)		(4,786)
Accounts payable		4,294		5,030		7,175
Accrued expenses and other		913		1,724		283
Unearned revenue		1,292		1,955		738
Net cash provided by (used in) operating activities		12,039		17,272		18,434
INVESTING ACTIVITIES:						
Purchases of property and equipment, including internal-use software and website development		(5,387)		(7,804)		(11,955)
Proceeds from property and equipment incentives		798		1,067		1,897
Acquisitions, net of cash acquired, and other		(795)		(116)		(13,972)
Sales and maturities of marketable securities		3,025		4,733		9.988
Purchases of marketable securities		(4,091)		(7,756)		(13,777)
Net cash provided by (used in) investing activities		(6.450)		(9.876)		(27,819)

What Amazon lists on its Cash Flow Statement as "Purchases of property and equipment, including internal-use software and website development" is its capital expenditures for the periods. On the cash flow statement, these investments are listed as negative numbers (outflows of cash), so in 2017 the company invested $11,955 million.

Research and Development Budget

The assembly of an R&D budget is a complicated process, often involving inputs from multiple organizations and/or departments. It also involves getting approvals from supervisors, from supervisors' supervisors, and from other people with whom you may not work outside budgeting times. There are multiple factors involved in creating an R&D budget, from revenue growth to operating costs to capital requirements and not least of all administrative support. Most components in an R&D budget require input from other areas where people have specific expertise. That expertise is essential for obtaining accurate data that will hold up to final "down the road" analyses and management approval. Guesswork and rough estimates will not work in the creation of a detailed R&D budget, no matter the size of the organization or the bottom-line final budget.

A starting point for an R&D budget is an evaluation of previous R&D budget submissions, an investigation of the comments provided at the time, and the final results and analysis. There is no need to recreate the wheel–previous budgets are an excellent place to start. A secondary area to evaluate is a breakdown of the overall components. The capital requirements, for example, are often created by specific divisions within the overall organization. These divisions will have details on how monies for specific capital are obtained, which often depends on the amount of the allocation required. They will also know how the capital is itemized and labeled for legal and tax purposes. A whole new research lab is entirely different than a magnetic resonance imaging instrument, yet both are large capital items that require extensive manufacturing and research engineering support.

Some organizations are more capital intensive than others and often the capital budget will be written separately from the R&D budget. Except for specific situations, such as instrumentation, what is capitalized and what is not capitalized should be left to those who are supremely experienced in it, as the rules and regulations can change annually. Capital also is defined differently between organizations, but it is generally one of the three factors of production, the other two being labor and land.

Other mostly independent financial factors in the R&D budget such as revenue growth, operating costs, inflation, and the general economy's effects on the R&D budget–are often delegated or heavily supported by the organization's financial and accounting divisions. The organization's R&D budget is often an interactive "live" document which requires extensive discussions between all parties, especially among R&D personnel who most-often have "corporate" ownership of the document and budget. Manufacturing, for example, is often responsible for pilot production of a new device or process. Yet, that function will rely on technical R&D personnel to provide detailed information on new materials, energy requirements, safety issues, regulatory concerns, sustainability potential, and legal ownership, among many other items that the manufacturing personnel (or most other organizational divisions) will not understand or be able to accurately address.

Always a concern for R&D is the shortening life cycles of technologies. R&D organizations have consistently been accused of taking the shorter route to new development because this path is easier and requires fewer resources. This premise may be valid, but the alternative working on technologies that are more complex has the disadvantage that once developed, they may be out-of-date technologically and no longer competitive. The "half-life" of new technologies shortening and researchers must factor that reality into their research plans. Another concerning facet of new technological development is that new technology, once fully developed and put into production, may have unforeseen negative effects or failure-modes. Researchers are notorious for pushing the limits of materials and stretching design capabilities. Aging infrastructures are another R&D concern, and here economics often rears its ugly head. Often failures result from a lack of maintenance and inspections, as in bridge structures.

Research and Development Funding Effects

Surely, technology issues can affect R&D funding, especially when the technology development is not completed on time or within expected limits. New technologies are the biggest issue that could affect R&D funding. Close behind are the organization's R&D strategy and overall growth. All three, individually or in concert, could work to boost R&D funding. When preparing an R&D budget, contingency plans or budget allocations should be provided for losses of R&D funding resources that were not expected or planned. A failed piece of essential equipment, the closure of a valued supplier, or the disruption of a needed facility can all be expensive-to-remedy losses for the R&D work flow.

Cash Budget

Cash budget is a written estimate of a firm's future cash position. It predicts for some future period the cash receipts from different sources, cash disbursements for different purposes and the resulting cash position generally on a monthly basis as the budget period develops. It is, thus, a formal presentation of-expected circular flow of cash through the business. The usual forecast period of a cash budget is one year broken down by monthly periods or weekly periods. This allows incorporation of seasonal variations in cash flow. When cash flows are relatively stable, the finance manager may prepare budget for full one year period. When the outlook is very uncertain, he may have to be satisfied with a projection for only quarterly.

Cash budget is different from income statement. The cash budget depicts movement of cash whereas the projected income statement presents account for all sources of income to be tapped and for all classes of expenses to be incurred during a stated period and shows how much profit, if any, is expected to be earned in a future period. Cash budget consists of all expected inflows of cash including income and non-income sources such as receipts from sale of stocks and bonds and receipts from sale of fixed assets. The later items (receipts from non-income sources) do not appear in the income statement. Likewise, cash budget provides for all types of cash outgo including payments of expenses accrued in the prior periods, the forecast period, or the subsequent periods (prepayments) or as payments not immediately related to expenses such as the purchase of fixed assets or dividend distribution to the stockholders. Disbursements in respect of purchase of fixed assets or dividend distribution would not find place in the income statement. Similarly, there are certain items that would appear in the income statement but are not included in the cash budget.

All appropriations such as depreciation and amortization of patents appear only in the anticipated income statement and are not shown in cash budget. In view of these reasons, cash budget should not be confused with income statement. The cash budget is also different from other budgets, in that the cash budget is concerned with the timing of receipts and disbursements of cash whereas the other budgets are concerned with the timing of transactions themselves. The cash budget consists of three parts:

- The forecast of cash inflows.
- The forecast of cash outflows.
- The forecast of cash balance.

Principal Objectives of Cash Budget

Cash budget in a firm is prepared to accomplish the following objectives:

- To project firm's cash position in future period.
- To predict cash surplus or deficit for the ensuing months.
- To permit planning for financing in advance of need. By indicating when cash will be required, the budget helps the management to arrange in advance bank loans or other short-term credits, to prepare for a sale of securities or to make other preparations for new financing.
- To help in selection of proper source of financing cash requirements of the firm.
- To permit proper utilisation of idle cash.
- To maintain adequate balance between cash and working capital, sales, investments and loans.
- To exercise control over cash expenditure by limiting the spending of various departments.

Utility of Cash Budget

Cash budget is an extremely important tool available in the hands of a finance manager for planning fund requirements and for controlling cash position in the firm.

As a planning device, cash budget helps the finance manager to know in advance the cash position of the firm in different time periods. The cash budget indicates in which months there will be cash surfeit and in which months the firm will experience cash drain and by how much. With the help of this information finance manager can draw up a programme for financing cash requirements. It indicates the most opportune time to undertake the financing process. There will be two advantages if the finance manager knows in advance as to when additional funds will be required. First, funds will be available in hand when needed and there will be no idle funds.

In the absence of the cash budget it may be difficult to determine cash requirements in different months. If cash required is not available in time it will entail the firm in a precarious position. The firm's output is reduced because of imbalance in financial structure and the rate of return consequently declines. If the firm is marginal, the decline in profits could lead to disaster. Further, it would be difficult for the firm to meet its commitments and would consequently lose its credit standing. A firm with a poor credit standing stands little chance of success. With the help of cash budget finance manager can determine precisely the months in which there will be cash surplus. Nevertheless, a reasonable amount of cash adds to a firm's debt paying power of the firm, holding excess cash for any period of time is largely a waste of resource yielding no return. This will result in the decline in profits.

The cash budget offsets the possibility of decline in profits because the finance manager in that case will invest idle cash in marketable securities. Thus, with the help of the cash budget, finance manager can maintain high liquidity without jeopardizing the firm's profitability. The cash budget, besides indicating cash requirements, reflects the length of time for which funds will be needed. This will help the finance manager to decide the most likely source from which the funds can be obtained. A firm which stands in need of funds for a short-term duration will use a source different from the one requiring funds for a long time.

Bank loan is most appropriate source to cover temporary cash requirements while permanent funds requirements are met by selling stock and bonds. If long-term cash requirements are met through short-term funds, this will leave the company in considerable financial predicament. The firm will have to either renew the loans to make it long-term or an entirely new loan must be negotiated. In either case the negotiations are on a much shorter notice than the original loan and the renewal or new loan will very likely be made with less favourable terms. Further, planning for cash may engender the confidence of suppliers of cash and credit to such an extent that they are more likely to grant loans on easier terms.

Usually bankers are loath to lend to companies which do not follow good managerial practices with respect to their financial requirements. However, when they grant loans they usually charge higher interest rates and place restrictive clauses in the loan contract. When funds are obtained for period longer than necessary, the cost of capital will go up resulting in decline in profits. Cash budget is also conducive to the formulation of sound dividend policy for the firm. Availability of adequate amount of cash is necessary for dividend payments. A firm may experience cash drain despite high earnings because of the fact that bulk of sales was effected through credit.

Even if the firm has sufficient cash in hand it may not be able to pay high dividends because of the need to repay loan or retire debt, to carry inventories and to meet other emergent requirements. Keeping the firm's cash position in mind finance manager can reach suitable dividend decision.

Cash budget is also a useful device to establish a sound basis for current control of the cash position. Cash budget sets the limitation on cash expenditure which must be observed by all those whose activities involve cash disbursements. With the help of cash budget reports which are prepared periodically finance manager can compare actual receipts and expenditure with the estimated figures.

With these reports finance manager can find out deviations and study reasons for variation and finally take steps to remedy the variations. But this tool is not devoid of its limitations. Errors in estimation anywhere along the logline of budget that must be prepared prior to the cash budget will obviously create inaccuracies in the cash forecast. This means that cash budget should be reviewed from time to time against actual performance so that corrections can be made and plans adjusted accordingly.

Another drawback of the cash budget is that it fails to indicate time segments of cash flows. For example, if company has planned to invest money in short-term securities in the month of April, the budget would not indicate when in April. Will it be early or late April? It is quite possible that the company could run out of cash altogether by April 10 leaving it without adequate cash balance with which to meet wages bills. Thus, the finance manager may find it useful to prepare more than one cash budget depending on how critical he feels his firm's cash position is. He may prepare a weekly forecast for the next 30 to 60 days, another for one year month by month and yet another long-range forecast for several years. This points up another reason for close administration of the cash budget.

Difference Between Cash Budget and Cash Flow Statement

Cash Budget:

- Purpose: Cash Budget reveals the surplus or deficit of cash for a particular period while carrying out planned activities and shows the ways of sources of cash in case of deficit, and ways of investing the idle cash, if there is a surplus of cash.
- Nature: It highlights the future cash position from the receipts and payments of cash under different heads for the budget period to indicate surplus or deficit.

- Applications: Cash Budget directly helps the management to know the estimated cash position and thereby the management may take important decisions in financial matters.
- Duration: Cash Budget is usually prepared for a short period, viz., daily, weekly, fortnightly, monthly, half-yearly etc.
- Basis of Preparation: Cash Budget actually depends on various functional budgets, viz., Purchase Budget, Sales Budget, Capital Expenditure Budget, for its preparation. Moreover, some useful information is also needed for various receipts and payments.

Cash Flow Statement:

- Purpose: Cash Flow Statement reveals the changes in cash position for various activities from the beginning to the end of the period by way of sources and applications.
- Nature: It highlights the analysis of various inflows and outflows of cash on the basis of past information.
- Applications: Cash Flow Statement helps the various interested persons relating to financial position viz., creditors, shareholders, bankers, investors etc. and in various areas of management viz., operating activities, investing activities and financing activities.
- Duration: Cash Flow Statement is prepared for a long period, usually yearly.
- Basis of Preparation: Cash Flow Statement is prepared on the basis of opening and closing balance of cash plus funds from operations and some other useful information relating to sources and applications of cash.

How to Prepare Cash Budget

There are three main components necessary for creating a cash budget.

- Time period.
- Desired cash position.
- Estimated sales and expenses.

Table: Here is an example of a cash budget for a small business:

Small Business Cash Budget			
For the three months ending March 31, 200X			
	January	February	March
Beginning Cash Balance	$15,000	-$13,500	$20,000

Expected Cash Receipts:			
Cash sales	20,000	25,000	30,000
Collection of accounts receivable	45,000	55,000	70,000
Other income	0	0	5,000
Total Cash	$80,000	$66,500	$125,000
Expected Cash Payments:			
Raw materials (or inventory)	50,000	11,000	5,000
Payroll	10,400	10,400	10,400
Other direct expenses	2,000	2,000	2,000
Advertising	10,000	0	0
Selling expenses	6,000	8,000	6,000
Administrative expenses	4,500	4,500	4,500
Plant and equipment expenditures	10,000	10,000	10,000
Other payments	600	600	600
Total Cash Expenses	$93,500	$46,500	$38,500
Ending Cash Balance	-$13,500*	$20,000*	$86,500

Time Period

The first decision to make when preparing a cash budget is to decide the period of time for which your budget will apply. That is, are you preparing a budget for the next three months, six months, twelve months or some other period? In this Business Builder, we will be preparing a three-month budget. However, the instructions given are applicable to any time period you might select.

Cash Position

The amount of cash you wish to keep on hand will depend on the nature of your business, the predictability of accounts receivable, and the probability of fast-happening opportunities (or unfortunate occurrences) that may require you to have a significant reserve of cash. You may want to consider your cash reserve in terms of a certain number of days' sales. Your budgeting process will help you to determine if, at the end of the period, you have an adequate cash reserve.

Estimated Sales and Expenses

The fundamental concept of a cash budget is estimating all future cash receipts and cash expenditures that will take place during the time period. The most important estimate you will make, however, is an estimate of sales. Once this is decided, the rest of the cash budget can fall into place. For example, if an increase in sales of 10 percent is desired and expected, various other accounts must be adjusted in your budget. Raw materials, inventory and the costs of goods sold must be revised to reflect the increase in sales. In addition, you must ask yourself if any additions need to be made to selling or general and administrative expenses, or can the increased sales be handled by current excess capacity. Also, how will the increase in sales affect payroll and overtime expenditures?

Instead of increasing every expense item by 10 percent, serious consideration needs to be given to certain economies of scale that might develop. In other words, perhaps, a supplier offers a discount if you increase the quantities in which you buy a certain item; or, perhaps, the increase in sales can be easily accommodated by the current sales force. All of these types of considerations must be taken into account before you start budgeting. Each type of expense must be evaluated for its potential to increase or decrease. Your estimates should be based on your experience running your business and on your goals for your business over the time frame for which the budget is being created. At a minimum, the following categories of expected cash receipts and expected cash payments should be considered:

- Expected Cash Receipts:
    - Cash balance.
    - Cash sales.
    - Collections of accounts receivable.
    - Other income.
- Expected Cash Expenses:
    - Raw material (inventory).
    - Payroll.
- Other Direct Expenses:
    - Advertising.
    - Selling expenses.
    - Administrative expense.
    - Plant and equipment expenditures.
    - Other payments.

Expected Cash Receipts

- Cash balance: The cash balance is your cash on hand. This includes what is in your checking accounts, savings accounts, petty cash and any other cash accounts that you might have.

- Cash sales: After arriving at a base figure of cash sales, it must be adjusted for any trade or other discounts and for possible returns. The base level of sales (and of accounts receivable) will be determined by the company's projections, goals and past experience.
- Collections of accounts receivable: After a base level of accounts receivable is established (based on sales projections), it must be adjusted to reflect the amount that will actually be paid during the time period. Typical adjustments for a small business might be to assume that 90 percent of accounts receivable will be collected in the quarter in which the sales occur, nine percent will be collected in the following quarter, and one percent will remain uncollectible. Of course, past experience will be the most reliable indicator for making these adjustments.
- Other income: Your cash position may be affected positively by income other than sales. Perhaps there are investments, dividends, or a loan that will be introducing cash to the company during the time period. These types of cash sources are referred to as "other income."

Expected Cash Expenses

- Raw materials (inventory): For small business retailers and manufacturers, the largest cash expense is usually the amount spent for inventory or raw materials. Again, past experience will be your best indicator of future cash outlays. But don't forget to factor in any necessary increases to keep up with projected sales. You may also want to consult with your suppliers as to whether any pricing changes are expected.
- Payroll: Salaries are commonly the second largest expense item during an accounting period. Don't forget to include estimates for all appropriate local, state, and federal taxes.

Other Direct Expenses

Use this line item for any additional expense that does not fit conveniently under the other headings. If you are making payments on a loan, include it here.

- Advertising: The role of advertising varies by type of business. If you are projecting an increase in sales, is there an accompanying marketing or advertising campaign? These costs must be budgeted. Include any expenses for print (brochures, mailers, and newspaper ads), radio, or other advertising services.
- Selling expenses: Typical selling expenses include salaries and commissions for sales personnel and sales office expenses. However, this line item can also include any traveling or other sales-related expense not covered elsewhere.

- Administrative expenses: General office expenses are included here. This will include your utilities, telephone, copying and day-to-day office expenses. Unless big changes are underway, past experience will guide you in evaluating future administrative expenses.
- Plant and equipment: Cash payments for equipment loans, mortgages, repairs, or other upkeep should be included here. Past experience will, again, be your guide.
- Other payments: If there are any cash payments you expect to make that are not covered in the above listing, include them here. (If they are repeatable, you may consider adding a separate line item.) However, typically, interest payments and taxes fall here.

Step 1: Create a cash flow budget for your company for a three–month period. Here is a cash flow budget worksheet for a small business:

Cash Flow Budget Worksheet				
For the three months ending March 31, 200X				
	January	February	March	Totals
Beginning Cash Balance				
Cash Inflows (Income):				
Accts. Rec. Collections				
Loan Proceeds				
Sales & Receipts				
Other:				
Total Cash Inflows				
Available Cash Balance				
Cash Outflows (Expenses):				
Advertising				
Bank Service Charges				
Credit Card Fees				
Delivery				
Health Insurance				
Insurance				
Interest				
Inventory Purchases				
Miscellaneous				
Office				
Payroll				
Payroll Taxes				
Professional Fees				

Rent or Lease				
Subscriptions & Dues				
Supplies				
Taxes & Licenses				
Utilities & Telephone				
Other:				
Subtotal				
Other Cash Outflows:				
Capital Purchases				
Loan Principal				
Owner's Draw				
Other:				
Subtotal				
Total Cash Outflows				
Ending Cash Balance				

How to Analyze a Cash Budget?

The preparation of a cash budget is only the first step toward good financial management. The next step is to analyze to see how close the company is performing to expectations. Have any unexpected cash outflows occurred? If so, is the company's financial position seriously affected? A simple method for monitoring the cash budget is to prepare a budget versus actual report of actual and budgeted expenses every month. This type of report consists of four columns. The first column shows the budgeted amounts, the second column shows actual company performance, and the third and fourth columns show the difference in terms of dollars and percent.

Step 2: If the data is available, construct a budget versus actual report for your business. Below is a sample month-end budget versus actual report for the fictional Turtle Company:

Budget vs. Actual Report			
	Budget	Actual	% Variance
Cash Balance	$5,000	$5,000	0%
Cash Receipts:			
Cash sales	20,000	22,000	110%
Collection of accounts receivable	15,000	13,500	90%
Other income	0	0	0%
Total Cash	$40,000	$40,500	101%
Expected Cash Payments:			
Raw materials (or inventory)	15,000	15,000	0%
Payroll	7,200	9,400	130%

Other direct expenses	500	500	0%
Advertising	500	1,000	200%
Selling expense	1,500	1,400	93%
Administrative expense	500	500	0%
Plant and equipment expenditures	5,000	7,500	150%
Other payments	0	0	0%
Total cash expenses	30,200	35,300	116%
Ending Cash Balance	$9,800	$5,200	53%

Cash expenses for payroll, advertising and plant and equipment exceeded the budgeted amounts for the Turtle Company. And because the company analyzes these figures monthly, changes can be made before the increased expenses become unmanageable. The use of a budget versus actual report allows owners to pinpoint how actual cash inflows and outflows vary from expectations and to make adjustments.

Budgeted Balance Sheet

Budgeted Balance Sheet is similar to a regular balance sheet and has the same line items as well. The only difference between the two is that the budgeted BS is for a future period. In other words, we can say it is the projection of the balance sheet for a future period. One generally prepares it at the beginning of a financial year. The company uses the balance sheet of the last year as the base for the budgeted BS and then makes relevant adjustments. Along with the previous year's balance sheet, a company also uses different budgets and budgeted income statement for its preparation.

Budgeted BS involves several calculations, and thus, one needs to be careful while preparing it. The accuracy of the balance sheet depends on the calculations, as well as the inputs and the base assumptions. One primary objective of preparing this balance sheet is to verify if the financial projections are at a reasonable and achievable level or not. Further, it also helps to identify scenarios that are not financially feasible, such as a large amount of Debt. A company should usually prepare a budgeted BS for every period for which it prepares a budget, and not just for the ending period. It would assist the company in determining any discrepancies in cash flows and the steps needed to address it.

Importance of Budgeted Balance Sheet

The following are the reasons why management will want to prepare a budgeted BS:

- It helps to identify any unfavourable financial transactions that a company may want to get rid of.
- It also ensures the mathematical accuracy of other schedules or inputs.
- A company can use it to calculate different ratios.

- For deciding future activities and actions, it becomes a guiding document.
- It can also trigger the areas where the company needs to work or change its strategies.
- It becomes the base for revisions or enhancements in the working capital limits.

Budgeted Balance Sheet and Master Budget

For every upcoming period, management usually prepares a master budget. It, in turn, includes many smaller budgets, such as sales, production, Cash, and more. After a company completes the master budget, it uses the master budget as an input for the comprehensive financial plan. In simple words, this comprehensive financial plan is nothing but the projections of the financial statements to know how the company would fare and how the financial status would look like at the end of the next financial period. For this, the company prepares the budgeted income or profit/loss statement, as well as the balance sheet. These two statements show the impact of all other budgets on the financial standing of the firm if the estimates meet the actual performance. One may also take it as a sanity check. Management wants to ensure if its plans are in-line with the long-term interest of the firm or not.

Let's take an example to know how the master budget and budgeted BS are related. Suppose in a production budget the manager includes a loan to buy new machinery. This new machinery will boost production while maintaining the cost, but will also increase the debt level. This debt level will reflect in the budgeted balance sheet, and then the management may decide if it wants to go ahead with it or not whether there is enough financial cushion available to take care of that extra loan. And whether the ROI of that machine is acceptable.

Steps to Prepare Budgeted Balance Sheet

Following are the steps to prepare a budgeted BS:

- Use Real Balance Sheet as Base: The first step is to take all the line items from the last years' real balance sheet.
- Collect the Data of All Budgets: The next step is to collect all the budgets that a company prepares at the start of the year. These budgets could be production budget, sales budget, cash budget, raw materials budget, salaries and wages budget, operating and financial expenses budget and more.
- Making Adjustments to Real Balance Sheet: Once we have all the data, including all the budgets and last year's balance sheet, we start to make adjustments. These adjustments are made to the real balance sheet using data from different budgets. For instance, we adjust last year's sales based on sales and production budget for the current year.

A company may also need to prepare schedules to overcome the complexities in preparing the budgets and budgeted BS and income statements. These schedules help with the calculation of accounts receivable, inventories, income tax, and more. Additionally, a company also needs to consider several policies such as tax, Credit, dividend, inventory, and more while finalizing the budgeted BS.

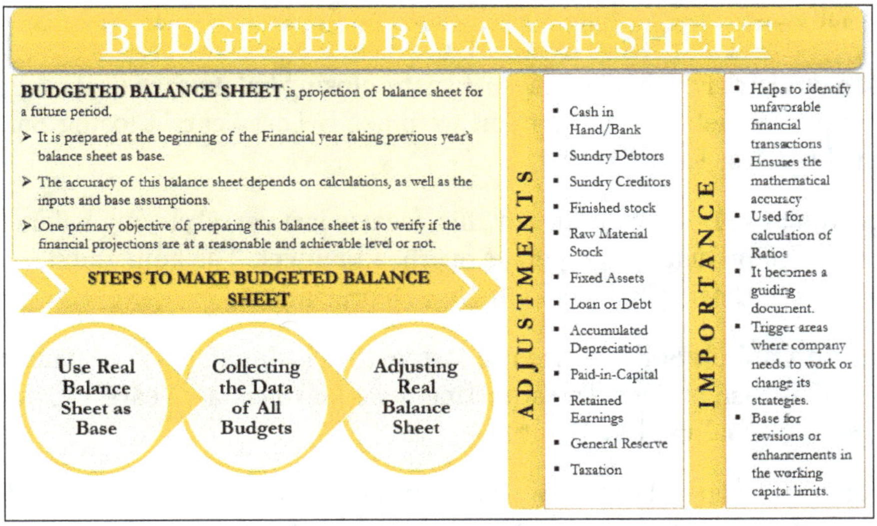

Adjustments

Under the steps to prepare the budgeted BS, the last step was to make adjustments. But, what adjustments one needs to make to the line items? Detailed below are some of the adjustments that a company needs to make to arrive at the budgeted BS:

- Cash in Hand/Bank: For this, we take the closing figure of Cash from the last year's real balance sheet and then use the cash budget to make the necessary adjustments.
- Sundry Debtors: For this, we use the closing balance and the data from the sales and cash budget. To get the balance we need Opening Debtors Balance plus New Credit Sale less Cash Received.
- Sundry Creditors: For this, we use their closing balance, as well as the purchase budget and cash budget. We use the following formula – Opening Creditors plus New Credit Purchases less New Payments Made.
- Finished stock: For calculating an estimate of the finished stock we use last years' closing balance, as well as the Production, Sales, and Cash Budgets. The adjustment we make is Opening Finished Stock plus New Production less New total Sales (Cash+ Credit).
- Raw Material Stock: For this, we use last years' closing balance, as well as

material, production, and Cash Budgets. The adjustment we make is Opening Raw Material Stock plus New Purchases (both Cash + Credit) less New Consumption.

- Fixed Assets: For this, we use last years' closing balance, as well as Cash Budget, Projected Plan Report, and Plant Utilization budget. The adjustment we make is Last Years' Closing Balance plus New Purchase less New Sale (Cost price).
- Loan or Debt: For this, we use last years' closing balance, as well as inputs from the cash budget. The adjustment we make is Last Years' Closing Balance plus New Loan less Repayments.
- Accumulated Depreciation: For this, we use last years' closing balance of accumulated depreciation, as well as overhead budget. The adjustment we make is Last Years' Closing Balance plus New Depreciation.
- Paid-in-Capital: For this, we use last years' closing balance of paid-in-capital, as well as cash budget. The adjustment we make is Last Years' Closing Balance plus Additional Paid-in-Capital.
- Retained Earnings: For this, we use last years' closing balance of retained earnings, as well as cash budget and budgeted income statement. The adjustment we make is Last Years' Closing Balance plus Estimate of Profit less Estimate of Dividend Paid.
- General Reserve: For this, we make an adjustment to last years' closing balance of general reserve for any change in the law regarding reserve requirements.
- Taxation: For this, we use last years' closing balance of tax, as well as tax returns, cash budget, and any regulatory change in tax rate or requirements. The adjustment we make is Last Years' Closing Balance plus New Payable Tax less.

Example of Budgeted Balance Sheet

The beginning balances for the long-term assets and stockholders' equity accounts are shown in the following table. The Pickup Trucks Company does not have any long-term liabilities.

Land	$ 45,000
Building	300,000
Equipment	60,000
Accumulated Depreciation	(50,000)
Common Stock	25,000
Additional Paid:	
Capital	350,000
Retained Earnings	89,799

Pickup Trucks Company Budgeted balance Sheet 20X1	
Assets	
Current Assets	
Cash	$ 20,527
Accounts Receivable	180,000
Finished Goods Inventory	27,844
Raw Materials Inventory	2,356
Total Current Assets	2,30,727
Property, Plant and Equipment	
Land	$ 30,000
Building	300,000
Equipment	136,000
Less: Accumulated Depreciation	(65,200)
Total Property, Plant and Equipment	4,00,800
Total Assets	$631,527
Liabilities and Stockholders' Equity	
Current Liabilities	
Notes Payable	$ 22,000
Accounts Payable	27,608
Income Taxes Payable	14,448
Total Current Liabilities	64,056
Stockholders' Equity	
Common Stock, $1 par value,1,000,000 shares authorized,25,000 shares issued and outstanding	25,000
Additional Paid-in-Capital	350,000
Retained Earnings	1,92,471
Total Stockholders' Equity	5,67,471
Total Liabilities and Stockholders' Equity	$631,527

Explanations for each balance are as follows:

- Cash: Ending balance per the cash budget.
- Accounts receivable: 30% of fourth quarter sales ($600,000 × 30%).
- Finished goods inventory: 2,475 units (15% of next quarter's sales of 16,500) times $11.25 per unit cost.
- Raw materials inventory: Materials for 1,683 units (10% of next quarter's production of 16,830 units) times $1.40 per unit cost of materials.
- Land: Sale of land with a cost of $15,000 (per cash budget information) deducted from beginning balance of $45,000.
- Building: No activity during the year.

- Equipment: Beginning balance of $60,000 plus purchases totaling $76,000.
- Accumulated depreciation: Beginning balance of $50,000 plus $15,200 additional depreciation per the manufacturing overhead budget.
- Notes payable: $72,000 in borrowings during the year minus $50,000 principal repayments per the cash budget.
- Accounts payable: 40% of fourth quarter purchases ($69,021 × 40%).
- Income taxes payable: Balance owed for current year taxes. Difference between estimated taxes paid (per cash budget for quarters two, three, and four) and the expense per budgeted income statement. The company did not make a payment of its 20X1 taxes in quarter one of 20X0; the payment in the cash budget quarter one is for 20X0 taxes.
- Common stock: No stock activity during the year.
- Additional paid-in-capital: No stock activity during the year.
- Retained earnings: Beginning balance $89,799 plus net income for the year of $102,672 per the budgeted income statement. Dividends were not declared and paid, and therefore none are deducted.

Budgeted Statement of Changes in Financial Position

A Statement of changes in financial position (funds statement) helps us to understands how and why a business enterprise has acquired its resources and what those resources were used for. The objectives of funds statement are:

- To summarise the financing and investing activities of the entity, including the extent to which the enterprise has generated funds from operations during the period.
- To complete the disclosure of changes of financial position during the period.

Preparation of Statement of Changes in Financial Position

Concept of Funds

A statement of changes in financial position can be prepared using different concepts of funds as a basis. For instance, statement of changes in financial position may focus on changes in working capital, cash, or total financial resources of a business enterprise. Accordingly, the preparation of the following types of statement of changes in financial position:

- Statement of changes in working capital, popularly known as Funds Flow Statement or Statement of Sources and Applications of funds.

- Statement of changes in cash popularly known as Cash Flow Statement.
- Statement of changes in Total Financial Resources.

Main Steps in Preparing the Statement

In order to prepare a statement of changes in financial position on a working capital basis, it is necessary to have balance sheets at two points in time and an income statement covering that span of time. The steps involved in preparing the statement are as follows:

- Determine the change (increase or decrease) in working capital.
- Determine the adjustments account to be made to net income.
- For each non-current account on the balance sheet, establish the increase or decrease in that account. Analyse the change to decide whether it is a source (increase) or use (decrease) of working capital.
- Be sure the total of all sources including those from operations minus the total of all uses equals the change found in working capital in step 1.

General Rules for Preparing Funds Flow Statement and Working Capital Basis

The following general rules should be observed while preparing funds flow statement:

- Increase in a current asset means increase (plus) in working capital.
- Decrease in a current asset means decrease (minus) in working capital.
- Increase in a current liability means decrease (minus) in working capital.
- Decrease in a current liability means increase (plus) in working capital.
- Increase in current asset and increase in current liability does not affect working capital.
- Decrease in current asset and decrease in current liability does not affect working capital.
- Changes in fixed (non-current) assets and fixed (non-current) liabilities affects working capital.

Significance of Statement of Changes in Financial Position —Working Capital Basis

A better understanding and analysis of the affairs of a business enterprise requires the knowledge about the movements in assets, liabilities and capital which have taken place during the year and their consequent effect on its financial position. This information is not specifically disclosed by a profit and loss account and balance sheet but can be made available in working capital based funds flow statement. The funds flow statement is in no way a replacement for the profit and loss account and balance sheet although the information which it contains is a selection, reclassification and summarisation of information contained in these two statements. The balance sheet gives a "snapshot" view at a point in time of the sources from which a firm has acquired its funds and the uses which the firm has made of these funds.

The equities side of the balance sheet delineates these sources, and the asset side shows the uses. The income statement is a flow statement; it explains changes that occurred in the profit and loss account by summarizing the increases (revenues) and decreases (expenses) in net profit during the accounting period. A funds flow statement explains the changes that took place in a balance sheet account or group of accounts during the period between dates of two balance sheets "snapshots." it shows the manner in which the operations of an enterprise have been financed and in which its financial resources have been used.

It also distinguishes the use of funds for the long-term from the short- term. For example, it distinguishes the use of funds for the purchase of new fixed assets from funds used in increasing the working capital of the company. Thus, it provides a meaningful link between the balance sheets at the beginning and at the end of a period and profit and loss account for that period. It should be understood, however, that a funds statement does not purport to indicate the requirements of a business for capital.

The concept of working capital is in conformity with normal accrual accounting procedures. Hence, a funs flow statement based on the concept of net working capital fits well with other statements. Above all, working capital is also a measure of the short-term liquidity of the firm. Therefore, an analysis of factors bringing about a change in the amount of net working capital is useful for decision-making by shareholders, creditors, lenders and management.

Limitation of Statement of Changes in Financial Position —Working Capital Basis

The working capital concept of funds enlarges the problem of valuation because it includes inventory and prepaid items. Thus, the measurement of working capital flows is less precise than for cash. A fund statement based on the working capital concept is usually a brief presentation, and many significant inter-firm transactions are not disclosed. For example, significant addition to inventories financed by short-term credits would not be shown because the two items are offset in the computation of the net change in working capital. Furthermore, transactions not affecting working capital, such as the acquisition of plant and equipment by the issuance of equity capital, would not be included in the statement. Therefore, the funds statement in this presentation would not disclose structural changes in the financial relationships in the firm or major changes in policy regarding investments in current assets and short-term financing.

Master Budget

The master budget is the aggregation of all lower-level budgets produced by a company's various functional areas, and also includes budgeted financial statements, cash forecast, and a financing plan. The master budget is typically presented in either monthly or quarterly format, and usually covers a company's entire fiscal year. An explanatory text may be included with the master budget, which explains the company's strategic direction, how the master budget will assist in accomplishing specific goals, and the management actions needed to achieve the budget. There may also be a discussion of the headcount changes that are required to achieve the budget.

A master budget is the central planning tool that a management team uses to direct the activities of a corporation, as well as to judge the performance of its various responsibility centers. It is customary for the senior management team to review a number of iterations of the master budget and incorporate modifications until it arrives at a budget that allocates funds to achieve the desired results. A company uses participative budgeting to arrive at this final budget, but it may also be imposed on the organization by senior management, with little input from other employees. The budgets that roll up into the master budget include:

- Direct labor budget.
- Direct materials budget.
- Ending finished goods budget.
- Manufacturing overhead budget.
- Production budget.
- Sales budget.
- Selling and administrative expense budget.

The selling and administrative expense budget may be further subdivided into budgets for individual departments, such as the accounting, engineering, facilities, and marketing departments. Once the master budget has been finalized, the accounting staff may enter it into the company's accounting software, so that the software can issue financial reports comparing budgeted and actual results. Smaller organizations usually construct their master budgets using electronic spreadsheets. However, spreadsheets may contain formula errors, and also have a difficult time constructing a budgeted balance sheet. Larger organizations use budget-specific software, which does not have these two problems.

Example of a Master Budget

Many lower-level budgets have specific formats that are used to arrive at certain outcomes, such as the fully absorbed cost of the finished goods inventory, or the number of units of products to be manufactured. This is not the case for the master budget, which looks very much like a standard set of financial statements. The income statement and balance sheet will be in the normal format mandated by Generally Accepted Accounting Principles or International Financial Reporting Standards. The primary difference is the cash budget, which does not usually appear in the standard format of the statement of cash flows. Instead, it serves the more practical purpose of identifying specific cash inflows and outflows that will result from the rest of the budget model. Here is an example of the cash budget:

Alpha Intergalactic Corporation				
Cash Budget				
For the Year Ended December 31, 20XX				
	Quarter 1	Quarter 2	Quarter 3	Quarter 4
Beginning cash	$100,000	$98,000	$95,000	$38,000
+/- Net profit (loss)	+25,000	+12,000	+40,000	+23,000
+ Depreciation	+15,000	+15,000	+22,000	+24,000
-Capital expenditures	-28,000	0	-80,000	-35,000
+/- Working capital changes	-14,000	-30,000	-39,000	-21,000
= Ending cash	$98,000	$95,000	$38,000	$29,000

The most difficult item to estimate in the cash budget is the net change in working capital from period to period. During periods of rapid growth, working capital can be a strongly negative number, since the company must invest in more accounts receivable than usual. If the amount of working capital appears to be holding steady despite rapid growth, then it is quite likely that management has built an unrealistic expectation into the budget to be able to collect accounts receivable more quickly than has been the case in the past.

A similar problem can arise with inventory, which is another component of working capital. It generally takes more inventory to support more sales, so the portion of working capital comprised of inventory can be expected to increase in conjunction with more sales. Thus, it is extremely likely that a company experiencing any amount of growth will forecast negative cash flows, because of the need to fund additional working capital.

Other Master Budget Issues

Another document sometimes included in the master budget is a set of key performance metrics that are calculated based on the information in the budget. For example, it may show accounts receivable turnover, or inventory turnover, or earnings per share. These metrics are useful for testing the validity of the budget model against actual results in the past. For example, if the accounts receivable turnover metric is much lower than historical results, that could mean that the company is over-estimating its ability to collect accounts receivable promptly, which means that the amount of accounts receivable shown in the balance sheet may be understated and the amount of cash may be overstated.

Problems with the Master Budget

When a company implements a master budget, there is a strong tendency for senior management to force the organization to closely adhere to it by including budget goals in employee compensation plans. Doing so has the following effects:

- When compiling the budget, employees tend to estimate low sales and high expenses, so that they can easily meet the budget and achieve their compensation plans.
- Forcing the organization to follow the budget requires a group of financial analysts who track down and report on variances from the plan. This adds unnecessary overhead expense to the business.
- Managers tend to ignore new business opportunities, because all resources are already allocated toward attaining the budget, and their personal incentives are tied to the budget.

Thus, enforcing a master budget can skew the operational performance of a business. Because of this problem, it may be better to employ the master budget as just a rough guideline for management's near-term expectations for the business.

Fixed and Flexible Budget

Fixed Budget

This budget is drawn for one level of activity and one set of conditions. It has been defined as a budget which is designed to remain unchanged irrespective of the volume of output or turnover attained. It is rigid budget and is drawn on the assumption that there will be no change in the budgeted level of activity. It does not take into consideration any change in expenditure arising out of changes in the level of activity. Thus, it does not provide for changes in expenditure arising out of change in the anticipated conditions and activity. A fixed budget will, therefore, be useful only when the actual level of activity corresponds to the budgeted level of activity.

A master budget tailored to a single output level of 20,000 units of sales is a typical example of a fixed budget. But, in practice, the level of activity and set conditions will change as a result of internal limitations and external factors like changes in demand and prices, shortages of materials and power, acute competition etc. It is hardly of any use as a mechanism of budgetary control because it does not make any distinction between fixed, variable and semi-variable costs and provides for no adjustment in the budgeted figures as a result of change in cost due to change in level of activity. It does not provide a meaningful basis for comparison and control. It is also not helpful at all in the fixation of price and submission offenders.

Flexible Budget

The Chartered Institute of Management Accountants, England, defines a flexible budget (also called sliding scale budget) as a budget which, by recognising the difference in behaviour between fixed and variable costs in relation to fluctuations in output, turnover, or other variable factors such as number of employees, is designed to change appropriately with such fluctuations. Thus, a flexible budget gives different budgeted costs for different levels of activity.

A flexible budget is prepared after making an intelligent classification of all expenses between fixed, semi-variable and variable because the usefulness of such a budget depends upon the accuracy with which the expenses can be classified. Such a budget is prescribed in the following cases:

- Where the level of activity during the year varies from period to period, either due to the seasonal nature of the industry or to variation in demand.
- Where the business is a new one and it is difficult to foresee the demand.
- Where the undertaking is suffering from shortage of a factor of production such as materials, labour, plant capacity etc. The level of activity depends upon the availability of such a factor of production.
- Where an industry is influenced by changes in fashion.
- Where there are general changes in sales.
- Where the business units keep on introducing new products or make changes in the design of its products frequently.
- Where the industries are engaged in make to order business like ship-building.

Distinction Between Fixed Budget and Flexible Budget

Table: Following are the main differences between these budgets:

Point of Distinction	Fixed Budget	Flexible Budget
Flexibility	It is inflexible and does not change with the actual volume of output achieved.	It is flexible and can be suitably recasted quickly accordingly to the level of activity attained.

Condition	It assumes that conditions would remain static.	It is designed to change according to changed conditions.
Classification of Costs	Costs are not classified according to their variability i.e. fixed, variable and semi-variable.	Costs are classified according to the nature of their variability.
Comparison	Comparison of actual and budgeted performance cannot be done correctly if the volume of output differs.	Comparisons are realistic as the changed plan figures are placed against actual ones.
Forecasting	It is difficult to forecast accurately the results in it.	It clearly shows the impact of various expenses on the operational aspect of the business.
Budget	Only one budget at a fixed level of activity is prepared due to an unrealistic expectation on the part of the management i.e. all conditions will remain unchanged.	Under it, series of budgets re prepared at different levels of activity.
Ascertainment of costs	It is not possible to ascertain costs correctly if there is a change in circumstances.	Costs can be easily ascertained at different levels under this type of budget.
Tool for cost control	It has a limited application and is ineffective as a tool for cost control.	It has more application and can be used as an effective as a tool for cost control.
Fixation of prices & submission of tenders	If the budgeted and actual activity levels vary, the correct ascertainment of costs and fixation of prices become difficult.	It helps in fixation of prize and submission of tenders due to correct ascertainment of costs.

Utility or Importance of Flexible Budget

- Flexible budget provides a logical comparison of budgeted allowances with the actual cost i.e., a comparison with like basis.
- Flexible budget reckons operational realities and streamlines control function and profit planning. It gives balanced perspective on comparison. When flexible budget is prepared, actual cost at actual activity is compared with budgeted cost at actual activity i.e., two things to a like basis.
- Flexible budget recognises concept of variability and provides logical comparison of expenditure with actual expenditure as a means of control.
- With flexible budget, it is possible to establish budgeted cost for any range of activity.
- A flexible budget is very useful for purposes of budgetary control because it corresponds with changes in the level of activity.
- It is helpful in assessing the performance of departmental heads because their performance can be judged in relation to the level of activity attained by the organisation.

- Cost ascertainment at different levels of activity is possible because a flexible budget is prepared for various levels of activity.
- It is helpful in price fixation and sending quotations.
- Other Types of Budgets:
    - Basic Budgets: A basic budget has been defined as a budget which is prepared for use unaltered over a long period of time. This does not take into consideration current conditions and can be attainable under standard conditions.
    - Current Budgets: A current budget can be defined as a budget which is related to the current conditions and is prepared for use over a short period of time. This budget is more useful than a basic budget, as a target it lays down will be corrected to current conditions.
    - Long-Term Budgets: A long-term budget can be defined as a budget which is prepared for periods longer than a year. These budgets help in business forecasting and forward planning. Capital Expenditure Budget and Research and Development Budget are examples of long-term budgets.
    - Short-term Budgets: This budget is defined as a budget which is prepared for period less than a year and is very useful to lower levels of management for control purposes. Such budgets are prepared for those activities, the trend in which is difficult to foresee over longer periods. Cash budget and material budget are examples of short-term budgets.

Performance Budgeting

Performance Budgeting had its origin in U.S.A. after the Second World War. It tries to rectify some of the shortcomings in the traditional budget. In the traditional budget amounts are earmarked for the objects of expenditures such as salaries, travel, office expenses, grant in aid etc. In such system of budgeting the money concept was given more prominence i.e. estimating or projecting dollar value for the various accounting heads or classification of revenue and cost. Such system of budgeting was more popularly used in government departments and many business enterprises. But is such system of budgeting control of performance in terms of physical units or the related costs cannot be achieved.

Performance oriented budgets are established in such a manner that each item of expenditure related to a specific responsibility centre is closely linked with the performance of that centre. The basic issue involved in the fixation of performance budgets is that of developing work programmes and performance expectation by assigned responsibility, necessary for the attainments of goals and objectives of the enterprise, it involves establishment of well-defined centres of responsibilities, establishment for each responsibility centre a programme of target performance in physical units, forecasting the amount of expenditure required to meet the physical plan laid down and evaluation of performance.

These days budgets are established in such a way so that item of expenditure is related to specific responsibility centre and is closely linked with the performance of that standard. Developing work programmes and performance expectations by assigned responsibility is the main issue involved in fixation of performance budgets and is necessary for the achievement and objects of the enterprise. Thus in performance budgeting classification of expenditure follows a three tier pattern viz. Function—Programme—Activity. Programme or production goals in physical and financial terms are established in accordance with this new classification and after the period, the actual performance is compared. Following matters will be specified very clearly in such bud getting:

- Objectives of the organisation and for which funds are requested.
- Cost of activities proposed for the achievement of these objectives.
- Quantitative measures to measure the performance.
- Quantum of work to be performed under each activity.

Thus performance budget follows a separate format laying down:

- Objectives and the organisation structure to achieve the same.
- Financial requirement table which gives details of programme activity classification, object wise classification and sources of funding.

Steps for System of Performance Budgeting

Following steps are necessary in the establishment of a successful system of performance budgeting:

- Establishment of well-defined responsibility centres or action points where operations are performed and financial transactions in terms of money take place.
- Establishment of each responsibility centre and a programme of expected performance in physical units of that centre. For example, the performance budget for a sales department may be units of goods sold and, for production department, units of products programmed to be manufactured and for capital works, quantum of work likely to be done during the budget period.
- To forecast the amount of expenditure under the various classification heads to

meet the physical plan. Then the procedure of budgeting could follow the usual routine.

- Evaluation performance is done under two stages i.e.:
    - The actual performance is compared with the physical target in order to determine the extent of deviation and adjusting the original dollar budget into a budget allowance for the actual physical work performed.
    - The actual expenditure is compared with the adjusted budget (or the budget allowance) to determine the monetary variances.
- Performance reporting indicating the result of analysis of the variance from the budget is done like that of variance reporting.

Difference Between Performance Budgeting and Traditional Budgeting

Performance Budgeting	Traditional Budgeting
1. In it, the flow of decision is upward.	1. In it, the flow of decision is downward.
2. It follows the function – programme – activity classification.	2. In it, the classification of expenses is by objects.
3. It makes a prospective approach with its focus on future markets.	3. The approach is retrospective in such budgeting.

Advantages of Performance Budgeting

Following are the main advantages of performance budgeting:

- It presents clearly the purposes and objectives for which funds are required.
- It gives better appreciation of budgeting by legislature.
- It improves budget formulation process.
- It enhances accountability of the executives.

Budgetary Control

Budgetary control involves establishment of budgets, continuous comparison of actual performance with budgets, finding out discrepancies, fixing the responsibilities, taking corrective measures and revising the budgets in the wake of change in circumstances.

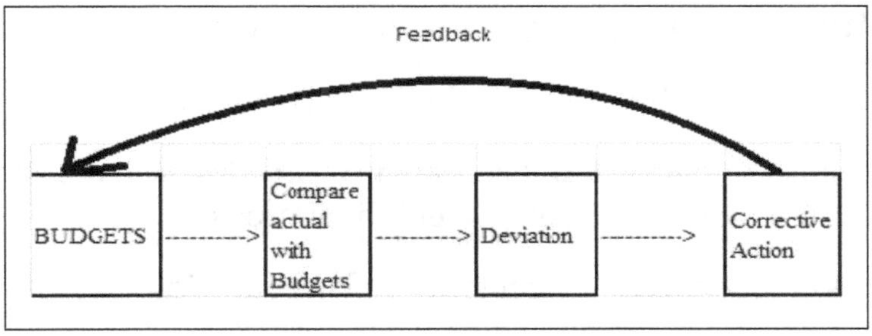

Budget, Budgeting and Budgetary Control

A Budget is the plan of estimated expenses and/or revenues associated with the operations of various departments of the organization. Budgeting may be said to be the process of preparing budgets while budgetary control embraces all this and in addition includes the science of devising the budgets themselves and using such budgets by the management for effecting overall control over the operations of the organization.

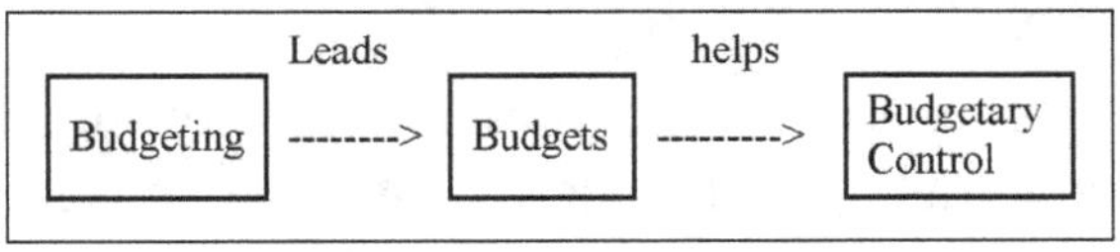

Objectives of Budgetary Control

The objectives of Budgetary Control are:

- Definition of goals i.e. to portray in clear-cut terms, the overall aims of the organization and breaking them down into target goals of each unit.
- Defining responsibilitiesi.e.to clearly specify the responsibilities of each person so that everybody knows what is expected of him and how will he be evaluated.
- Optimum use of resources i.e. to use the human, financial and material resources in best possible manner and reducing wastages.
- Coordination and cooperation: to integrate different units and departments so that they work with harmony in a unified manner.
- Proper execution i.e.to ensure that all activities are proceeding in the manner envisaged in the budget.
- Ease in comparison i.e. to compare the actual performance against the budget and draw attention to the deviations observed.
- Prompt remedial measures i.e. to take proper measures in case deviations are noticed to prevent discrepancies in future.
- Revision i.e. to revise the budget in the light of changed circumstances.

Characteristics of a Budgetary Control System

A budgetary control system has the following characteristics:

- Establishment of budgets: Budgets are prepared for each department and then they are presented to the management for approval.
- Coordination among departments: The plans of various departments are coordinated and finally integrated into the master budget.
- Comparison: Under budgetary control, the actual performance is compared with the budgetary estimates on a continuous basis to discover the variations and fix responsibilities.
- Revision: The budgets are revised in the light of changes in the conditions and circumstances.

Advantages of Budgetary Control System

The advantages of budgetary control are numerous. It prevents the occurrence of the deviations from the preplanned path through the media of observation, research, planning, control and decision making and thus helps in the performance of future activities in an orderly manner. Some of the advantages are:

- Efficiency and economy: Budgetary Control reveals the faults in the operations, weaknesses in the organizational structure and minimizes wasteful spending.
- Fixation of responsibilities: Budgetary control prevents "buck passing" and exposes those who are at fault/deviation.
- Coordination: It coordinates the production, marketing, financial, administrative and other dimensions and forces them to work in totality rather than in isolation and operate as a group in harmony.
- Pre determination of financing: Because the organization has a blue print of activities to be undertaken in the coming period, funds and finances can be arranged well in advance preventing the financial crisis.
- Management by exception: Budgetary control exposes the deviations and only variances and discrepancies are reported to the superiors. This enables them to concentrate on these issues seriously enabling management by exception.
- Forerunner of standard costing: A budgetary control makes available budgeted figures which can be used as a benchmark for variance analysis paving way for the adoption of standard costing principle in the organization.
- Objectivity in evaluation: Since everyone's performance is assessed on the basis of pre-set criterion, assessment is objective without any bias.

Essentials of a Successful Budgetary Control System

For an effective system of budgetary control, the presence of following elements is necessary:

- The budgetary control system should have the full support of the top management as well as the co- operation of all the employees.
- There should be well planned organizational set up in which responsibility and authority of each one should be clearly demarcated.
- The accounting system should provide accurate and timely information.
- There should be proper system of communication and reporting and all the participants of the organization must be involved in budget setting process.
- There should be an efficient system of feedback which reports variances fairly and promptly.
- The staff should be highly motivated and have faith in the budgetary control system.
- Budget should be used as a coordinating device rather than a control device.

Budgetary Control Process

The method by which a budget is prepared differs from organization to organization. While some organizations may have well organized, well documented procedures, others may not have any formal procedure and so in their case, budgeting process proceeds in a haphazard and disorganized manner. But since budgeting is an important planning exercise, it is suggested that it should be carried out in a systematic manner to avoid the conflicts and frustration at a later stage. Differences in the management styles, organizational objectives, size of organization, nature of business and similar factors have bearing on the procedures to be adopted by an organization in the budgeting process:

- Specification and communication of organizational objectives: A budget is a medium through which an organization's objectives and policies are reflected. The budgeting exercise starts in the light of these objectives plus policies and guidelines issued by top management to govern budget preparation. Detailed information and guidance is given on matters such as projected general economic conditions, allowances to be made for price increase and wage increases, changes in the scale of operations and so on. Further instructions are issued as to what information is required from each responsibility center for the budget and how this information is to be recorded in the budget form. In the absence of statements to the Contrary, it is assumed that factors affecting operations in the budget year will be similar to those in the current year.

- Preparing well defined organizational chart: An organization should have a well-defined organizational chart depicting the hierarchal position of each executive in the organizational and his functional responsibility. Such a chart will clearly show the lines of authority, the authority delegated and relative position of each in relation to others.
- Consideration of certain key issues:
  - Principal budget factor/critical success factors: Every organization has certain critical success factors or key factors that can influence the activities of an undertaking and can limit the volume of output. They impact the profitability of the organization. Critical success factors could be -specified raw material, a specific type of skilled labor, floor space, cash resources etc. These limiting factors may shift from time to time due to external and internal circumstances. So, care must be taken for their identification and the ways of overcoming key factors. In majority of the organizations, the most critical factor is consumer demand or expected level of reserves/sales. That's why, sales budget is usually prepared first of all followed by other related budgets.
  - Budget centers: A budget center is the lowest unit in the organization for which detailed costs are budgeted, separately from those of other budget centers. It is a center of organization for which separate budgets can be prepared and control can be exercised. The entire organization should be clearly divided into different sections as budget centers for enabling budgetary control and fixing responsibilities of departmental heads.
  - Budget period: A budget period a period for which the budget is prepared. This is the period for which forecasts can reasonably be made and estimates can be given. Budget period could be short range or long range. Short range budget may cover period of 3 months or 6 months or12 months while long range budget covers period more than one year. Capital expenditure budget and R & D budget are examples of long range budget. Sales budget or Income &Expenditure budget are examples of short range budget. In preparing short range budgets, certain factors must be kept in mind, like; budget period should have a term enough to complete production cycle of various products. In case of seasonal businesses, the budget period should cover one entire season cycle.It should be long enough to provide adequate time to arrange funds for production and should coincide with the financial accounting period to facilitate comparison of actual with budget estimates.
  - Budget Committee: It is the body entrusted with the responsibility of overseeing the proper formulation and implementation of the budget. The budget involves the various functional activities and so the association of various functional managers is desirable. The budget committee is composed of

all the major functional heads and acts as a forum where communication, coordination and discussion among them is facilitated. The main functions of the budget committee are to assist functional managers in preparation of budget, receive and review their budget estimates and recommend changes if any, resolve conflicts between departments on budget matter, to prepare master budget on the basis of functional budgets, to compare budget with actual performance and recommend action to be taken on the basis of variance analysis and make recommendations for the budget manual.

- Budget manual: It is a document which contains standing instructions with respect to the procedures to be followed and the time schedules to be observed while making budgets. It acts as a guide in the hands of the budget officers and all the functional heads and prevents the need of frequent instructions from the top management. The budget manual provides instructions such as time limit for submission of preliminary forecasts, person to whom this has to be submitted, important items for each forecast, categorization of expenses, prescribed forms to make reports, listing the matters to be decided only with the approvals of the top management etc.

Initial Preparation of Budget Components

The budget guidelines prepared by top management together with the sales plan are disseminated down through the successive levels in the organization. Managers at each level add more details for the guidance of their subordinates. When the guidelines arrive at the lowest responsibility centers, the concerned managers prepare the budget plans for the items falling within their sphere, keeping in mind the constraints specified in the guidelines. These estimates are made by them by combining specific analytical techniques with their judgment.

Negotiation

Negotiation between a superior and subordinate (budgeted) is a very crucial stage in the budgeting process. If budget is too tight, it becomes unattainable and leads to frustration. On the other hand, if it is too loose, it leads to complacency. The budgetee and his superior, therefore, seek to arrive at a desirable middle path by means of slacks and cuts. The subordinates generally resort to slack or padding i.e. overstate their budgeted costs or understate their budgeted revenues to create a budgeted profit at the level that is easier to achieve. Budgetary slack provides protection against cost increase or revenue short falls due to unforeseen events. But it leads to budget cuts imposed by the superior who is aware of slack, padding and other similar tactics of the subordinates. In order to address this issue, instead of resorting to arbitrary cuts, superior should require a full explanation of why costs may be expected to increase. Subordinates on his part must justify increase in cost by explaining underlying causes such as cost of inflation, need for better quality and so on. The end product of the negotiation process is an agreement which represents a commitment by each party, the budgetee and his superior. The nature of the commitment could one of three types:

- It may represent a ceiling (e.g. "Not more than $ 10,000 should be spent for employee training").
- It may represent a floor (e.g. "At least $ 10,000 should be spent for employee training").
- It may represent a guide (e.g. "Approximately $ 10,000 should be spent for employee training").

Coordination and Review

The negotiation process is repeated successfully at higher levels of the organizational hierarchy up to the very top. Negotiations at higher levels result in changes in the detailed budget that have been agreed to at the lower levels. As the individual budgets move up in the organizational hierarchy in the negotiation and review process, they are also examined in terms of the compatibility (i.e. in relationship to one another) and potentiality (whether in the overall interest of the company). If they are found out of balance, some of the underlying budgets/figures may be modified. Major unresolved issues are submitted to the budget committee.

Final Approval and Distribution

Just prior to beginning of the budget year, the proposed budget is submitted to the top management for approval. If the proper procedure is followed and there are no great surprises in the proposed budgets, they are approved. The budgets are then communicated to the department/responsible managers. Modifications incorporated in the final budget should be particularly made known to managers to seek their cooperation and support for the budget.

Implementing the Budget Plan

The final budget is presented to the managers concerned and adopted as the plan of operation for the forthcoming budget period. The various service units in the organization are required to release the necessary materials, labor, facilities, finances and other resources to carry out the budget.

Revision

A budget is formulated in accordance with certain assumptions as to conditions that will prevail during the budget period. If the actual conditions turn out to be different from those assumed, differences may be significant. This may call for revision in the budget during the year. Some organizations instead of revising their budget, take account of changes in conditions when they analyze the differences between the budgeted and actual performance. Other companies may solve this problem of revision by having two budgets- a baseline budget set at the beginning of the year and a current budget reflecting the best current estimates of revenue and expenses. A comparison of actual performances with the baseline shows the extent of deviation from the original plan and a comparison of the current budget with the baseline budget shows how much of this deviation is attributable to changes in the current conditions from those originally assumed.

Budget Reports

Budget report is like a report card of a budget center. In this report, the actual figure and the budgeted figures are reported side by side to facilitate comparison and determine deviation or variations. In the report, both favorable and adverse variations should be reported with necessary comments/reasons. These reports form the basis for fixing the responsibility and taking corrective action. The budget report follows the principle of management by exception.

Zero-Based Budgeting

Zero-based budgeting (ZBB) is a budgeting technique that allocates funding based on efficiency and necessity rather than budget history. Management starts from scratch and develops a budget that only includes operations and expenses essential to running the business; there are no expenses that are automatically added to the budget.

All expenses must be justified in order to qualify to be placed in the budget. For example, if a company expects to incur $100,000 in salaries and wages expenses, and believes that the full $100,000 is necessary to operate the business smoothly, then it will be included in the budget – however, each individual allotment of salary/wages has to be examined and justified in order to be included. If instead of paying some salaries, the company's management determines that it can substitute technology at a lower cost, then adjustments to the budget are made accordingly.

Zero-Based Budgeting vs. Traditional Budgeting

All businesses use budgets to keep track of spending and improve ways to minimize costs and maximize profit. Budget planning for the current/next year is usually based on budgets from previous years. In fact, traditional budgeting begins with the previous year's budget and usually implements incremental percentage increases or decreases to meet new goals. These percentages usually range anywhere from 1% to 10%.

Sometimes, budgets can get out of control, or in some years, may show significantly higher or lower costs, depending on the overall market outlook and other external factors. In such scenarios, it does not make sense to look at last year's budget because significant changes in the company's situation have taken place. The entire budget needs to be redone from scratch. Hence, a zero-based budget. In a zero-based budget, the company analyzes every expense/aspect of the business one by one. This is referred to as starting from a "zero base." While zero-based budgeting examines all expenses, traditional budgeting only examines proposed new expenses.

Advantages of Zero-Based Budgeting

- The final output is well justified and is aligned with the company's overall business strategy or business plan.
- Encourages more collaboration throughout the company.
- Improves performance and operating efficiency by challenging assumptions and examining expenditures.
- By avoiding traditional budgeting percentage increases, there is a significantly better chance of making cost reductions.

Disadvantages of Zero-Based Budgeting

- Implementing a zero-based budget requires qualified personnel and specialized training, which can be time-consuming and costly.
- May harm the company's overall culture or brand image.
- May be cost-prohibitive (because of time, research, and analysis required) for companies with minimal available funding.
- It is substantially more complex and tedious to start from a zero base. Traditional budgeting is much simpler, faster, and easier to implement.

Performance Budgeting

Performance Budget is "A budget that reflects the input of resources and the output of services for each unit of an organization. This type of budget is commonly used by the government to show the link between the funds provided to the public and the outcome of these services.

Scope, Merits and Demerits of Performance Budgeting

Models of Performance Budgeting

There is not just one model of performance budgeting, but a range of different models.

The various models of PBB, link, funding and results, but they do so in different ways. Some performance budgeting models, such as program budgeting and zero-base budgeting, are government-wide systems. On the other hand, some are only intended to apply to particular sectors of expenditure or categories of organization, for instance, a formula funding model will normally apply to schools.

A common tool used for this purpose is program budgeting, in which expenditure is classified in the budget by objectives, rather than solely by economic categories such as salaries, supplies and communication costs and organizational categories. The primary objective of program budgeting is improved expenditure prioritization & Effectiveness and/or efficiency of the services which they delivery. To achieve these, they rely on three mechanisms, used either in isolation or in combination.

- The first of these mechanisms is linking budgets to performance targets.
- The second mechanism used to creating a tighter link between funding and results is formula funding.
- The third mechanism used by the newer performance budgeting models is performance funding incentives to departments.

Advantages of PBB

There are several merits of Performance Budgeting such as transparency, quantitative analysis, setting budgeting priorities, organic integration of the process of planning and budgeting, improving public relations and brings financial and expected results aspects in sync.

- Transparency of performance budgets is one major advantage because taxpayers see results during every budgeting cycle when good programs get funding, whereas bad programs are dropped.
- Another advantage is quantitative analysis and input from employees that have a vested interest in their departments.
- Workers and program managers know what budgeting priorities are needed to further the goals of the agency when their performance is examined.
- It improves legislative review by presenting a comprehensive picture of the various departments.
- This system ensures the advantages that are likely to accrue from an organic integration of the process of planning and budgeting.
- It helps to improve public relations by providing clearer information for a rational public appraisal of responsible government.

- It brings the financial and expected results aspects together, which is missing in the traditional planning, programming and budgeting process.

Disadvantages of PBB

PBB is not devoid of limitations; it suffers from disadvantages like, focus on quantitative rather than a qualitative evaluation, and without decentralized accounting and systematic reporting mechanisms it would be ineffective and inefficient.

- One major disadvantage to performance budgeting is the relative cost between two divisions.
- Supplies, workload and office needs may differ from one department to the other, which makes larger budgets more challenging.
- Some department heads may inflate or bloat their successes to ensure better funding during the next budget cycle.
- Performance budgets are great for routine programs, but if emergency needs arise there may be difficulties in getting more funding.
- The programme and activity classifications developed are sometimes too broad to reveal the significant activities of the department to serve as a basis for budgetary decisions and management.
- Due to its goal-oriented nature, PBB technique focuses on quantitative rather than a qualitative evaluation.
- PBB without decentralized accounting and systematic reporting mechanisms would be ineffective and inefficient.

Despite its difficulties and limitations, PBB provides a meaningful basis for administrative planning, executive coordination, legislative scrutiny and administrative accountability. Most importantly, a progressive budget based on PBB would strengthen the democratic process and evoke meaningful participation of the personnel in the implementation of the tasks set out in the budget.

Obstacles and Challenges to a Successful PBB Implementation can be, however, overcome by bringing about changes in culture and policies of the organization. Efforts should be made to include everyone to become a performance manager. The Top Level Management must also Define SMART Performance Measures to enable the personnel to know, what is expected of them. Finally a successful PBB will require enterprise-wide collaboration & commitment.

Steps Involved in PBB

The most important requirement for PBB is a programme of action for any given year with specific indications regarding the tasks and the costs of achieving them. Programme formulation, allocation of resources and budget execution are the core steps giving effect to PBB.

- Establishing a meaningful functional classification of public expenditure.
- Establishment, improvement and extension of activity schedules for all measurable activities.
- Establishment of work output, employee utilization, standard or unit costs by objective methods, that is, bringing the system of accounting and financial management into accord with the classification.
- Creation of related cost and performance recording and reporting system.

Programmed Budgeting and Performance Budgeting

The name "Program Budget" is derived from the simple fact that the planning process is organized by program rather than by department of fiscal input or output. Program budgeting has passed through several distinct evolutionary periods. The First was the developmental period, which was borne out of the need for a national budget. Accounting Act of 1921 was such that it was virtually impossible for any appropriating body or the public to know where its money was going. The budgeting practice of lumping expenditures had been consistent with the planned purpose of the appropriation. Budgeting procedures basically consisted of revising estimates. The most significant change in budgeting occurred in 1907 under the leadership of Frederick A. Cleveland, when New York City's Bureau of Munical Research adapted this method. Shortly thereafter, other cities followed New York's leadership in budget.

Currently, no standard definition of program budgeting exists. Program budgeting is generally described as a planning oriented procedure. According to Schick, the main objective of Programme Budgeting is to rationalize policy-making by:

- Providing Data on the costs and benefits of alternative ways of attaining proposed public objectives.
- Providing Output measurements to facilitate the effective attainment of chosen objectives.

Program budgeting can be described as an approach and a process that relates resources to proposed and actual results. Program budgeting includes: concepts; techniques and a structure. The Overall Structure of Program Budgeting consists of programs, subprograms and activities. In order to measure results program budgeting requires Outcomes which include measurable and specific Outputs and performance indicators. It is also referred to as 'Output Budgeting'& is being mainly used by Central & State Governments in India.

Unique Features of Programme Budgeting

- Profit orientation is missing.
- Objectives laid & their achievement targets are not laid down in terms of money.
- Targets are in physical units.
- Success here is measured in terms of over/under achievement of targets & resources spent in achieving such targets.

Advantages of Program Budgeting

- Program budgets present more useful information on service delivery & allow for transparency and accountability in service delivery.
- PBB's are more useful for determining whether allocations reflect priorities in planning the delivery of services.
- PBB helps in monitoring the use of resources within each program identifying areas where savings can be made or where more funds are needed.
- It helps in providing a systematic & sound system of Performance reporting evaluation of each programme.
- It encourages decision making at all levels of management in the organization.
- It facilitates introduction of the versatile tool "management by objectives".
- It leads to improvement of financial control.

Limitations of Programme Budgeting

- It fails to reflect the operation & execution process of the programme.
- It has no relevance to actual budget.
- It does not serve as an operating tool for managers.
- Evaluation of activities & operations of on-going programme is not focused & the emphasis is on the new programmes.

Programme Budgeting vs. Performance Budgeting

Programme budgeting, developed by U.S. president Lyndon Johnson, and was first introduced by the United States Secretary of Defence- Robert S. McNamara in the Pentagon in the 1960s. It is the budgeting system that, , describes and gives the detailed costs of every activity or programme that is to be carried out in detail along with their necessary resource costs, for example, raw materials, equipment and staff. The sum of all activities or programmes constitutes the Programme Budget. Thus, when looking at a Programme Budget, one can easily find out what precisely will be carried out, at what cost and with what expected results in considerable detail. The system was taught at the John F. Kennedy School of Government of Harvard University but it evoked little interest except from critics. Whereas Performance Budgeting is an "adjusted budget prepared after operations to compare actual results with costs that should have been incurred at the actual level attained".

- A performance budget allocates money to various programs within an organization and also details the service level on which the budget is predicated. The service level is identified by the use of performance measures. In addition to controlling costs, the primary orientation of the performance budget is that of improving the internal management of the program.
- The program budget allocates money to major program areas, focusing on the expected results of services and activities to be carried out. Program areas often utilized by government entities include public safety, public works, human services, leisure services, and general government. The emphasis of program budgeting is on the attainment of long-term goals.
- Both the program and performance budget use indicators to measure financial and operational performance, but the budgets have a different focus. A performance budget emphasizes management efficiency, whereas a program budget emphasizes the benefits that the departments gain from overall expenditures.
- Performance Budgeting aims to simplify the budget formulation process.
- Performance Budgeting serves as a controlling tool for financial operations & makes management more accountable for its actions but same is not the case with Programme Budgeting.

What is Program Budget?

Program budget is a budget that is prepared specifically for a project or program. This type of budget includes expenses and revenues related to a specific project only.

Advantages

- It helps in determining the priority of the projects.
- It helps in planning and managing the delivery of services in the future.
- It helps in spotting the areas where higher funds are required.

Disadvantages

- If the program budget is incorrect, it can lead to increase in costs.
- It requires lot of information so takes ample time to find out exact financial resources required.

References

- Cost-accounting-budgeting-analysis, accounting-basics: tutorialspoint.com, Retrieved 18, February 2020
- Capital-expenditures, accounting, knowledge, resources: corporatefinanceinstitute.com, Retrieved 25, July 2020
- Budgeted-balance-sheet: efinancemanagement.com, Retrieved 14, January 2020
- Statement-of-changes-in-financial-position-an-overview, financial-statement-5584: accountingnotes.net, Retrieved 03, April 2020
- Fixed-and-flexible-budget-meaning-difference-and-utility-73918: yourarticlelibrary.com, Retrieved 10, June 2020
- Zero-based-budgeting, accounting, knowledge, resources: corporatefinanceinstitute.com, Retrieved 17, March 2020

3

Standard Costing

The practice which is associated with the estimation of a production process is termed as standard costing. It involves variance analysis which compares actual and budgeted costs of raw materials and labor during production. This chapter discusses in detail the different types of variance which are studied in relation to standard costing.

The word standard means a 'norm' or a 'criterion'. Standard cost is thus a criterion cost which may be used as a yardstick to measure the efficiency with which actual cost has been incurred. There is a constant process of development effected in business through the help of standard costing method since the standard costs set in are sensible, capable of being attained and are revised from time to time in accord with needs and requirements of the business enterprise.

Standard Cost

- Standard cost is a figure which represents an amount that can be taken as a typical of the cost of an article or other cost factor. It is established on the basis of planed operations, planed cost efficiency levels, and expected capacity utilization.
- Standard cost is a predetermined calculation of the presumed cost under the specified conditions. It is built up from an assessment of the value of cost elements. It correlates technical specification of material, labour and other cost to the price or wage rate which have occurred during the period in which the standard cost is to be determined. For example, wages or machine hour per unit of product.
- The standard cost is a predetermined cost which is calculated from management standard of efficient operation and relevant necessary expenditure.

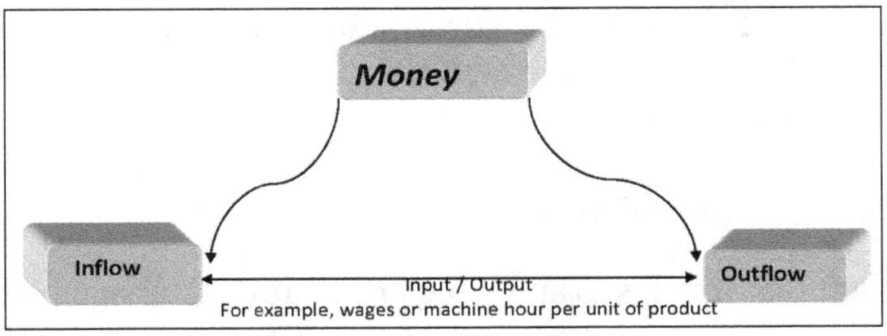

Historical Costing

- The term 'Historical Cost' is also known as Actual Cost. The meaning of this cost suggests the actual costs of products which have been incurred in their production.

- The experts maintain that, the production of products, the expenses like material, labour, overheads etc. should be paid first and then they should be recorded in books. So these total expenses are called historical costs or past costs.
- The figures relating to costs obtained at the end of the production process may have some definite value in rectifying past practices if they are properly analyzed.

Concepts of Standard Cost and Standard Costing

- Standard Cost: Standard costs are called pre-determined costs. The different standards regarding all the elements of costs, i.e., material, labor and overheads, are determined on the basis of historical cost and many other factors. These factors are cautiously studied before determining the standards. The standard committee will generally consist of production manager, purchase manager, personal manager, and other functional heads. It is possible that the standard cost decided by the manager could be idle, normal or expected. The idle standard cost may refer to an estimate of the cost under perfect competition. It is competed on the basis that there is no scrap, no idling of machinery or breakdown and so on. On the other hand, expected standard cost is based upon the attainable result. Standard Costs are not simple average but they are set with due care after careful study and observation of production activity in the past and the present.
- Standard Costing: Standard costing is a perfect system of controlling the costs and measuring efficiency and its development. It is a technique of cost reduction and cost control. It helps to provide valuable guidance in several management functions such as formulating policies, determining price level, etc. The essence of standard costing is to set objectives and targets to achieve them, to compare the actual costs with these targets. Standard Costing is used to ascertain the standard cost under each element of cost, i.e., materials, labours, overhead. It can eliminate all kinds of waste. Through the application of this costing it can be ascertained whether or not the activities of production are going on according as the pre-determined plan.

Advantages of Standard Costing

- Proper Planning: It helps to apply the principle of "Management by exception". That is, the management need not worry over those activities which proceed in tandem plans. It is only on the issues of exceptions that they have to concentrate.
- Efficient Cost Control: Standard Costing is a tool for the management to gain

reduction in the cost and control over it. Under this technique, differences are analyzed and responsibilities are determined.

- Motivational Factor: Labour efficiency is promoted and they are destined to be cost conscious. Standards provide incentives and motivation to work with greater effort. This increases efficiency and productivity.
- Comparison of Forecasting and Outcome: A target of efficiency is set for the employees and the cost consciousness is stimulated. Since the process of standard costing allow an appraisal to be made of personnel, machines and method of working, current inefficiencies come to the notice and get eliminated.
- Inventory Control: Standard costing facilitates inventory control and simplifies inventory valuations. This ensures uniform pricing of stocks in the form of raw materials, work-in-progress and finished goods.
- Economical System: Standard costing system is economical system from the viewpoint that it does not require detailed records. It also does not require a big staff. It results in the reduction in paper work in accounting and needs very few records. Thus, there is saving of time as well as money.
- Helpful in Budgeting: Budgets are prepared on the basis of standard costing. Standards which are set up in respect of materials, labour and overheads are helpful in preparing various budgets. For example, flexible budget, sales budget, etc.
- Helps Formulate Policies: This technique is a valuable aid to the management in determining prices and formulating production policies. Standard costing equips cost estimates while planning the production of new products.
- Helps Distinguish Activities: Standard costing helps in distinguishing between skilled and unskilled activities. So the skilled worker only gives pays attention to improving the activities of the unskilled workers.
- Eliminates Wastage: Through fixing standard, certain waste such as material wastage, idle time, lost machine hours, etc. are reduced.

Limitations of Standard Costing

- Costly System: Because the Standard Costing requires highly skillful and competent personnel, it becomes a costly system too. For the same experts are paid high remuneration.
- Difficulties in Fixation of Standard: It is always difficult to determine precise standard costs in a given situation which will coincide with actual cost when operations are over. Standard cost are determined partly by the past experience

and partly by the cost projections based on advanced statistical techniques. Thus, uncertainties revolve around standards.

- Constraint for Service Industry: Standard costing is applied for planning and controlling manufacturing costs. Thus, it cannot be applied in a service industry.
- Consistency of Standard: because the standards of marginal costing fluctuate and vary time to time, it is difficult to always sustain and continue the same standards.
- Unsuitable for Non-standardized Products: Standard costing is expensive and unsuitable for job manufacturing industries as they manufacture non standardized products such as catering, tailoring, printing, etc.
- Relatively Fixed Standards: A business may not be able to keep standards up-to-date. In other words, a business may not revise standards to keep pace with the frequent changes in manufacturing conditions. Firms may avoid revising standards as it is a costly affair.
- Difficulties for Small Industries: Establishment of standards and their implementation involve initial high costs. Standards have to be revised and new standards be fixed involving larger costs. Thus, small firms find it expensive to operate standard costing system. This system is not fit for each type of industries.
- Discouragement for Workers: Sometimes the employees and workers are discouraged when the standards are fixed at a high level. The unreal high standards may adverse by effect the morale of workers rather than working as an incentive for better efficiency.
- Inaccurate Diverse Results: Inaccurate and unreliable standards cause misleading results and thus may not enjoy the confidence of the users of this system.

Objectives of Standard Costing

- To institute a control mechanism on all the elements of costs that affect production and sales.
- To measure different operational efficiencies and check the wastages.
- To improve the delegation of authority and generate a sense of responsibility among the employees.
- To develop a cost consciousness in the employees.
- To presume the production costs, sales and profit.
- To avail the benefits of 'Management by exception.
- To bring about a vivid progressive vision and sagacious decision making at each managerial level.

Preliminaries of Establishment of Standard Cost System

The following four points are usually considered for setting up a standard cost system in a business:

- Setting up cost center.
- Classification of Accounts.
- Types of Standards.
- Settings the Standards.

Setting up Cost Center

Introducing Standard Cost System is requires first of all to establish cost centers with their well-designed ambit of work. In the process there should be no ambiguity about the responsibility of each cost center so that their responsibility may be identified. A cost center is a location; people or item of equipments for cost may be ascertained and used for the purpose of cost control.

Classification of Accounts

Accounts are classified in order to assist collection and analysis. To use the system of standard costing effectively, all accounts have to be classified on the basis of their functions, items of revenue nature, assets and liabilities, etc. Codes are given for each item and each account along with elements of cost with this end in view, codes may be used. A code is a symbolic representation of any particular item of information. For example:

Direct Material	01-19
Direct Labour	20-29
Direct Expense	30-39
Indirect Expense	40-49
Indirect Labour	50-59
Indirect Expense	60-69

Types of Standards

Basically, there are two types of standard, Current Standard and Basic Standard.

- Current Standard: It is established for the use over a diminutive period of time and is related to current circumstances. Such a standard remains in operation for a limited period and belongs to the current conditions. These standards are revised at regular intervals. Current standard are of three types like Ideal standards, Expected standards, and Normal standards.

- Ideal Standards: This is a hypothetical standard which is rather not practicable to attain. This ideal is clearly unrealistic and unattainable. It pre- supposes that the performance of men, materials and machines is perfect and thus makes no allowance for the loss of time, accident, wastage of materials and any other type of waste of materials and any other type of waste or loss. Such standards have the advantage of establishing a goal which, however, is not always attainable in practice. As such it is having a little practical value. The standard which can be attained under the most favourable condition possible.
- Expected or Practical Standards: Such standards are likely to be expected or utilized in the future period. Such standards are based on expected performance after making a reasonable allowance for unavoidable losses and other inevitable lapses from perfect efficiency. So it is most generally used standard and is best suited for cost control. This standard can be anticipated as well as attained in future in sync with the specified budget.
- Normal Standards: It is also known as 'Past Performance Standard' because it is based on the average performance in the past. It should be attainable and it provides a challenge to the staff. The aim of such a standard is to eliminate the variations in the cost which arise out of trade cycle. The average standard can be anticipated as well as attained in a future period of time. Preferably, it should be long enough to cover one trade- cycle.

- Basic Standards: This is a standard which is established for use unaltered for an indefinite time. It is similar to an index number against which all results are measured. Variances from basic standards show trends of deviations of the actual cost. However, basic standards are of no practical utility from the point of view of cost control and cost ascertainment. This standard is set on a long-term basis and seldom revised. It is an underlying standard from which current standard can be developed.

Setting the Standard

The process of setting standard is a valuable activity in itself. The success of standard costing system depends on the reliability, accuracy and acceptance of the standards. If standards have been properly set and maintained, they are a sound basis for determining cost for various purposes. While setting the standards, the following points should be taken into consideration: duration of use of standard, reasonable standard of performance, level of activity. For the given units standard sets for the following items are direct material cost, direct wage cost, direct expense, factory variable overhead cost, selling and distribution variable cost and selling price and sales margin.

- Standards for Material: It includes determination of standard quantity of material required, and determination of standard price per unit of material.

- Material Quantities: After establishing the standard quality of material, it is more important and necessary to establish the standard regarding quantity of each material. Generally, quantities are expressed in terms of kilograms, feet, units and so forth.
- Standards for Labour: This standard is determined with regard to the current rate of pay and any anticipated variations. It should be fixed for each grade of labour and for each operation involved. The standard hours are fixed for all categories of labour i.e., for skilled and unskilled labour. In these standards, number of hours and workers are established.
- Material Prices: This is a forecast of the average prices of material during the future period. This standard is quite difficult to establish because prices are regulated more by the external factors than by the company management. While setting standard prices, the past experiences, existing prices and anticipations should closely examine. Price of material in the past, current prices and fluctuating trends are the base for determining standard of price.
- Setting for Overheads: Setting standard for overheads is more complex than the development of material and labour standards. It is estimated for variable overheads and fixed overheads.
    - Variable Overheads: Variable overhead has been defined as a cost which tends to vary directly with the volume of output. It is assumed that the overhead rate per unit is invariable, irrespective of the quantity produced, so it is necessary to calculate only a standard cost per unit or per hour.
    - Fixed Overheads: Fixed overhead tends to be unaffected by variations in the volume of output. Therefore it is required to determine total fixed overhead for the period and budgeted production in units.
- Standard Hour: Production is usually articulated in physical units such as tons, pounds, gallons, numbers, kilograms, liters, etc. When a company is manufacturing different types of products, it is almost impossible to increase the production, which cannot be expressed in the same unit. Standard hour means a hypothetical hour, which represents the amount of work that should be performed in one hour under standard conditions.

Difference Between Standard Cost and Historical Cost

No.	Historical Cost	Standard Cost
1.	Historical costs are the actual cost.	Standard costs are the pre- determined cost.
2.	It only informs the total cost of a Product or service.	Its function is to evaluate managerial performance and deficiency.

3.	Historical costs are ascertained after they have been incurred, and therefore are experienced costs of decisions previously made.	Standard costs are anticipated costs which tend to state what the cost of production should be.
4.	It is related to past.	It is related to future.
5.	It cannot do the role of Planning and Budgeting.	Budgets are prepared on the basis of Standard costs.

Difference Between Standard Cost and Estimated Cost

No.	Standard Cost	Estimated Cost
1.	Standard cost aims at what the cost should be.	Estimated cost is an assessment of will be.
2.	Standard costs are planned cost which is determined on a scientific basis after taking into account certain level efficiency.	It is based on the average of past figures, taking into consideration anticipated charges in future.
3.	It lays emphasis on cost control, on setting the target against which actual performance is measured and if need be, corrective measures are sought.	Estimated costs are used by the undertakings for fixing the selling price of the product.

Difference Between Standard Cost and Budgetary Cost

No.	Standard Cost	Budgetary Cost
1.	Standard costing is intensive in application as it calls for a detail analysis variance.	Budgetary control is extensive in nature and the intensity of analysis tends to match less than that in standard costing.
2.	Standard cost represents realistic yardsticks and, therefore, more useful for controlling and reducing cost.	Budgets usually represent an upper limit on spending without considering the effectiveness of the expenditure in terms of output.
3.	Standard cost is a projection of cost account.	Budget is a projection of financial accounts.
4.	Standard cost are developed mainly for the manufacturing function and sometimes also for marketing and administration.	Budgets are compiled for different functions of the business such as sales, purchase, cash, production, etc.
5.	Standard costs are usually established after considering such vital matters as production capacity, methods employed and other factors which require attention when determining an acceptable level of efficiency.	Budgets may be based on previous year's costs without any attention being paid to efficiency.

Difference Between Cost Centre and Profit Centre

No.	Cost Centre	Profit Centre
1.	A cost centre may be a location, person or item of equipment for which cost center may be ascertained and used for the purpose of cost control.	Profit center is the cost center which shows profit.
2.	Cost center is necessary for fixing responsibilities for unfavorable variances.	Profit center does not show for fixing responsibilities for unfavorable variance.

Standard Cost Card/Standard Cost Sheet

The standards established for each element of cost (such as of material, labor and overhead) for a product are recorded in a statement form known as "Standard cost card or sheet". It shows the time and rate of each category of labor, the overhead rate and the cost per unit. This information, however, is specific with number of production, quantity and price of each type of material required. Such a card is maintained for all kinds of products or services. The build-up of the standard cost of each item is recorded in standard cost card. Cost shown in the card should be approved by the person who will be responsible for the operation concerned. A sample of such standard cost card is given below:

Sample of Standard Cost Card/Sheet Format			
Standard cost card/Sheet			
No...............		Date of setting standard............	
Product..............			

Elements of Cost	Quantity	Amount (in $)	Standard Cost
1)Direct material:			
Material X	10 units	5.00	50.00
Material Y	20 units	10.00	200.00
	30 units		250.00
Less: Normal wastage @10%	5 units	Scrap unit	50.00
Normal Output	25 units		200.00
2) Direct Labour	10 hours	2.00	20.00
3) Overheads			
- Variable	10 hours	1.00	10.00
- Fixed	10 hours	2.00	20.00
Total Cost			250.00
Add: Profit 10% on cost			25.00
Sales price			275.00

Setting Up of Standards and their Revision

Different elements or variables which influence the setting up of standards are Material, Labour and Overheads.

Setting Standards for Direct Materials

There are several basic principles which ought to be appreciated in setting standards for direct materials. If material is used for a product, it is known as direct material.

On the other hand, if the material cost cannot be assigned to the manufacturing of the product, it will be called indirect material. Therefore, it involves two things:

- Quality of material.
- Price of the material.

When the organization wishes to purchase material, the quality and size should be determined. The standard quality to be maintained should be decided. The quantity is determined by the production department. This department makes use of historical records, and an allowance for changing conditions will also be given for setting standards. A number of test runs may be undertaken on different days and under different situations, and an average of these results should be used for setting material quantity standards. The second step in determining direct material cost will be a decision about the standard price. Cost of Material will be decided in consultation with the purchase department. The cost of purchasing and store keeping of materials should also be taken into consideration. The procedure for purchase of materials, minimum and maximum levels for various materials, discount policy and means of transport are the other factors which have bearing on the materials cost price. It includes the following:

- Cost of materials.
- Ordering cost.
- Carrying cost.

The purpose should be to increase efficiency in procuring and store keeping of materials. The type of standard used, for example ideal standard or expected standard, would also affect the choice of standard price.

Setting Direct Labour Cost

If the organization wishes to engage a labour force for manufacturing a product or a service for which some amount is to be paid, this is called wages. If the labour is engaged directly to produce the product, this is known as direct labour. The second largest amount of cost is the labour cost. The benefit derived from the workers can be assigned to a particular product or a process. If the wages paid to workers cannot be directly assigned to a particular product, these will be known as indirect wages. The time required for producing a product would be ascertained and labour should be properly graded. Different grades of workers will be paid different rates of wages. The times spent by different grades of workers for manufacturing a product should also be studied for deciding upon direct labour cost. The setting of standard for direct labour will be done basically on the following parameters:

- Standard labour time for producing a unit.
- Labour rate per hour.

Standard labour time indicates the time taken by different categories of labour force which are as under:

- Skilled labour.
- Semi-skilled labour.
- Unskilled labour.

For setting a standard time for labour force, previous experience, past performance records, test run result, work-study etc. are taken into consideration. The labour rate standard refers to the expected wage rates to be paid for different categories of workers. Past wage rates and demand and supply principle may not be a safe guide for determining standard labour rates. The anticipation of expected changes in labour rates will be an essential factor. In case there is an agreement with workers for payment of wages in the coming period, these rates should be used. If a premium or bonus scheme is in operation, then anticipated extra payments should also be included. Where a piece rate system is used, standard cost will be fixed per piece. The object of fixed standard labour time and labour rate is to device maximum efficiency in the use of labour.

Setting Standards of Overheads

The next important element comes under the head overheads. The very purpose of setting standard for overheads is to minimize the total cost. Standard overhead rates are computed by dividing overhead expenses by direct labour hours or units produced. The standard overhead cost is obtained by multiplying standard overhead rate by the labour hours spent or number of units produced. The determination of overhead rate involves three things:

- Determination of overheads.
- Determination of labour hours or units manufactured.
- Calculating overheads rate by dividing determination of overheads by determination of labour hours or units manufactured.

The overheads are classified into fixed overheads, variable overheads and semi-variable overheads. The fixed overheads remain the same irrespective of level of production, while variable overheads change in the proportion of production. The expenses increase or decrease with the increase or decrease in output. Semi-variable overheads are neither fixed nor variable. These overheads increase with the increase in production but the rate of increase will be less than the rate of increase in production. The division of overheads into fixed, variable and semi-variable categories will help in determining overheads.

Method of Setting Standards

It is pertinent to note that a single standard set may not be suitable for all purposes and all situations. Realistic and rational standards only help to take good decisions. These standards help in taking pricing and capital expenditure decisions which are critical to very survival of the organization.

- High Standards: A high standard is helpful in cost reduction and motivating employees to try to reach the targets. As high standards are not realistic they are not helpful in product costing, inventory valuation, capital expenditure decisions etc.
- Low standards: A standard which is low or loose can be attained by poor performance. It defeats the very purpose of standard costing & fails to disclose inefficiencies. These standards are not helpful in cost control as they are not accurate measures to compare actual results.
- Current Standards; A current standard is a standard which is established for use over a short period of time and is related to current condition. It reflects the performance that should be attained during the current period. The period for current standard is normally one year. It is presumed that conditions of production will remain unchanged. In case there is any change in price or manufacturing condition, the standards are also revised.

Circumstances Under which Standards are Revised and Meaning of Standard Cost Card

Revision of Standards

It is a difficult situation and decision for any organization to contemplate revision of standards. Some experts argue that frequent revisions in standards would defeat the purpose of setting standards and destroy the effectiveness. Conversely, other experts are of the opinion that if the standards are not revised they destroy the utility in inventory valuation & cost control. Therefore, the standards require a continuous review and frequent change, at times. In this volatile world of fierce competition, changing technology, advent of multinational companies, new machineries, better quality labour, increased awareness of labour in terms of their rights etc., all these factors render the set standards obsolete and unfit for use. Under these circumstances, if old standards are used then it would result in poor cost control, unrealistic budgets and unreasonable unit cost for inventory.

Circumstances Under which Standards are Revised

A company must make a plan or programme for revision of budgets so that standards can be set at a current attainable level. Hence the following must be done for revision of standards:

- Labour rate standards should be revised for any change in labour rates.

- Material standards should be revised for any change in the types of material, quality of material or method of production.
- If a new machine is purchased to replace the old one, then labour time standards material quantity standards must be updated.
- In every company, there should be a system in force to revise standards, at least, every year.

Therefore, a periodic review or revision is not only desirable but also necessary, in order to accomplish the objectives of Standard Costing. For effective use of this technique, sometimes there is a need to revise the standards which follow for better control. Even standards are also subjected to change like the production method, environment, raw material, and technology. Standards may need to be changed to accommodate changes in the organization or its environment. When there is a sudden change in economic circumstances, technology or production methods, the standard cost will no longer be accurate.

Standards that are out of date will not act as effective feed forward or feedback control tools. They will not help us to predict the inputs required nor help us to evaluate the efficiency of a particular department. If standards are continually not being achieved and large deviations or variances from the standard are reported, they should be carefully reviewed. Also, changes in the physical productive capacity of the organization or in material prices and wage rates may indicate that standards need to be revised. In practice, changing standards frequently is an expensive operation and can cause confusion. For this reason, standard cost revisions are usually made only once a year.

Revision Variance

When a budget is revised, but the change discussed as above, is not incorporated in the standard cost rate, a variance would arise, which is known as the Revision Variance. Revision variance is the difference between basic standard cost and the revised standard cost.

Variance Analysis

Every business owner must have a budget which lays out the company's future course of activities. A budget helps to showcase from where the sales would come and how the funds would be spent to achieve those sales, with the key objective of generating a profit. While budgeting is a great planning tool, it is also a useful management tool for keeping the business on track for meeting its objectives. For accomplishing this goal, budgeting and variance analysis provides key insights to help the management in taking prompt and feasible decisions.

Budgeting

Preparing a budget at the commencement of the year is a critical exercise for a business and is known as budgeting. It helps in gathering the input from various departments and brings every stakeholder on the same page. It also works as an excellent medium of communication conveying to everyone where the organization wishes to go and how it plans to get there.

After the year gets going and the actual results start coming, the management starts comparing the actuals with the budgets. At this time variances from the budget are identified, and the management has to dig deep to find out the reasons for such variances. This analysis is used for maintaining a control over the business. For instance, if the budget for sales is USD 1,00,000 and the actual sales are USD 80,000, variance analysis produces a difference of USD 20,000. This analysis is effective when the management reviews the variance on a trend line. Sudden changes in a month to month (MoM) variance are clearly visible. This analysis also requires investigation of these variances which helps the management to interpret as to why such variance or differences occurred.

How Companies Apply Variance Analysis?

Most of the companies are concerned with business planning and meeting their financial commitments. Ultimately all want growth. Accordingly, they analyze the variances between:

- Previous-year actual results and current year's budget, which helps them in planning and this is also a part of the budgeting process.
- Existing budget (current financial year) and current-year actuals, which helps them in meeting their commitments. This activity is performed at regular intervals throughout the year like at close of every quarter and at year-end.
- Previous-year actual and current-year actual for analyzing growth. This is done at year-end.

Application of Variance Analysis

- Comparing Budget with Actual: Variance analysis helps in managing the annual budgets by monitoring the budgeted figures and comparing it with the actual revenue/cost. In case of companies which are project or program driven, the financial data are evaluated at key intervals such as month close, quarter end, etc. For example, the month end reports can just provide quantitative data with respect to revenue and expenses or inventory levels. However, variance analysis would help to understand the reasons behind the variances between planned and actual revenue/cost which could lead to adjustments in the business strategies and end objectives.

- Identifying Relationships: Relationship between a pair of variables/elements/ items could also be identified with the help of variance analysis. Correlations (both positive and negative) are critical in business planning. For instance, variance analysis could reveal that when the sale for Product A rises there's a correlated rise in the sales for Product B. Thereby, revealing a positive correlation between 2 products.
- Forecasting: Forecasting uses patterns of the past data for developing a theory about the future business performance. Variances are placed into the context which helps analysts in identifying factors. For example, seasonal change holidays could be a major cause of positive/negative variances.

Most Commonly used Variances

- Purchase price variance: Purchase Price Variance results when actual price which is paid for materials is different from the budgeted cost for such materials. It is usually used as a lagging indicator for quantifying the efficiency of the procurement function. (How efficiently can you procure/purchase required material).
- Labor rate variance: This variance shows the variance between the actual price which is paid for direct labor that is used in the process of production and its standard labor cost (the cost that is acceptable and usually a standard price). Unfavorable variances mean that cost of labor exceeds the budgeted value, while favorable variances mean that labor cost was less than planned. Such information could be used for the planning and budgeting for future periods, and also works as a feedback for employees responsible for direct labor component of the business.
- Material yield variance: This variance is the difference between actual quantity of material used and the standard quantity expected to be used in course of production, multiplied by the standard cost of such materials.
- Volume Variance: Volume variance measures the difference between actual quantities sold or consumed and budgeted quantity expected to be consumed or sold, multiplied by the standard price per unit. The volume variance is a general measure of whether the business is generating the volume of products that it had planned.

Benefits of using Variance Analysis

Using variance analysis in the decision-making process renders the following positive impacts:

- Competitive advantage: Variance analysis helps an organization to be proactive in achieving their business targets, helps in identifying and mitigating any potential risks which eventually builds trust among the team members to deliver what is planned.

- Identifying the changes required in the business strategy: In some of the cases, comparing budget with actual results may point out the requirement for re-evaluating the target customer base or product line of the company. Several assumptions go into developing a budget. In case those assumptions are blowing up the budget, it could be because the budget-related projections are wrong for a variety of reasons. It could also be due to changes in the economy or delays in getting the products/services sent to end customers.
- Identifying any managerial concerns: At times, variance analysis could also provide insight as to how well an organization is being managed. For instance in the case of purchasing, the inability to negotiate volume discounts or securing the competitive bids could indicate managerial problems within the purchasing department. Moreover, weak sales could also be an indication that the salespersons are not trained properly or they lack motivation. By addressing such issues, the variances could disappear as the organization gets on track.
- Managing risk: With the help of variance analysis, the finance heads gather insights which they require to understand the reasons for controllable and uncontrollable variances. Once they're aware of such variance, they're in a position to implement policies to mitigate such risks arising from such variances.
- Creating shareholder value: When an organization brings in proper internal controls, a cross-functional environment, efficient internal audit process, and the culture of meeting commitments, it increases the chances that the variances would be favorable which means that the business commitments would be met or even exceed the expectations.

Problems Associated with Variance Analysis

- Timing delay: The accounting staff gathers variances at end of every month before providing results to the management. In most of the cases, management requires the feedback much faster, and so it tends to rely on warning flags or measurements which are generated on spot.
- Source of variance: Most of the reasons for the variances aren't available in accounting records, so accounting personnel needs to go through the information like labor routings, bills of material, and overtime records for determining the reasons for such variances. Such add-on activity is cost-effective only when the management could actively fix the problems based on the information provided.
- Detailed analysis: If budgeting isn't performed considering the detailed analysis

of every factor, the budgeting process might be loosely done that would deviate from actual numbers. Analyzing variances might not make sense in such scenario.

Material Cost Variance

Material cost variance is the difference between the standard cost of material allowed for the actual output achieved and the actual cost of material used. It is favourable when the actual cost of material is less than the standard cost of material for actual output and adverse when actual cost is higher than the standard cost.

$$\text{MCV} = \text{Standard Cost of Material for actual output} - \text{Actual Cost of Material used}$$

$$\text{Or, MCV} = [\text{Standard quantity for actual output} \times \text{Standard Price}] -$$

$$[\text{Actual quantity} \times \text{Actual price}]$$

$$\text{Or, MCV} = (\text{SQ} \times \text{SP}) - (\text{AQ} \times \text{AP})$$

The standard quantity for actual output (and not standard output) is to be taken which can be calculated as:

$$\text{Standard quantity for actual output} = \text{Actual Output} \times \text{Standard quantity of material per unit.}$$

Example: The Standard quantity of material to produce one unit of Product Y is 8 kg and the standard price per kg of material is $5. However, it is observed that the actual material used for production of 2000 units of Product Y is 18,000 kg and actual price paid per kg of material is $6. Calculate Material Cost Variance.

Solution:

Standard quantity of material per unit = 8 kg

Standard Price = $5

Actual quantity used of material = 18,000 kg

Actual Output = 2000 units

Actual Price = $6

Standard quantity for actual output= Actual Output × Standard quantity of material per unit

= 2000 × 8

= 16,000

Material cost variance= Standard Cost of Material for actual output – Actual Cost of Material used

= [Standard quantity for actual output × Standard Price] – [Actual quantity × Actual price]

= (16,000 × 5) – (18,000 × 6)

= 28,000 (A)

Material Cost Variance can be further sub divided into Material Price Variance and Material Usage/Quantity Variance.

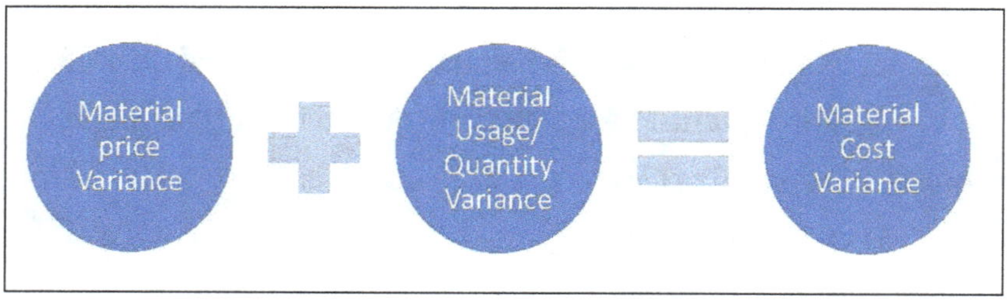

Material Price Variance (MPV)

Material price variance arises when the firm purchases the raw material at a price different than the standard price. "Material Price Variance is that portion of material cost variance which is due to the difference between the standard price specified and the actual price paid."

Material price Variance = (Standard price – Actual price) ×Actual Quantity

= (SP – AP) × AQ

Thus, MPV is the difference between the Standard price and the Actual price multiplied by actual quantity. It is favorable when the actual price paid is less than the standard price set to purchase the material and adverse when the actual price paid is more than the standard price. The quantum of variance is calculated by multiplying this difference of actual and standard price with the actual quantity used for the production of finished goods. It is advisable to calculate MPV in advance that is at the time of purchase of material rather than to wait and look for the other material variances in terms of usage and total cost. The idea is what can be calculated earlier, to be presented faster for early feedback and remedial measures. Let's continue with our example to calculate MPV.

Material price Variance = (Standard price – Actual price) × Actual Quantity

= (5 – 6)×18,000

= 18,000 (A)

Material Usage/Quantity Variance (MUV/MQV)

Material Usage variance arises when there is a difference between the actual quantities of raw material and standard quantities of raw material to produce the output achieved. "Material Usage Variance is that portion of the material cost variance which is due to the difference between the standard quantity specified and the actual quantity used."

Material Usage/Quantity Variance= (Standard quantity for actual output - Actual quantity) × Standard Price

MUV/MQV= (SQ – AQ) ×SP

It is favourable when the actual quantity used is less than the standard quantity specified to produce the actual output and adverse when the actual quantity used is more than the specified standard. Continuing the example, we can calculate Material Usage Variance as follows:

MUV/MQV = (SQ – AQ) × SP

= (16,000 – 18,000) ×5

= 10,000 (A)

Check: The total of MPV and MUV should be equal to MCV.

MCV = MPV + MUV

28,000 (A) = 18,000 (A) + 10,000 (A)

The Material Usage Variance is sub divided into Material Mix Variance and Material Revised Usage Variance or Material sub- usage Variance.

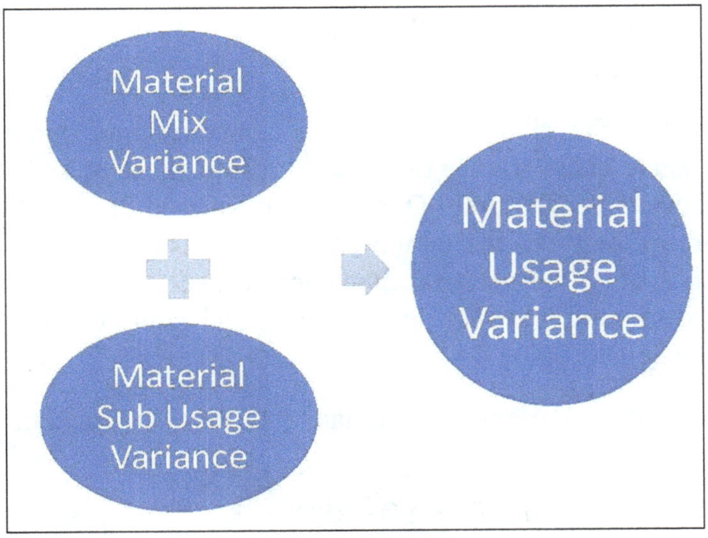

Material Mix Variance

Material Mix Variance may arise in a situation where the firm uses different proportion (mix) of raw material to produce the finished product. The firm pre determines the standard mix to be used for production but its actual mix may differ than expected because of many reasons like, price rise in the cost of material, delay in purchasing the material etc. For instance, if one unit of finished product X should be produced by 20 kg of raw material A and 40 kg of raw material B, the standard mix is 1: 2. If the actual mix is not 1: 2 them it will result into MMV. Therefore, the difference between the actual and standard composition of materials results in Material Mix Variance. It is calculated as follows:

Material Mix Variance = [Revised Standard Quantity – Actual Quantity] × Standard Price

$$MMV = (RSQ - AQ) \times SP$$

where, the Revised standard Quantity (RSQ) is the standard proportion of total of actual quantities of all the materials. RSQ takes into account the increase or decrease in the pre- determined consumption of material that leads to different actual consumption. RSQ is calculated as follows:

$$RSQ = \frac{\text{Standard quantity of one material}}{\text{Total of standard quantities of all materials}} \times \text{Total of actual quantities of all materials}$$

If the total actual quantities of all the material are equal to total standard quantities of all the material, the Revised Standard quantity would be same as Standard quantity.

Material Sub – Usage (Revised Usage) Variance (MSUV/MRUV)

There can be reasons other than those of material mix variance that attributes to material Usage Variance. This variance takes into account those reasons and undertakes the difference between the Standard Quantity and Revised Standard Quantity. When there is no difference between the total actual quantities of all the material and total standard quantities of all the material then the Revised Standard quantity would be same as Standard quantity resulting into no Material Revised Usage Variance. It is calculated as follows:

$$\text{Material Revised Usage Variance} = (\text{Standard Quantity - Revised Standard Quantity}) \times \text{Standard Price}$$

$$MRUV = (SQ - RSQ) \times SP$$

The sum total of MMV and MRUV must be equal to MUV. Check: MUV = MMV + MRUV.

Example: From the data given below, calculate Material Mix variance and Material Revised Usage Variance.

Raw material	Standard	Actual
A	30 units @ $50 per unit	40 units @$50 per unit
B	70 units @ $40 per unit	80 units @ $45 per unit
Total	100	120

Material Mix Variance = [Revised Standard Quantity – Actual Quantity] × Standard Price

$$MMV = (RSQ - AQ) \times SP$$

$$RSQ_A = \frac{30}{100} \times 120 = 36 \text{ units}$$

$$RSQ_B = \frac{70}{100} \times 120 = 84 \text{ units}$$

$$MMV_A = (RSQ - AQ) \times SP$$
$$= (36 - 40) \times 50 \quad = 200(A)$$
$$MMV_B = (RSQ - AQ) \times SP$$
$$= (84 - 80) \times 40 \quad = 160(F)$$
$$MMV \quad = 40(A)$$

Material Revised Usage Variance =
(Standard Quantity - Revised Standard Quantity) × Standard Price

$$MRUV = (SQ - RSQ) \times SP$$

$$MRUV_A = (SQ - RSQ) \times SP$$
$$= (30 - 36) \times 50 \quad = 300(A)$$
$$MRUV_B = (SQ - RSQ) \times SP$$
$$= (70 - 84) \times 40 \quad = 560(F)$$
$$MRUV \quad = 860(A)$$

Let us also calculate Material Cost Variance, Material price Variance and Material Usage Variance in this example.

$$MCV = [\text{Standard quantity for actual output} \times \text{Standard Price}] - [\text{Actual quantity} \times \text{Actual price}]$$

$$\text{Or, } MCV = (SQ \times SP) - (AQ \times AP)$$

$$MCV_A = (SQ \times SP) - (AQ \times AP)$$

$$= (30 \times 50) - (40 \times 50) \quad = 500(A)$$

$$MCV_B = (SQ \times SP) - (AQ \times AP)$$

$$= (70 \times 40) - (80 \times 45) \quad = 800(A)$$

$$MCV \quad = 1{,}300(A)$$

$$\text{Material price Variance} = (\text{Standard price} - \text{Actual price}) \times \text{Actual Quantity}$$

$$= (SP - AP) \times AQ$$

$$MPV_A = (SP - AP) \times AQ$$

$$= (50 - 50) \times 40 \quad = \text{Nil}$$

$$MPV_B = (SP - AP)$$

$$= (40 - 45) \times 80 \quad = 400(A)$$

$$MPV \quad = 400(A)$$

$$\text{Material Usage / Quantity Variance} = (\text{Standard quantity for actual output} - \text{Actual quantity}) \times \text{Standard Price}$$

$$MUV / MQV \quad = (SQ - AQ) x SP$$

$$MUV_A = (SQ - AQ) \times SP$$

$$= (30 - 40) \times 50 \quad = 500(A)$$

$$MUV_B = (SQ - AQ) \times SP$$

$$= (70 - 80) \times 40 \quad = 400(A)$$

$$MUV \quad = 900(A)$$

$$\text{Check}: MCV = MPV + MUV$$

$$= 400(A) + 900(A)$$

$$= 1{,}300(A)$$

$$\text{Check}: MUV = MMV + MRUV$$

$$= 40(A) + 860(A)$$

$$= 900(A)$$

Material Yield Variance (MYV)

The word 'Yield' in the material Yield variance denotes the output. This variance measures the difference in actual output/yield for a given set of inputs and the standard output/yield for a given set of inputs. For example, the 10 kg of inputs A and B together should produce 8 kg of final product. Here, the loss rate is 20% and standard yield is 80%. It implies that the input of both the raw material of, say, 2,000 kg will produce 1,600 units of actual output. The actual yield may differ than the standard yield because the actual loss may differ than the standard loss. Therefore, the material Yield variance is that part of material usage variance that measures the difference between the standard yield and the actual yield.

$$\text{Material Yield Variance} = (\text{Actual Yield} - \text{Standard Yield on actual input})$$
$$\times \text{Standard Output Price}$$
$$\text{MYV} = (\text{AY} - \text{SY}) \times \text{SOP}$$

where, the Standard Output Price is the standard material cost per unit of output,

$$\text{Or, SOP} = \frac{\text{Standard Material Cost}}{\text{Net Standard Output (i.e., Gross output - Standard Loss)}}$$

MYV is favourable when the Actual Yield is more than the Standard Yield and vice-versa. Out of Material Revised Usage Variance and Material Yield Variance, only one has to be calculated. The difference between the two is MRUV is an input variance and undertakes gain or loss in the input quantities of the raw material whereas; the MYV is an output variance as it represents the loss on output of the finished product.

Example: Calculate Material Yield Variance from the following information:

Raw material	Standard Amount		Actual Amount	
A	40 units @ $50 per unit	2,000	45 units @$50 per unit	2,250
B	60 units @ $40 per unit	2,400	55 units @ $45 per unit	2,475
Total	100	4,400	100	4,725
Less: Loss	20		35	
Yield	80		65	

Solution:

$$\text{Material Yield Variance} =$$
$$(\text{Actual Yield} - \text{Standard Yield on actual input}) \times \text{Standard Output Price}$$
$$\text{MYV} = (\text{AY} - \text{SY}) \times \text{SOP}$$
$$= (65 - 80) \times \frac{4{,}400}{80}$$
$$= 825(\text{A})$$

It is important to note here that the material input of standard and actual is same, that is, 100 units, that makes the yield comparable. However, if it is not same then the standard yield should be revised as per the actual input.

Example:

Raw material	Standard Amount		Actual Amount	
A	40 units @ $50 per unit	2,000	200 units @$50 per unit	10,000
B	60 units @ $40 per unit	2,400	300 units @ $45 per unit	3,500
Total	100	4,400	500	23,500
Less: Loss	20		120	
Yield	80		380	

Solution:

Material Yield Variance =

$$(\text{Actual Yield} - \text{Standard Yield on actual input}) \times \text{Standard Output Price}$$

$$MYV = (AY - SY) \times SOP$$

$$AY = 380$$

$$SOP = \frac{4{,}400}{80} = 55$$

Standard Loss = 20% of 100 units = 20 units

$$\text{Standard yield for actual material mix}(500 \text{ units}) = \text{Actual material mix} - \text{Standard Loss}$$

$$= 500 - 20\% \text{ of } 500$$

$$= 400$$

$$MYV = (380 - 400) \times 55$$

$$= 1{,}100 \text{ (A)}$$

Labour Cost Variance

Labour cost variance is the difference between the standard cost of labour allowed for the actual output achieved and the actual cost of labour used. It is favourable when the actual cost of labour is less than the standard cost of labour for actual output and adverse when actual cost is higher than the standard cost.

$$LCV = \text{Standard Labour Cost for actual output} - \text{Actual Labour Cost}$$

$$LCV = [\text{Standard hours for actual output} \times \text{Standard rate per hour}] - [\text{Actual hours} \times \text{Actual rate per hour}]$$

$$\text{Or, } LCV = (SH \times SR) - (AH \times AR)$$

Example: Calculate Labour Cost Variance from the following information:

Standard hours per unit = 20

Standard Rate = \$5

Actual hours used = 15,000 kg

Actual Output = 1000 units

Actual Rate = \$6

Standard hours for actual output	= Actual Output × Standard hours per unit = 1000 x 20 = 20,000
Labour cost variance	= Standard Cost for actual output – Actual Labour Cost =(SH × SR) – (AH × AR)
LCV	= (20,000 × 5) – (15,000 × 6) = 1,00,000 – 90,000 = 10,000 (F)

Labour Cost Variance can be further sub divided into Labour Rate Variance and Labour Time/Efficiency Variance.

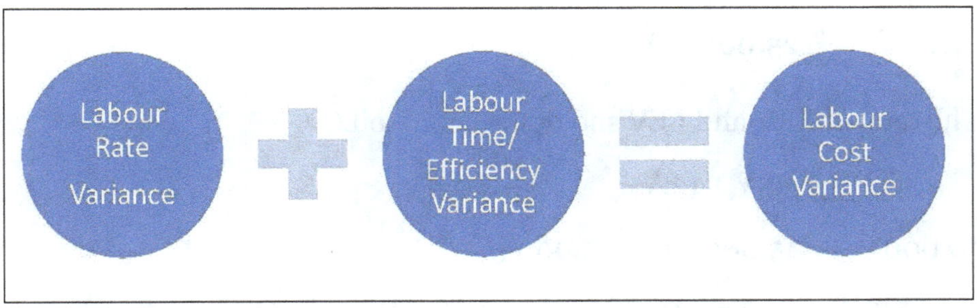

Labour Rate Variance (LRV)

Labour rate variance arises when the firm pays the wages at a rate different than the standard wage rate. LRV is that portion of Labour cost variance which is due to the difference between the standard rate specified and the actual rate paid.

$$\text{Labour Rate Variance} = (\text{Standard Rate} - \text{Actual Rate}) \times \text{Actual Hours}$$
$$= (SR - AR) \times AH$$

It is favourable when the actual rate paid is less than the standard rate set to pay the labour and adverse when the actual rate paid is more than the standard rate. The quantum of variance is calculated by multiplying this difference of actual and standard rate with the actual hours used for the production of finished goods.

Let's continue with our previous example to calculate LRV.

Labour Rate Variance	= (Standard Rate – Actual Rate) × Actual Hours = (SR – AR) × AH = (5 – 6) × 15,000 = 15,000 (A)

Labour Time/Efficiency Variance (LTV/LEV)

Labour Efficiency variance is that part of the labour cost variance which is due to the difference between the actual labour hours and standard labour hours specified to produce the output achieved.

$$\text{Labour Efficiency Variance} = (\text{Standard Hours for actual output} - \text{Actual Hours}) \times \text{Standard Rate per hour}$$

$$\text{LEV} = (\text{SH} - \text{AH}) \times \text{SR}$$

It is favourable when the actual labour hours used is less than the standard labour hours specified to produce the actual output and adverse when the actual labour hours used is more than the specified standard. Continuing the example, we can calculate Labour Time/Efficiency Variance as follows:

$$\text{LTV / LEV} = (\text{SH} - \text{AH}) \times \text{SR}$$
$$= (20{,}000 - 15{,}000) \times 5$$
$$= 25{,}000\ (\text{F})$$

Check: The total of LRV and LEV should be equal to LCV.

LCV = LRV + LEV

10,000 (F) = 15,000 (A) + 25,000 (F)

The Labour Efficiency/Time Variance is sub divided into Idle Time Variance, Labour Mix Variance and Labour Sub-Efficiency Variance.

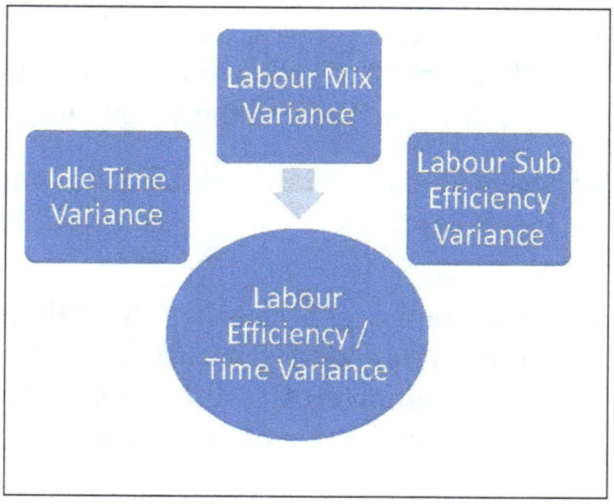

Idle Time Variance (ITV)

Idle time means the workers are not able to utilise the total time for which they are paid for and sitting idle for some time. It can be because of any reason, like, strike, power failure, shortage in supply of material etc. Idle Time Variance is that part of Labour Efficiency Variance which is unproductive due to idle time. It is calculated as follows:

$$\text{Idle Time Variance} = \text{Idle Hours} \times \text{Standard Rate}$$
$$\text{ITV} = \text{IH} \times \text{SR}$$

Idle time represents the unproductive time which is a loss for any organisation. Therefore, it is always unfavourable. Let us assume in the above example that the idle time due to power failure is 100 hours then the Idle Time Variance would be calculated as follows:

$$\begin{aligned} \text{ITV} &= \text{IH} \times \text{SR} \\ &= 100 \times 5 = 500(\text{A}) \end{aligned}$$

It should be mentioned here that some accountant take ITV as part of labour Cost Variance. In that case, the total actual hours available to compute the labour efficiency variance will be reduced by 500 hours, 15,000 – 100 = 14,900 hours.

$$\begin{aligned} \text{LEV} &= (\text{SH} - \text{AH}) \times \text{SR} \\ &= (20{,}000 - 14{,}900) \times 5 \\ &= 25{,}500(\text{F}) \end{aligned}$$

Hence, LCV = LRV + LEV + ITV

10,000 (F) = 15,000 (A) + (25,500 (F) + 500 (A)

Labour Mix Variance (LMV)/Gang Composition Variance

Labour Mix Variance may arise in a situation where the firm uses different proportion (mix) of labour to produce the finished product. The firm pre determines the standard mix to be used for production but its actual mix may differ than expected because of many reasons like, price rise in the cost of labour, delay in engaging the labour etc. For instance, if one unit of finished product X should be produced by 20 hours of Grade A labour and 40 hours of Grade B labour, the standard mix is 1: 2. If the actual mix is not 1: 2 them it will result into LMV. Therefore, the difference between the actual and standard composition of different grades of labour results in Labour Mix Variance. It is calculated as follows:

$$\text{Labour Mix Variance} = [\text{Revised Standard Hours - Actual Hours}] \times \text{Standard Rate per hour}$$

$$\text{LMV} = (\text{RSH} - \text{AH}) \times \text{SR}$$

where, the Revised standard Hours (RSH) is the standard proportion of total of actual hours of all the labour. RSH takes into account the increase or decrease in the pre- determined labour hours consumption that leads to different actual consumption. RSH is calculated as follows:

$$RSH = \frac{\text{Standard Hours of one grade of labour}}{\text{Total of standard hours of all labour}} \times \text{Total of actual hours of all labour}$$

If the total actual hours of all the labour are equal to total standard hours of all the labour, the Revised Standard hours would be same as Standard hours. This Variance would be adverse when the Actual hours are more than the Revised Standard hours and vice- versa.

Labour Revised Efficiency Variance (LREV)/Labour Sub-Efficiency Variance (LSEV)

There can be reasons other than those belongs to Idle time variance and Labour Mix variance that attributes to Labour Usage Variance. This variance takes into account those reasons and undertakes the difference between the Standard Hours and Revised Standard Hours. When there is no difference between the total actual hours of all the labour and total standard hours of all the labour then the Revised Standard hours would be same as Standard hours resulting into no Labour Revised Efficiency Variance. It is calculated as follows:

$$\text{Labour Revised Efficiency Variance} = (\text{Standard Hours} - \text{Revised Standard Hours}) \times \text{Standard Rate}$$

$$LREV = (SH - RSH) \times SR$$

This variance would be adverse when the Revised Standard hours are more than the Standard hours and vice- versa. The sum total of ITV, LMV and LREV must be equal to LEV.

$$\text{Check}: LEV = ITV + LMV + LREV$$

Example: From the data given below, calculate Labour Mix variance and Labour Sub Efficiency Variance.

Grades of Workers	Standard Cost for one unit	Actual Output = 100 units
A	20 hours @ $50 per unit	2,500 hours @$40 per unit
B	40 hours@ $40 per unit 6	6,500 hours @ $35 per unit
Total	60	9,000

Solution: Let us make the basic calculation by making the labour input cost comparable for the actual output produced.

Grades of Workers	Standard Cost for one unit			Actual Output = 100 units		
	Hours	Rate	Amount	Hours	Rate	Amount
A	2,000	50	1,00,000	2,500	40	1,00,000
B	4,000	40	1,60,000	6,500	35	2,27,500
Total	6,000		2,60,000	9,000		3,27,500

$$\text{Labour Mix Variance} = [\text{Revised Standard Hours - Actual Hours}] \times \text{Standard Rate}$$

$$LMV = (RSH - AH) \times SR$$

$$RSH_A = \frac{2{,}000}{6{,}000} \times 9{,}000 = 3{,}000 \text{ hours}$$

$$RSH_B = \frac{4{,}000}{6{,}000} \times 9{,}000 = 6{,}000 \text{ hours}$$

$$LMV_A = (RSH - AH) \times SR$$

$$= (3{,}000 - 2{,}500) \times 50 \qquad = 25{,}000(F)$$

$$LMV_B = (RSH - AH) \times SR = (6{,}000 - 6{,}500) \times 40 = 20{,}000(A)$$

$$LMV = 5{,}000(F)$$

$$\text{Labour Revised Efficiency Variance} = (\text{Standard Hours - Revised Standard Hours}) \times \text{Standard Rate}$$

$$LREV = (SH - RSH) \times SR$$

$$LREV_A = (SH - RSH\ ) \times SR$$

$$= (2{,}000 - 3{,}000) \times 50 \quad = 50{,}000(A)$$

$$LREV_B = (SH - RSH) \times SR$$

$$= (4{,}000 - 6{,}000\ ) \times 40 \quad = 80{,}0000(A)$$

$$LREV \qquad = 1{,}30{,}000(A)$$

Let us also calculate Labour Cost Variance, Labour Rate Variance and Labour Efficiency Variance in this example.

$$LCV = [\text{Standard hours for actual output} \times \text{Standard rate per hour}] - [\text{Actual hours} \times \text{Actual rate per hour}]$$

$$\text{Or, } LCV = (SH \text{ x } SR) - (AH \text{ x } AR)$$

$$= \text{Standard Labour Cost} - \text{Actual Labour Cost}$$

$$= 2{,}60{,}000 - 3{,}27{,}500$$

$$= 67{,}500(A)$$

$$\text{Labour Rate Variance} = (\text{Standard Rate} - \text{Actual Rate}) \times \text{Actual Hours}$$
$$= (SR - AR) \times AH$$

$$LRV_A = (SR - AR) \times AH$$
$$= (50 - 40) \times 2{,}500 \quad = 25{,}000(F)$$
$$LRV_B = (SR - AR) \times AH$$
$$= (40 - 35) \times 6{,}500 \quad = 32{,}500(F)$$
$$LRV \quad = 57{,}500(F)$$

$$\text{Labour Efficiency Variance} = (\text{Standard Hours for actual output} - \text{Actual Hours}) \times \text{Standard Rate per hour}$$
$$LEV = (SH - AH) \times SR$$

$$LEV_A = (SH - AH) \times SR$$
$$= (2{,}000 - 2{,}500) \times 50 \quad = 25{,}000(A)$$
$$LEV_B = (SH - AH) \times SR$$
$$= (4{,}000 - 6{,}500) \times 40 \quad = 1{,}00{,}000(A)$$
$$LEV \quad = 1{,}25{,}000(A)$$

$$\text{Check}: LCV = LRV + LEV$$
$$= 57{,}500(F) + 1{,}25{,}000(A)$$
$$= 67{,}500(A)$$
$$\text{Check}: LEV = LMV + LSEV$$
$$= 5{,}000(F) + 1{,}30{,}000(A)$$
$$= 1{,}25{,}000(A)$$

Labour Yield Variance (LYV)

The Labour Yield Variance is just like Material yield Variance. The LYV measures the difference in actual output/yield for a given set of labour inputs and the standard output/yield for a given set of labour inputs. The actual yield may differ than the standard yield because the actual loss may differ than the standard loss. Therefore, the Labour Yield variance measures the difference between the standard yield and the actual yield.

$$\text{Labour Yield Variance} = (\text{Actual Yield} - \text{Standard Yield on actual input}) \times \text{Standard Output Price}$$
$$MYV = (AY - SY) \times SOP$$

where, the Standard Output Price is the standard labour cost per unit of output.

$$\text{Or, SOP} = \frac{\text{Standard Labour Cost}}{\text{Net Standard Output (i.e., Grossoutput - Standard Loss)}}$$

LYV is favourable when the Actual Yield is more than the Standard Yield and vice- versa.

Example: Calculate Labour Yield Variance from the following information:

Labour	Standard labour cost for 400 units	Actual Labour cost for 600 units
A	40 hours @ $15 per hour	60 hours @ $17 per hour
B	60 hours @ $10 per hour	60 hours @ $12 per hour

Solution: Let us do the basic calculations by making Standard hours for actual output.

Labour	Standard labour cost for 400 units			Actual Labour cost for 600 units		
	Hours	Rate	Amount	Hours	Rate	Amount
A	60	15	900	60	17	1,020
B	90	10	900	60	12	720
Total Cost/Hrs	150		1,800	120		1,740

$$\text{Labour Yield Variance} = (\text{Actual Yield} - \text{Standard Yield on actual input}) \times \text{Standard Output Price}$$

$$\text{MYV} = (\text{AY} - \text{SY}) \times \text{SOP}$$

$$= (600 - \frac{600}{150} \times 120) \times \frac{1{,}800}{600}$$

$$= 360 (\text{F})$$

Overhead Variance

1. Calculation of Overheads when Overhead rate per hour is used:

- $\text{Standard overhead rate per hour} = \frac{\text{Budgeted overheads}}{\text{Budgeted hours}}$
- $\text{Standard hours for actual output} = \frac{\text{Budgeted hours}}{\text{Budgeted output}} \times \text{Actual output}$
- $\text{Absorbed / Recovered Overheads} = \text{Standard hours for actual output} \times \text{Standard overhead rate per hour}$
- $\text{Standard Overhead} = \text{Actual hours} \times \text{Standard overhead rate per hour}$

- Budgeted Overhead = Budgeted hours × Standard overhead rate per hour
- Actual Overhead = Actual hours × Actual overhead rate per hour

2. Calculation of Overheads when Overhead rate per unit is used:

- Standard overhead rate per unit = $\frac{\text{Budgeted overheads}}{\text{Budgeted output}}$
- Standard output for actual hours = $\frac{\text{Budgeted hours}}{\text{Budgeted output}} \times \text{Actual hours}$
- Absorbed Overheads = Actual output × Standard overhead rate per unit
- Standard Overhead = Standard output for actual hours × Standard overhead rate per unit
- Budgeted Overhead = Budgeted output × Standard overhead rate per unit
- Actual Overhead = Actual output × Actual overhead rate per unit

Total Overhead Cost Variance (TOCV)

The total Overhead Cost Variance results whenever there is a difference between the actual overhead cost incurred and the standard overhead cost for the actual output achieved. TOCV undertakes the under and over absorption of overheads. The standard overhead cost for the actual output can be calculated either by applying the formula of standard overhead rate per hour or by standard overhead rate per unit.

$$\begin{aligned}\text{TOCV} &= \text{Absorbed Overheads - Actual Overheads}\\ &= (\text{Standard hours for actual output} \times \text{Standard overhead rate per hour})\\ &\quad \text{- Actual Overhead incurred}\\ &= (\text{Actual Output} \times \text{Standard overhead rate per unit})\\ &\quad \text{- Actual Overhead incurred}\end{aligned}$$

$$\text{where, Standard overhead rate per hour} = \frac{\text{Budgeted overheads}}{\text{Budgeted hours}}$$

$$\text{Standard overhead rate per unit} = \frac{\text{Budgeted overheads}}{\text{Budgeted output}}$$

When the actual overhead cost is less than the absorbed overhead cost, the variance is favourable and vice- versa.

Example: Calculate total Overhead Cost variance from the following information:

Budgeted Overheads = \$25,000

Budgeted Hours = 12,500

Budgeted output = 5,000 units

Actual overheads = $30,000

Actual output = 7,000 units

Solution:

$$\text{TOCV} = \text{Absorbed Overheads - Actual Overheads}$$
$$= (\text{Standard hours for actual output} \times \text{Standard overhead rate per hour}) - \text{Actual Overhead incurred}$$

$$\text{Standard overhead rate per hour} = \frac{\text{Budgeted overheads}}{\text{Budgeted hours}}$$
$$= \frac{25{,}000}{12{,}500} = 2$$

$$\text{Standard hours for actual output} = \frac{12{,}500}{5{,}000} \times 7{,}000 = 17{,}500$$

$$\text{TOCV} = (17{,}500 \times 2) - 30{,}000$$
$$= 5{,}000(\text{F})$$

should be computed for Fixed and Variable Overhead Variances respectively.

Variable Overhead Variances

The Variable Overhead Variance is bifurcated between Variable overhead cost variance, Variable overhead Expenditure/Spending/Budget Variance and Variable Overhead Efficiency Variance.

Variable Overhead Cost Variance (VOCV)

Variable overhead Cost Variance measures the difference between Absorbed Variable overhead and Actual Variable Overhead.

$$\text{VOCV} = \text{Absorbed Variable Overhead} - \text{Actual Variable Overhead}$$

Example: Calculate Variable Overhead Cost Variance from the following data.

	Actual	Budgeted
Outputs (units)	9,000	10,000
Hours	2,000	2,500
Variable Overhead	5,500	5,000
Fixed Overhead	8,000	9,000

Solution:

$$\text{Standard overhead rate per hour} = \frac{\text{Budgeted overheads}}{\text{Budgeted hours}}$$

$$= \frac{5{,}000}{2{,}500} \quad = \$2 \text{ per hour}$$

$$\text{Standard hours for actual output} = \frac{\text{Budgeted hours}}{\text{Budgeted output}} \times \text{Actual output}$$

$$= \frac{2{,}500}{10{,}000} \times 9{,}000 = 2{,}250 \text{ hours}$$

$$\text{Absorbed / Recovered Overheads} = \text{Standard hours for actual output} \times \text{Standard overhead rate per hour}$$

$$= 2{,}250 \times 2 = \$4{,}500$$

$$\text{VOCV} = \text{Absorbed Variable Overhead} - \text{Actual Variable Overhead}$$

$$= \$4{,}500 - \$5{,}500$$

$$= \$1{,}000(\text{A})$$

The Variable Overhead Cost Variance is sub divided into Variable Overhead Expenditure/Spending/Budget Variance and Variable Overhead Efficiency Variance.

$$\text{Variable Overhead Cost Variance} = \text{Variable Overhead Expenditure Variance} + \text{Variable Overhead Efficiency Variance}$$

Variable Overhead Expenditure/Spending/Budget Variance

This Variance arises when there is a difference between standard variable overhead and actual variable overhead incurred. The formula is as follows:

$$\text{Variable Overhead Expenditure Variance} = \text{Standard variable overhead} - \text{Actual variable overhead}$$

Variable Overhead Efficiency Variance

This variance arises when there is a difference between adsorbed variable overhead and standard variable overhead. It is calculated as follows:

$$\text{Variable Overhead Efficiency Variance} = \text{Absorbed variable overhead} - \text{Standard variable overhead}$$

Example: Continuing with the same example, let's calculate Variable Overhead Expenditure Variance and Variable Overhead Efficiency Variance.

Solution:

We know,

Standard overhead rate per hour = \$ 2 per hour

Standard hours for actual output = 2,250 hours

Absorbed/Recovered Overheads = \$ 4,500

$$\text{Standard Variable Overhead} = \text{Actual hours} \times \text{Standard overhead rate per hour}$$
$$= 2{,}000 \times 2 = \$4{,}000$$

$$\text{Variable Overhead Expenditure Variance} = \text{Standard variable overhead} - \text{Actual variable overhead}$$
$$= 4{,}000 - 5{,}500 = \$1{,}500(A)$$

$$\text{Variable Overhead Efficiency Variance} = \text{Absorbed variable overhead} - \text{Standard variable overhead}$$
$$= 4{,}500 - 4{,}000 = \$\ 500(F)$$

$$\text{Variable Overhead Cost Variance} = \text{Variable Overhead Expenditure Variance} + \text{Variable Overhead Efficiency Variance}$$
$$1{,}000(A) = 1{,}500(A) + 500(F)$$

Fixed Overhead Variances

We will divide the fixed overhead variance into Expenditure variance, volume variance, efficiency variance, capacity variance and calendar variance.

Fixed Overhead Cost Variance (FOCV)

It is that portion of total overhead cost variance that arises due to difference between standard fixed overhead cost for actual output and actual fixed overhead.

$$\text{Fixed Overhead Cost Variance} =$$
$$\text{Absorbed Fixed Overhead} - \text{Actual Fixed Overhead}$$

Example: Calculate Fixed Overhead Cost Variance continuing with example.

Solution:

$$\text{Standard overhead rate per hour} = \frac{\text{Budgeted Fixed overheads}}{\text{Budgeted hours}}$$

$$= \frac{9{,}000}{2{,}500} = 3.6$$

$$\text{Standard hours for actual output} = \frac{\text{Budgeted hours}}{\text{Budgeted output}} \times \text{Actual output}$$

$$= \frac{2{,}500}{10{,}000} \times 9{,}000 = 2{,}250 \text{ hours}$$

$$\text{Absorbed / Recovered Overheads} = \text{Standard hours for actual output} \times \text{Standard overhead rate per hour}$$

$$= 2{,}250 \times 3.6$$

$$= \$\ 8{,}100$$

$$\text{FOCV} = \text{Absorbed Fixed Overhead} - \text{Actual Fixed Overhead}$$

$$= \$8{,}100 - \$8{,}000$$

$$= \$100(\text{F})$$

FOCV is divided into two variances, that is, Fixed Overhead Expenditure Variance and Fixed Overhead Volume Variance.

$$\text{Fixed Overhead Cost Variance} = \text{Fixed Overhead Expenditure Variance} + \text{Fixed Overhead Volume Variance}$$

Fixed Overhead Expenditure/Spending/Budget Variance

It is that portion of fixed overhead cost variance which arises due to the difference between budgeted fixed overhead and actual fixed overhead. If the actual fixed overhead is more than the budgeted, the expenditure would be adverse and vice- versa.

$$\text{Fixed Overhead Expenditure Variance} = \text{Budgeted Fixed Overhead} - \text{Actual Fixed Overhead}$$

Fixed Overhead Volume Variance

It is that portion of fixed overhead cost variance which arises due to the difference between standard cost of overhead absorbed by actual production and the budgeted overhead. If the actual output is more than the budgeted output, the volume variance would be favourable and vice- versa. It is calculated as follows:

$$\text{Fixed Overhead Volume Variance} = \text{Absorbed fixed Overhead} - \text{Budgeted Fixed Overhead}$$

Example: Calculate Fixed Overhead Expenditure Variance and Fixed Overhead Volume Variance in the example.

Solution: We have calculated the following in the previous example.

Standard overhead rate per hour = \$ 3.6 per hour

Standard hours for actual output = 2,250 hours

Absorbed/Recovered Overheads = \$ 8,100

$$\text{Standard Fixed Overhead} = \text{Actual hours} \times \text{Standard overhead rate per hour}$$
$$= 2{,}000 \times 3.6 = \$7{,}200$$

$$\text{Fixed Overhead Expenditure Variance} = \text{Budgeted Fixed Overhead} - \text{Actual Fixed Overhead}$$
$$= 9{,}000 - 8{,}000 = \$1{,}000(\text{F})$$

$$\text{Fixed Overhead Volume Variance} = \text{Absorbed fixed Overhead} - \text{Budgeted Fixed Overhead}$$
$$= 8{,}100 - 9{,}000 = \$\ 900(\text{A})$$

Let us check.

$$\text{Fixed Overhead Cost Variance} = \text{Fixed Overhead Expenditure Variance} + \text{Fixed Overhead Volume Variance}$$
$$100(\text{F}) = 1{,}000(\text{F}) + 900(\text{A})$$

Fixed Overhead Volume Variance is sub- divided into Efficiency Variance, Capacity Variance and Calendar Variance.

Fixed Overhead Efficiency Variance

It is that portion of Fixed overhead volume variance that arises due to the difference between the actual output and the standard output expected, arising from the efficiency of workers or plant. It is measured by the difference between absorbed fixed overhead and standard fixed overhead.

$$\text{Fixed Overhead Efficiency Variance} = \text{Absorbed fixed Overhead} - \text{Standard Fixed Overhead}$$

Fixed Overhead Capacity Variance

It is that portion of fixed overhead volume variance that arises due to difference in standard and actual output because of under and over capacity utilisation of plant and equipment attributing to factors like idle time, lockouts and strikes, material shortage, machinery break down, labour turnover. It results due to the difference in actual working hours than budgeted. It is expressed as:

Fixed Overhead Capacity Variance = Standard fixed Overhead - Budgeted Fixed Overhead

Fixed Overhead Calendar Variance

The Fixed Overhead Calendar Variance arises when there is a difference between the number of working days in the budgeted period and actual number of working days to which the budget is applicable. The organization takes into account all the normal holiday in due course of business in a particular country while laying down the standard. However, the difference may arise between the actual working days and the budgeted working days because of unexpected and exceptional circumstances, like, national tragedy, death of national leader etc.

$$\text{Fixed Overhead Calendar Variance} = \begin{pmatrix}\text{Actual number of working days -} \\ \text{Standard number of working days}\end{pmatrix} \times \text{Standard rate per day}$$

$$= (\text{Revised Budgeted hours - Budgeted hours}) \times \text{Standard rate per hour}$$

This variance would be adverse when there are extra holidays and favourable in case of extra working days. However, the probability of extra working days is very less. Whenever calendar variance is calculated, the calculation of capacity variance has to be modified and thereby, Revised Capacity Variance should be calculated.

$$\text{Revised Capacity Variance} = (\text{Actual hours - Revised Budgeted hours}) \times \text{Standard rate per hour}$$

Let us calculate Efficiency Variance and Capacity Variance in example.

$$\text{Fixed Overhead Efficiency Variance} = \text{Absorbed fixed Overhead - Standard Fixed Overhead}$$

$$= 8{,}100 - 7{,}200 = \$900\,(F)$$

$$\text{Fixed Overhead Capacity Variance} = \text{Standard fixed Overhead - Budgeted Fixed Overhead}$$

$$= 7{,}200 - 9{,}000 = \$1{,}800\ (A)$$

Check:

$$\text{Volume Variance} = \text{Efficiency Variance} + \text{Capacity Variance}$$
$$= 900(F) + 1{,}800(A)$$
$$= 900(A)$$

References

- Standard-Costing-Variance-Analysis: sajaipuriacollege.in, Retrieved 21, July 2020
- Variance-analysis: cleartax.in, Retrieved 07, May 2020

4

Marginal Costing

The change in cost which occurs when the quantity produced of a particular product increases, is known as marginal cost. Some of the major concepts which are studied under marginal costing are break even analysis and decision regarding sales mix. The diverse aspects of marginal costing have been thoroughly discussed in this chapter.

By analyzing the behaviour of costs in relation to changes in volume of output it becomes evident that there are some items of costs which tend to vary directly with the volume of output, whereas there are others which tend to vary with volume of output, are called variable cost and those remain unaffected by change in volume of output are fixed cost or period costs. Marginal costing is a study where the effect on profit of changes in the volume and type of output is analysed. It is not a method of cost ascertainment like job costing or contract costing. It is a technique of costing oriented towards managerial decision making and control.

Marginal costing, being a technique can be used in combination with other technique such as budgeting and standard costing. It is helpful in determining the profitability of products, departments, processes, and cost centres. While analyzing the profitability, marginal costing interprets the cost on the basis of nature of cost. The emphasis is on behaviour of costs and their impact on profitability. Marginal costing is defined as "the ascertainment of marginal costs and of the effect on profit of changes in volume or type of output by differentiating between fixed costs, and variable costs".

Features of Marginal Costing

The following are the special features of Marginal Costing:

- Marginal costing is a technique of working of costing which is used in conjunction with other methods of costing (Process or job).
- Fixed and variable costs are kept separate at every stage. Semi – Variable costs are also separated into fixed and variable.
- As fixed costs are period costs, they are excluded from product cost or cost of production or cost of sales. Only variable costs are considered as the cost of the product.
- As fixed cost is period cost, they are charged to profit and loss account during the period in which they incurred. They are not carried forward to the next year's income.

- Marginal income or marginal contribution is known as the income or profit.
- The difference between the contribution and fixed costs is the net profit or loss.
- Fixed costs remains constant irrespective of the level of activity.
- Sales price and variable cost per unit remains the same.
- Cost volume profit relationship is fully employed to reveal the state of profitability at various levels of activity.

Assumptions in Marginal Costing

The technique of marginal costing is based on the following assumptions:

- All elements of costs can be divided into fixed and variable.
- The selling price per unit remains unchanged at all levels of activity.
- Variable cost per unit remains constant irrespective of level of output and fluctuates directly in proportion to changes in the volume of output.
- Fixed costs remain unchanged or constant for the entire volume of production.
- Volume of product is the only factor which influences the costs.

Characteristics of Marginal Costing

The essential characteristics and mechanism of marginal costing technique may be summed up as follows:

- Segregation of cost into fixed and variable elements: In marginal costing, all costs are segregated into fixed and variable elements.
- Marginal cost as product cost: Only marginal (variable) costs are charged to products.
- Fixed costs are period costs: Fixed cost are treated as period costs and are charged to costing profit and loss account of the period in which they are incurred.
- Valuation of inventory: The work in progress and finished stocks are valued at marginal cost only.
- Contribution is the difference between sales and marginal cost: The relative profitability of the products or departments is based on a study of "contribution" made by each of the products or departments.

Advantages of Marginal Costing

Marginal costing is an important technique of managerial decision making. It is a tool for cost control and profit planning. The following are the advantages of marginal costing technique:

- Simplicity: The statement propounded under marginal costing can be easily followed as it breaks up the cost as variable and fixed.
- Stock Valuation: Stock valuation cab be easily done and understood as it includes only the variable cost.
- Meaningful Reporting: Marginal costing serves as a good basis for reporting to management. The profits are analyzed from the point of view of sales rather than production.
- Effect on Fixed Cost: The fixed costs are treated as period costs and are charged to Profit and Loss Account directly. Thus, they have practically no effect on decision making.
- Profit Planning: The Cost–Volume Profit relationship is perfectly analysed to reveal efficiency of products, processes, and departments. Break-even Point and Margin of Safety are the two important concepts helpful in profit planning.
- Cost Control and Cost Reduction: Marginal costing technique is helpful in preparation of flexible budgets as the costs are classified into fixed and variable. The emphasis is laid on variable cost for control. The constant focus is on cost and volume and their effect on profit pave the way for cost reduction.
- Pricing Policy: Marginal costing is immensely helpful in determination of selling prices under different situations like recession, depression, introduction of new product, etc. Correct pricing can be developed under the marginal costs technique with the help of the cost information revealed therein.
- Helpful to Management: Marginal costing is helpful to the management in exercising decisions regarding make or buy, exporting, key factor and numerous other aspects of business operations.

Limitations of Marginal Costing

Following are the limitations of marginal costing:

- Classification of Cost: Break up of cost into fixed and variable portion is a difficult problem. More over clear cost division of semi–variable or semi–fixed cost is complicated and cannot be accurate.
- Not Suitable for External Reporting: Since fixed cost is not included in total cost, full cost is not available to outsiders to judge the efficiency.
- Lack of Long – term Perspective: Marginal costing is most suitable for decision

making in a short term. It assumes that costs are classified into fixed and variable. In the long term all the cost are variable. Therefore it ignores time element and is not suitable for long term decisions.

- Under Valuation of Stock: Under marginal costing only variable costs are considered and the output as well as stock are undervalued and profit is distorted. When there is loss of stock the insurance cover will not meet the total cost.
- Automation: In these days of automation and technical advancement, huge investments are made in heavy machinery which results in heavy amount of fixed costs. Ignoring fixed cost in this context for decision making is irrational.
- Production Aspect is ignored: Marginal costing lays too much emphasis on selling function and as such production aspect has been considered to be less significant. But from the business point of view, both the functions are equally important.
- Not Applicable in all Types of Business: In contract type and job order type of businesses, full cost of the job or the contract is to be charged. Therefore it is difficult to apply marginal costing in all these types of businesses.
- Misleading Picture: Each product is shown at variable cost alone, thus giving a misleading picture about its cost.
- Less Scope for Long – term Policy Decision: Since cost, volume, and profits are interlinked in price determination, which can be changed constantly, development of long term pricing policy is not possible.

Marginal Costing and Absorption Costing

Absorption costing charges all the costs i.e., both the fixed and variable fixed to the products, jobs, processes, and operations. Marginal costing technique charges variable cost. Absorption is not any specific method of costing. It is common name for all the methods where the total cost is charged to the output. Absorption Costing is defined as "the practice of charging all costs, both fixed and variable to operations, processes, or products" From this definition it is inferred that absorption costing is full costing. The full cost includes prime cost, factory overheads, administration overheads, selling and distribution overheads.

Table: Distinction between Absorption Costing and Marginal Costing.

Absorption Costing	Marginal Costing
1. Total cost technique is the practice of charging all cost, both variable and fixed to operations, process or products.	1. Marginal costing charges only variable cost to products, process, or operations and excludes fixed cost entirely.
2. It values stock at the cost which includes fixed cost also.	2. It values stock at total variable cost only. This results in higher value of stock under absorption costing than in marginal costing.

3. It is guided by profit which is the excess of sales over the total costs in solving managerial problems.	3. It focuses its attention on Contribution which is excess of sales over variable cost.
4. In total cost technique; there is a problem of apportionment of fixed costs which may result in under or over recovery of expenses.	4. It excludes fixed cost. Therefore, there is no question of arbitrary apportionment.

Illustration of Marginal Costing and Absorption Costing

Income Statement Under Marginal Costing

Sales [A]	--------------------
--	
Less: variable cost of production	
Direct material Direct labour Variable manufacturing overheads	----------- ----------- ------------
	--
Cost of goods manufactured	-------------------
Add: beginning inventory	-------------------

Cost of goods available for sale	--------------------------
Less: closing inventory	--------------------------
	--
Cost of goods sold [B]	-------------------------
	--
[C] Marginal contribution [A – B]	---------------------

Less: fixed manufacturing overhead Variable selling and administrative expenses Fixed selling and administrative expenses	------------- ------------- -------------
	---
Total non-production cost [D]	--------------------
Net income [C-D]	---------------------
--	

Income under marginal costing technique can be computed by following these steps:

- Sales value can be computed by multiplying units sold and price per unit.

- Variable production cost includes costs for direct material, direct labour and variable overhead. This can be computed by multiplying per unit material, labour cost and labour overhead cost with units produced respectively.
- By adding all the variable costs we shall get cost of production.
- In cost of production we shall add value of opening inventory to get cost of goods available for sale.
- From, cost of goods available for sale, we shall deduct value of closing inventory to get cost of goods sold.
- Valuation of opening as well as closing inventory is done through including only variable production cost, which is considered to be product cost. Here with variable production cost we mean direct material, direct labour and variable manufacturing overheads.
- Now, next step is to get marginal contribution i.e. sales value minus variable cost of goods sold.
- Now, to get net income we need to deduct all period costs from the marginal contribution. With period cost here we mean by fixed manufacturing cost, fixed and variable administrative cost and fixed and variable selling & distribution costs.

Illustration for Projected Income Statement Under Marginal Costing

Year	2013	2014
Selling price	$15/unit	$15/unit
Quantity sold	20,000	23,000
Production actual	25,000	19,000
Budgeted production	30,000	30,000
Costs:		
Direct material	$3/unit	$ 3/unit
Direct labour	$2/unit	$2/unit
Variable manufacturing expense	$1/unit	$1/unit
Fixed manufacturing cost	$ 90,000p.a	$ 90,000p.a
Variable administrative cost	$ 0.50/unit	$ 0.50/unit
Fixed administrative cost	$ 25,000p.a	$ 25,000p.a
Variable selling and distribution cost	$ 1.50/unit	$ 1.50/unit
Fixed selling and distribution cost	$ 35,000p.a	$ 35,000p.a

Compute, under marginal costing actual income for 2013 and projected income for 2014.

Income statement under marginal costing:

Year	2013	2014
Sales [A]	3,00,000	3,45,000
Less: variable cost of production		
Direct material Direct labour Variable manufacturing overheads	75,000 50,000 25,000	57,000 38,000
19,000	-- ---------------------------	
Cost of goods manufactured	1,50,000	
1,14,000		
Add: beginning inventory	NIL	30,000
-------------------------------- --	-------- -------- -------- -----	
Cost of goods available for sale	1,50,000	
1,44,000		
Less: closing inventory	30,000	
6,000		

Cost of goods sold [B]	1,20,000	
1,38,000		
[C] Marginal contribution [A – B]	1,80,000	
2,07,000		

Less: Variable administrative expenses Variable selling expenses Fixed manufacturing overhead 90,000 Fixed administrative expenses 25,000 Fixed selling expenses 35,000	10,000 30,000 90,000 25,000 35,000	11,500 34,500

Total non-production cost [D]	1,90,000	1,96,000
Net income [C-D]	(10,000)	
11,000		
--		

Working notes:

	2013	2014
1) Sales value	20,000 X 15 = 3,00,000	23,000 X 15 = 3,45,000
2) Direct material	25,000X3 =75,000	19,000X3 =57,000
3) Direct labour	25,000X2 = 50,000	19,000X2 = 38,000
4) Variable manufacturing exp.	25,000x1 = 25,000	19,000X1 = 19,000
5) Opening inventory* 20,000	NIL	25,000 + 0
		= 5,000 units
6) Closing inventory* 23,000	25,000 + 0-20,000 = 5,000 units	5,000+19,000– = 1,000 units
7) Value of opening inventory	NIL	5,000x (3+2+1) = 30,000
8) Value of closing inventory	5,000 X (3+2+1) =30,000	1,000 X (3+2+1) = 6,000
9) Variable administrative cost	20,000 X.50 = $10,000	23,000 X.50 = $11,500
10) variable selling cost	20,000X1.50 = $ 30,000	23,000X1.50 = $ 34,500
*closing inventory= opening inventory + production – sale		

Income Statement Under Absorption Costing

Sales [A]	--------------------
--	
Less: cost of production	
Direct material Direct labour Variable & fixed manufacturing overheads	----------- ----------- ------------
	-- --------------
Cost of goods manufactured	-------------------
Add: beginning inventory	-------------------

Cost of goods available for sale	--------------------------
Less: closing inventory	--------------------------
	--
Cost of goods sold Add: under absorbed fixed manufacturing overhead Less: over absorbed fixed manufacturing overhead	------------------------- ------------ ------------

[B]Cost of goods sold at actual	-------------------------

[C] Gross profit [A – B]	---------------------

Less: Variable selling and administrative expenses Fixed selling and administrative expenses	------------- -------------
	--
[D] Total non-production cost	--------------------
Net income [C-D]	---------------------
--	

Income under absorption costing technique can be computed by following these steps:

- Sales value can be computed by multiplying units sold and price per unit.
- Production cost includes costs for direct material, direct labour and fixed & variable overhead. This can be computed by multiplying per unit material, labour cost and manufacturing overhead cost with units produced respectively.
- By adding all the production costs we shall get cost of production.
- In cost of production we shall add value of opening inventory to get cost of goods available for sale.
- From, cost of goods available for sale, we shall deduct value of closing inventory to get cost of goods sold.
- Valuation of opening as well as closing inventory is done through including both fixed & variable production cost, which is considered to be product cost. Here with fixed & variable production cost we mean, direct material, direct labour and fixed & variable manufacturing overheads.
- Fixed manufacturing overheads for the number of units produced through some absorption rate, it can be over absorbed or under absorbed depending on the positive or negative deviation from the budgeted output. So, if there is over production then we shall have over absorption which we shall deduct from cost of goods sold on the other hand if production is less than the budgeted production, then we shall have under absorption, which we shall add in cost of goods sold.
- Now, next step is to get gross profit i.e. sales value minus cost of goods sold actual.
- Now, to get net income we need to deduct all period costs from the gross profit.

With period cost here we mean by fixed and variable administrative cost and fixed and variable selling & distribution costs.

Illustration for Projected Income Statement Under Absorption Costing

Year	2013	2014
Selling price	$15/unit	$15/unit
Quantity sold	20,000	23,000
Production actual	25,000	19,000
Budgeted production	30,000	30,000
Costs:		
Direct material	$3/unit	$ 3/unit
Direct labour	$2/unit	$2/unit
Variable manufacturing expense	$1/unit	$1/unit
Fixed manufacturing cost	$ 90,000p.a	$ 90,000p.a
Variable administrative cost	$ 0.50/unit	$ 0.50/unit
Fixed administrative cost	$ 25,000p.a	$ 25,000p.a
Variable selling and distribution cost	$ 1.50/unit	$ 1.50/unit
Fixed selling and distribution cost	$ 35,000p.a	$ 35,000p.a

Compute, under marginal costing actual income for 2013 and projected income for 2014.

Income statement under marginal costing:

Year	2013	2014
Sales [A]	3,00,000	3,45,000
Less: variable cost of production		
Direct material Direct labour Variable manufacturing overheads Fixed manufacturing overhead	75,000 50,000 25,000 75,000	57,000 38,000 19,000 57,000
	--	
Cost of goods manufactured	2,25,000	
1,71,000		
Add: beginning inventory	NIL	45,000
---------------------------- -------	-------------------------- ----	
Cost of goods available for sale	2,25,000	
2,16,000		
Less: closing inventory	45,000	
9,000		

Cost of goods sold	1,80,000	
2,07,000		
Add: under absorption of fixed manufacturing exp.	15,000	33,000
[B]Cost of goods sold (actual)	1,95,000	2,40,000
[C] Gross Profit [A – B]	1,05,000	
1,05,000		

Less: Variable administrative expenses Variable selling expenses Fixed administrative expenses 25,000 Fixed selling expenses 35,000	10,000 30,000 25,000 35,000	11,500 34,500

Total non-production cost [D]	1,00,000	1,06,000
Net income [C-D]	5,000	
(1,000)		
--		

Working notes:

	2013	2014
1) Sales value	20,000 X 15 = 3,00,000	23,000 X 15 = 3,45,000
2) Direct material	25,000X3 =75,000	19,000X3 =57,000
3) Direct labour	25,000X2 = 50,000	19,000X2 = 38,000
4) Variable manufacturing exp.	25,000x1 = 25,000	19,000X1 = 19,000
5) Fixed manufacturing exp.*	25,000 X 3 = $ 75,000	19,000 X 3 = $ 57,000
6) Under/over absorption	$90,000-$75,000 = $ 15,000	$90,000- $57,000 = $33,000
7) Opening inventory*	NIL	25,000 + 0 - 20,000 = 5,000 units
8) Closing inventory*	25,000 + 0-20,000 = 5,000 units	5,000+19,000 – 23,000 = 1,000 units
9) Value of opening inventory	NIL	5,000x (3+2+1) = 30,000

10) Value of closing inventory	5,000 X (3+2+1) =30,000	1,000 X (3+2+1) = 6,000
11) Variable administrative cost	20,000 X.50 = $10,000	23,000 X.50 = $11,500
12) variable selling cost	20,000X1.50 = $ 30,000	23,000X1.50 = $ 34,500
*closing inventory= opening inventory + production – sale *Absorption rate for fixed manufacturing overhead= total fixed manufacturing expenses/budgeted units 90,000/30,000= $ 3/unit		

Evaluation of Differences in Profit Under Marginal and Absorption Costing

To understand why there is difference in profit under marginal and absorption costing, we need to fully understand the process of ascertaining cost of production and net income. Both marginal and absorption costing technique had different profit figures. If we carefully check out for the difference in the process we will find, that the difference lies in the cost of production under the two methods. For marginal costing cost of production is being calculated without including fixed manufacturing cost while, under absorption costing, fixed manufacturing cost is not included in cost of production. Due to this inclusion of fixed manufacturing cost in cost of production under absorption costing, there are differences in value of opening and closing inventory as value of inventory is dependent on cost of production. Under marginal costing for valuation of inventory we take only variable production cost on the other hand, under absorption costing we take all production cost whether fixed or variable. Now, we can evaluate the difference in profit under both the methods and relate it to the value of inventories, which is different under both the methods. We can make three scenarios, namely:

Scenario / Technique	Production=-Sales	Production>Sales	Production<Sales
Marginal costing	Equal profit	Lesser profit	Higher profit
Absorption costing	Equal profit	Higher profit	Lesser profit
Reason	Value of opening and closing inventory is same.	As production is higher than sales so, inventories are being build up and under absorption costing, a part of fixed manufacturing cost is being carried forward to next period, which causes decrease in the actual cost of production as compared to marginal costing. So, profit is higher under absorption costing and vice versa when sale is greater than production.	

Marginal costing rewards sales as it shows higher profit as compared to absorption costing when sale is greater than production, while absorption costing rewards production as it shows higher profit when production is greater than sale.

Marginal and Direct Costing

Direct costing is the technique where only direct costs are considered while calculating the cost of the product. Indirect costs are met against the total margin (excess of selling price over direct costs) given by all the products taken together. Many accountants use 'Direct Costing' and 'Marginal Costing' as synonymous terms. This is unfortunate, because all direct costs need not be variable costs. A direct cost is a cost that can be identified readily with a department, a function, a unit of product or some other relevant unit. Direct cost can be fixed as well as variable. For example, if rent is paid for a factory building in which only one product is being manufactured, the rent paid will be taken as a direct cost but not as a variable cost. Thus, the cost of the product under Direct Costing and Marginal Costing will be different. Though, most of the direct costs are variable costs but, all direct costs may not be variable. The term 'Variable Costing' should be preferred to marginal costing as compared to 'Direct Costing'.

On the other hand, under variable costing we consider only the variable cost for calculating the cost of production and inventory valuation. So, we can say that both marginal costing and direct costing are different. Both are technique of costing, which can be used with different processes of costing like job costing, process costing etc.

Marginal Costing and Differential Costing

Marginal Costing is sometimes confused with Differential Costing. The term 'Differential Costing' means 'a technique used in the preparation of ad hoc information in which only cost differences between alternative courses of action is taken into consideration. Thus, in case of differential costing a comparison is made between the cost differential between two or more situations and decision regarding adopting a particular course of action is taken if it is on the whole profitable. The cost difference which, is being taken under differential costing may be because of variable costs or fixed costs or both. So, differential costing takes into consideration all type of costs but on the other hand, marginal costing takes into consideration only variable cost. This is illustrated with the following illustration:

Pioneer Manufacturing Company, makers of a specialized line of toys, receives an order for 2,000 units of toy battle tanks, from a large mail-order house at a price of $ 3 per unit. The company sells this type of toy to its other customers at $ 5 each but it has surplus capacity and can take the special order without adversely affecting its regular operations for the coming month. The income statement of the company for the preceding month is as follows:

Net Sales—10,000 units @ $ 5	50,000
Costs:	
Direct Material: $ 1.50 per unit	15,000
Direct Labour: $ 1 per unit	10,000
Factory Overhead	10,000
Selling and Administration Expenses	10,000
Total Costs	45,000
Net Profit	5,000

Direct material and direct labour costs to be incurred on the special order are estimated to be of the same amount per unit as for the regular business. Special tools costing $ 500 would be required to meet the specifications of the mail-order house.

Differential cost statement:

	Situation	Situation	Existing Proposed Net Increase/ Decrease
	10,000 Units	12,000 units	2,000 units
Sales (i)	50,000	56,000	6,000
Cost:			
Direct Materials	15,000	18,000	3,000
Direct Labour	10,000	12,000	2,000
Factory Overhead	10,000	10,000	—
Selling & Adm. Expenses	10,000	10,000	—
Special Tools —		500	500
Total Costs (ii)	45,000	50,500	5,500
Profit (i) – (ii) = (iii)	5,000	5,500	500

Differential costs are $ 5,500 while differential sales are $ 6,000. Thus, acceptance of order from a large mail order house gives an extra profit of $ 500. The order may be accepted provided it does not adversely affect the present sales at $ 5 per unit. Thus, in case of Differential Costing, the change in total costs (both fixed and variable) is taken into account. The term 'Differential Cost' means the net increase or decrease in total cost resulting from a variation in production. The differential cost is termed as 'Incremental Cost' when the cost increases and 'Decremental Cost' when the cost decreases. Thus, Incremental Costing and Decremental Costing are two variants of Differential Costing which are different from Marginal Costing and Direct Costing. The difference between Marginal Costing and Differential Costing can be summarized as follows:

- Differential Costing can be used both in case of Absorption Costing and Marginal Costing.

- In case of Marginal Costing, the entire fixed costs are excluded while in the case of Differential Costing such fixed costs which are relevant for decision making are considered.
- Differential costs are worked out separately as analysis statements while marginal costs may be embodied in the accounting system itself.
- In Marginal Costing, the contribution and the profit-volume ratio are the main yardsticks for the purposes of performance evaluation and decision-making. While in case of Differential Costing, the differential costs are compared with incremental or decremental revenue as the case may be.

The manner of application of Differential Costing is somewhat different from that of Marginal Costing. Under Differential Costing, differential costs of various alternatives are compared with the differential revenues and the decisions are taken on the basis of maximum net gain. While evaluating the viability of different projects, making a choice out of several alternative proposals, Differential Costing helps in a better way than Marginal Costing. If under Marginal Costing, while deciding about the profitability of products for making cost benefit analysis, fixed costs are also considered at some stage, it takes the shape of Differential Costing. Hence practically, the purpose of applying the two techniques is the same and here too, we have not made any difference in the application of these techniques to the problems which management has to face in its routine or otherwise decision making process.

Concept of Cost Behaviour and Various Types of Costs

Cost behaviour means the reaction of expenses to alteration in the amount of some business activity. In simple words, how cost is changing when there is some change in the output. Here we can divide the period of operation that is short term and long term. In long term all the costs are variable and changes with the alteration in level of operation but in short term, all cost does not vary as there is change in activity within a relevant range. In short term, we have three different kind of costs namely, variable, semi-variable and fixed cost.

- Fixed cost: The definition of a fixed cost is one which does not vary in total when the level of output by the business does vary. In other words, when the operating level within a business increases fixed costs in, does not increase. It also follows that when the operating level in a business decreases, the fixed costs would not decrease. An example of a fixed cost for a business making a product such as a bakery would be the any costs associated with the rent or ownership of premises, insurance, and costs associated with the ownership of equipment. As fixed costs are not dependent upon the level of output (sales), they are often expressed as being per period of time, for example annually, weekly or monthly. It can be helpful to picture costs in the form of a chart.

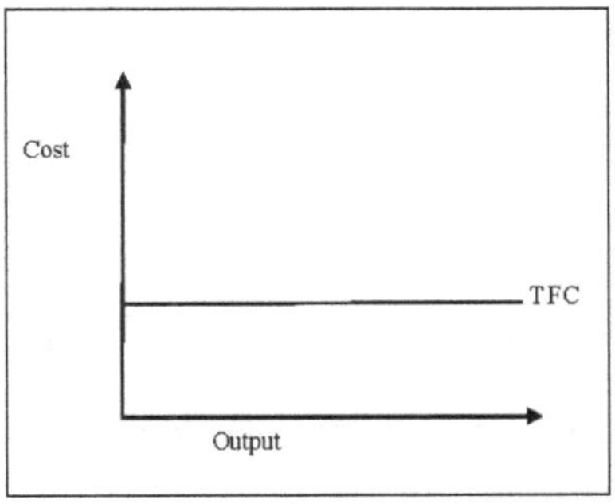

- Variable cost: Variable costs are those which do vary as a total cost to the organisation when output (number of items or services produced) varies. In fact a true variable cost will vary in exactly the same proportion as the output. In other words, as sales increase the variable costs increase. An example of a variable cost for a bakery would be the cost of flour.

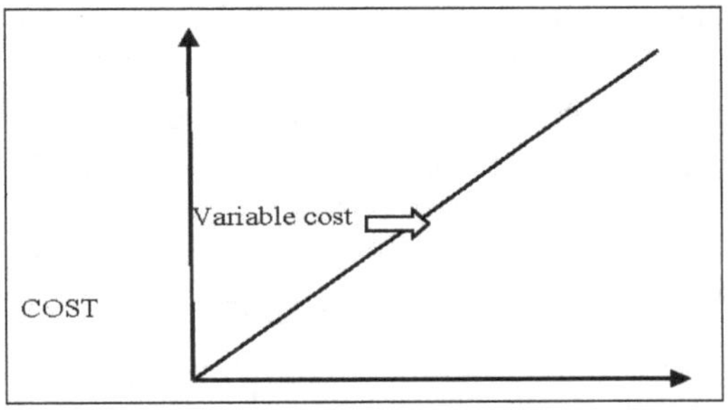

- Semi-variable cost: These are the costs which have the feature of both fixed and variable cost. It is incurred even when there is no activity as fixed cost and also increases proportionately as the level of activity increases like variable cost.

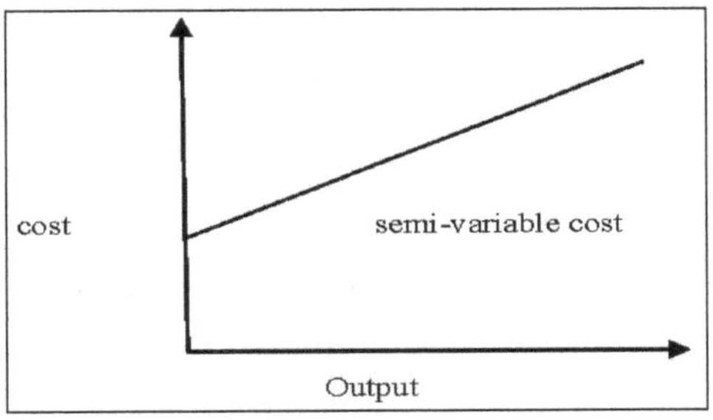

Segregation of Cost

Marginal costing requires segregation of all costs between two parts, fixed and variable. This means that the semi-variable cost will have to be segregated into fixed and variable elements. This may be done by any one of the following methods:

- Levels of output compared to levels of expenses method.
- Range method.

- Degree of variability method.
- Scatter graph method.
- Least squares method.

Levels of Output Compared to Levels of Expenses Method

According to this method, the output at two different levels is compared with corresponding level of expenses. Since the fixed expenses remain constant, the variable overheads are arrived at by the ratio of change in expense to change in output.

Example: Find the fixed cost per month and variable cost per unit.

Month	January	February
Output	5000 UNITS	6500 UNITS
Total cost	1,10,000	1,25,000

Number of units is being increased by 1500 and cost is being increased by \$ 15,000. By following the level of output method we can find out per unit variable cost change in cost/change in output.

So, variable cost would be 15000/1500 = \$ 10/unit.

Now as we have variable cost we can compute fixed cost by deducting total variable cost from total cost.

Fixed cost= total cost – total variable cost.

Fixed cost for January = 1, 10,000 – 10 × 5000= 1, 10,000 – 50,000 = 60,000

In the same manner we can get fixed cost for February.

Range Method

Only the highest and lowest points of output are considered out of various levels. This method is also designated as 'high and low' method.

Example: Find the fixed cost per month and variable cost per unit.

	Lowest output	Highest output
Output	5000 UNITS	6500 UNITS
Total cost	1,10,000	1,25,000

Number of units is being increased by 1500 and cost is being increased by \$ 15,000. By following the level of output method we can find out per unit variable cost change in cost/change in output.

So, variable cost would be 15000/1500 = \$ 10/unit

Now as we have variable cost we can compute fixed cost by deducting total variable cost from total cost.

Fixed cost= total cost – total variable cost.

Fixed cost = 1, 10,000 – 10 × 5000= 1, 10,000 – 50,000 = 60,000.

Degree of Variability Method

In this method, degree of variability is noted for each item of semi-variable expense. Some semi-variable items may have 30% variability while others may have 70% variability. The method is easy to apply but difficulty is faced in determining the degree of variability.

Scattergraph Method

In this method the given data is plotted on a graph paper and line of best fit is drawn. The method is explained below:

- The volume of production is plotted on the horizontal axis and the costs are plotted on the vertical axis.
- Corresponding to each volume of production costs are then plotted on the paper, thus, several points are shown on it.
- A straight line of best fit is then drawn through the points plotted. This is the total cost line. The point where this line intersects the vertical axis is taken to be the amount of fixed element.
- A line parallel to the horizontal axis is drawn from the point where the line of best fit intersects the vertical axis. This is the fixed cost line.
- The variable cost at any level can be known by noting difference between fixed cost and total cost lines.

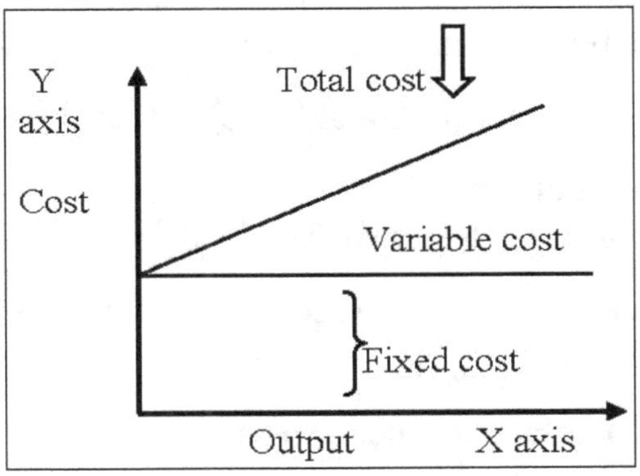

Method of Least Squares

This method is based on the mathematical technique of fitting an equation with the help of observations. The linear equation, i.e., a straight line equation, can be assumed as: y = a + bx and the various sub-equations shall be:

$$\sum y = na + b\sum x$$

$$\sum xy = a\sum x + b\sum x^2$$

Cost-Volume-Profit Method

Cost–volume–profit (CVP) analysis is a model to analyze the behaviour of net income in response to changes in total revenue, total costs, or both. In reality, businesses operate in a complex environment; a model reduces that complexity by using simplifying assumptions to focus on only the relevant relationships. The most important elements in a model affect one another in a predictable way. The breakeven point (BEP) is the point at which total revenue minus total business function costs is $0.

Essentials of CVP Analysis

The CVP model depends on understanding the effects of cost behaviour on profit, and identifies only the relevant relationships. The following assumptions identify relevant information required to complete a CVP analysis:

- Changes in the sales volume and production (or purchase) volume are identical (purchase volume would apply to a merchandiser). The ending balances in all inventories are zero. Everything purchased is used in production; everything produced is sold. For a merchandiser, the sales volume of finished goods purchased for resale is identical to the sales volume sold.
- All costs are classified as either fixed (FC) or variable (VC). All mixed costs are broken into their respective fixed and variable components. The fixed costs include both manufacturing and non-manufacturing fixed costs. The total variable costs include both manufacturing and non-manufacturing variable costs.
- All cost behaviour is linear (a straight line) within the relevant volume range.
- The sales price per unit, variable costs per unit, and total fixed costs and sales (or production) volume are known. The MIS provides all of this information.
- Either the product sold or the product mix remains constant, although the volume changes.
- All revenue and costs can be calculated and compared without considering the time value of money.

Total revenue is the product of total sales volume or quantity (Q) of units sold multiplied by the price per unit. Total variable cost is the product of total Q units produced multiplied by the cost per unit, and together with fixed costs (constant cost regardless of production volume) comprise total costs. Based on the simplifying assumption that Q sold = Q produced, the relationship among relevant elements of the CVP model upon which the BEP can be calculated is:

Operating income = (Unit sales price × Q) - (Unit variable cost × Q) - (Fixed costs)

At break even, operating income is zero. So for the break-even point, we can rearrange above equation to be:

(Unit sales price × Q) = (Unit variable cost × Q) + (Fixed costs)

Example of CVP Analysis

Decision Framework

We will begin by looking at an example based on known information about operating income (net income before interest and taxes). In the CVP analysis, only one factor, sales volume (Q), changes.

Example: Wei Shao is considering selling Do-All Software, a home-office software package, at a computer convention in Vancouver. Wei knows she can purchase this software from a computer software wholesaler at $120 per package, with the privilege of returning all unsold packages and receiving a full $120 refund per package. She also knows that she must pay Computer Conventions, Inc. $2,000 for the booth rental at the convention. She will incur no other costs. Should she rent a booth?

Wei faces an uncertain future as she analyzes the information she has at hand. A decision framework can be applied in this situation:

- Identify the problem and uncertainties. Wei has to resolve two important uncertainties the unit sales price she can charge and the number of packages (Q) she can sell at that price.
- Obtain information. Wei obtains the relevant information on the variable and fixed costs to attend the conference and purchase the software. She uses her own information on sales volume and her previous experience at a similar convention in Seattle four months ago. Wei also gathers published industry information. She realizes that customers may purchase their software from competitors and wants to match her volume and purchase price to customer demand.
- Predict the future. Wei predicts that she can charge $200 for Do-All Software. She is confident of the straight line or linear relationship between volume, price, and total revenue within her relevant range of 30 to 60 units. However, Wei

remains uncertain. Have there been important changes in customer demand over the last four months? Her regular sales in the last couple of months have been lower than she expected. Is she too optimistic or biased in her predictions?

- Make decisions by choosing among alternatives. Wei will use the CVP relationship to help her decide among alternatives available for pricing and quantity sold.
- Implement the decision, evaluate performance, and learn. If Wei attends the convention then she will know her outcome or actual profit. This is important feedback to compare with her predicted profit. Wei can learn from this comparison how to make better decisions in the future.

Cost–Volume–Profit Analysis

Wei knows that the booth-rental cost of $2,000 is a fixed cost because it must be paid even if she sells nothing. Wei's variable cost per Do-All Software package is $120 for quantities between 30 and 60 packages. Wei sorts her data into classifications of revenue and total variable cost, and then tests two volumes of sales shown in a spreadsheet:

	Wei Sells 5 Packages	Wei Sells 40 Packages
Revenue	$ 1,000 ($200 per package × 5 packages)	$8,000 ($200 per package × 40 packages)
Total variable cost	600 ($120 per package × 5 packages)	4,800 ($120 per package × 40 packages)
Contribution margin	$ 400	$3,200

The only numbers that change from selling different quantities are total revenues and total variable costs. The difference between total revenues and total variable costs is called the contribution margin. That is:

Revenue - Total variable cost = Contribution margin

What is the breakeven price (BEP) in sales volume Q, where operating income = $0? Wei does not yet know her predicted operating income, nor does she know what her minimum Q must be to cover her costs. By including the fixed cost of $2,000 in her analysis, Wei can calculate how operating income changes as Q changes. If she sells only 5 packages, then she will suffer an operating loss of $1,600 (= $400 – $2,000) and operating income < $0. If she sells 40 packages then she will enjoy a positive operating income of $1,200 (= $3,200 – $2,000) and operating income > $0.

	Wei Sells 5 Packages	Wei Sells 40 Packages
Revenue	$ 1,000 ($200 per package × 5 packages)	$8,000 ($200 per package × 40 packages)

Total variable cost	600 ($120 per package × 5 packages)	4,800 ($120 per package × 40 packages)
Contribution margin	$ 400	$3,200
Fixed cost	2,000	2,000
Operating income	$(1,600)	$ 1,200

But rather than simply using trial and error, Wei can use the CVP model:

Q sold = Q purchased for sale

If Wei assumes that operating income = $0, she can easily calculate the sales volume Q at which she will break even:

$$\$0 = Q \times (\text{Unit price - Unit variable cost}) - \text{Fixed cost}$$

Based on the information she has, Wei can substitute the financial values and complete her calculation as follows:

$$\$0 = Q \times (\$200 - \$120) - \$2{,}000$$

$$\$0 = Q \times (\$80) - \$2{,}000$$

$$\$2{,}000 = \$80Q$$

$$\frac{\$2{,}000}{\$80} = Q$$

$$25 = Q$$

Contribution margin per unit is the difference between selling price and variable cost per unit. In the Do-All Software example, contribution margin per unit is $80 per unit (= $200 price per unit – $120 variable cost per unit). Simplifying her model further:

$$\$0 = Q \times \text{Contribution margin per unit} - \text{Fixed cost}$$

When the unit sales price is $200, Wei knows that each unit sold covers the variable cost of $120 per unit and provides $80 (= $200 – $120) that can be used to cover her fixed cost of $2,000. By substituting the known amounts into the formula, Wei can calculate the BEP of 25 units (= $2000 ÷ $80):

$$\$0 = Q \times (\$80) - \$2{,}000$$

$$\$2{,}000 = \$80Q$$

$$\frac{\$2{,}000}{\$80} = Q$$

$$25 = Q$$

Table shows the result of calculating the BEP in two formats. On the right is the familiar financial statement of comprehensive income format. On the left is a contribution statement of comprehensive income, which groups costs as either variable or fixed according to their behaviour. The format of the report does not affect the dollar value of the operating income, since the revenue and total costs are identical. What has changed is the classification system used to report the results.

Expressing CVP Relationships

To make good decisions using CVP analysis, we must understand these relationships and the structure of the contribution statement of comprehensive income in table.

Table: Contribution Statement Compared to Financial Statement Format.

Quantity Purchased and Sold = 25			
Contribution Format		Financial Statement of Comprehensive Income Format	
Revenue ($200 × 25)	$5,000	Revenue ($200 × 25)	$5,000
– Total variable cost ($120 × 25)	3,000	– Total cost of sales (COS)	3,000
Total contribution margin	2,000	Gross margin	2,000
– Fixed costs (always a total)	2,000	– Total period cost	2,000
Operating income	$ 0	Operating income	$ 0

Table: Contribution Statement of Comprehensive Income for Different Quantities of Do-All Software Packages Sold.

	A	B	C	D	E	F	G	H
1				Number of Packages Sold				
2				0	1	5	25	40
3	Revenues	$ 200	per package	$0	$200	$1,000	$5,000	$8,000
4	Variable costs	120	per package	0	120	600	3,000	4,800
5	Contribution margin	80	per package	0	80	400	2,000	3,200
6	Fixed costs	2,000		2,000	2,000	2,000	2,000	2,000
7	Operating income			$(2,000)	$(1,920)	$(1,600)	$ 0	$1,200

There are three related ways to think more deeply about and model CVP relationships:

- The equation method.
- The contribution margin method.
- The graph method.

The equation method and the contribution margin method are most useful when managers want to determine operating income at a few specific levels of sales (for example, in Table, there is 1, 5, 25, and 40 units sold). The graph method helps managers visualize the relationship between units sold and operating income over a wide range of quantities of units sold.

Equation Method

Each column in table is expressed as an equation.

Revenues - Variable costs - Fixed costs = Operating income

How are revenues in each column calculated?

Revenues = Selling price (SP) * Quantity of units sold (Q)

How are variable costs in each column calculated?

Variable costs = Variable cost per unit (VCU) × Quantity of units sold (Q)

So,

$$\left(\text{Selling price} \times \text{Quantity of units sold}\right) - \left(\text{Variable cost per unit} \times \text{Quantity of units sold}\right) - \text{Fixed costs} = \text{Operating income}$$

Equation becomes the basis for calculating operating income for different quantities of units sold. For example, if you go to cell F7 in table, the calculation of operating income when Wei sells 5 packages is:

($200 × 5) - ($120 × 5) - $2,000 = $1,000 - $600 - $2,000 = - $1,600

Contribution Margin Method

Rearranging equation,

$$\left(\text{Selling price} - \text{Variable cost per unit}\right) \times \left(\text{Quantity of units sold}\right) - \text{Fixed costs} = \text{Operating income}$$

$$\left(\text{Contribution margin per unit} \times \text{Quantity of units sold}\right) - \text{Fixed costs} = \text{Operating income}$$

In our Do-All Software example, contribution margin per unit is $80 (= $200 - $120), so when Wei sells 5 packages, Operating income = ($80 × 5) - $2,000 = - $1,600.

Above equation expresses the basic idea we described earlier each unit sold helps Wei recover $80 (in contribution margin) of the $2,000 in fixed costs. The calculation for the contribution margin method can also be rearranged to show the breakeven point

(BEP) in relation to fixed costs and the contribution margin per unit.

$$\text{BEP} = \frac{\text{Total fixed costs}}{\text{Contribution margin per unit}}$$

Graph Method

In the graph method, we represent total costs and total revenues graphically. Each is shown as a line on a graph. Figure illustrates the graph method for Do-All Software sales. Because we have assumed that total costs and total revenues behave in a linear fashion, we need only two points to plot the line representing each of them.

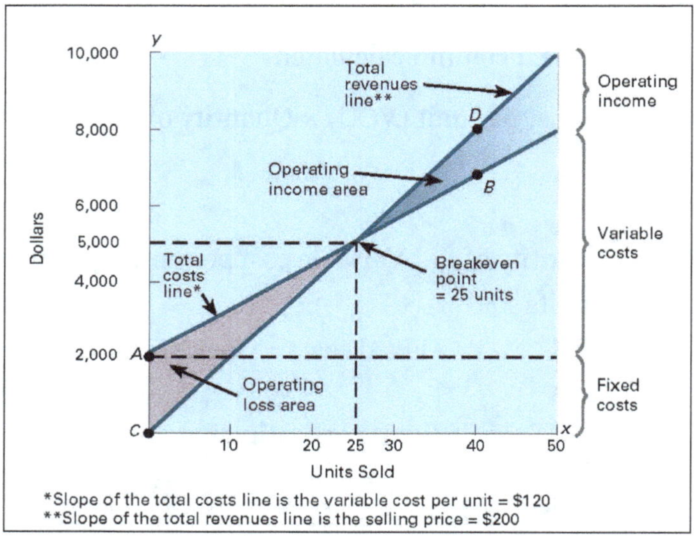

Cost– Volume–Profit Graph for Do-All Software Sales.

- Total costs line: The total costs line is the sum of fixed costs and variable costs. Fixed costs are $2,000 for all quantities of units sold within the relevant range. To plot the total costs line, use as one point the $2,000 fixed costs at zero units sold (point A) because variable costs are $0 when no units are sold. Select a second point by choosing any other convenient output level (say, 40 units sold) and determine the corresponding total costs. Total variable costs at this output level are $4,800 (= 40 units × $120 per unit). Remember, fixed costs are $2,000 at all quantities of units sold within the relevant range, so total costs at 40 units sold equal $6,800 (= $2,000 + $4,800), which is point B in figure. The total costs line is the straight line from point A through point B.

- Total revenues line: One convenient starting point is $0 revenues at 0 units sold, which is point C in figure. Select a second point by choosing any other convenient output level and determining the corresponding total revenues. At 40 units sold, total revenues are $8,000 (= $200 per unit × 40units), which is point D in figure. The total revenues line is the straight line from point C through point D. Profit or loss at any sales level can be determined by the vertical distance between the two lines at that level in figure. For quantities fewer than 25 units sold, total costs exceed total revenues, and the purple area indicates operating losses. For quantities greater than 25 units sold, total revenues exceed total costs, and the blue-green area indicates operating incomes. At 25 units sold, total revenues equal total costs. Wei will break even by selling 25 packages.

Contribution Margin Percentage: Break-even Point in Revenue

Instead of expressing contribution margin as a dollar amount per unit, we can also express it as a percentage. Contribution margin percentage (also called contribution margin ratio) equals the contribution margin per unit divided by the selling price per unit:

$$\text{Contribution margin percentage} = \frac{\$80}{\$200} = 0.40, \text{or } 40\%$$

The contribution margin percentage tells us how many pennies per $1.00 of revenue contribute to paying fixed costs. For example, a contribution margin percentage of 40% means for each $1.00 a customer pays for Do-All Software, $0.40 contributes to paying fixed cost. The contribution margin percentage enables us to solve for values with partial data. For example, how do you calculate the breakeven point in revenue when you do not know the sales price per unit? The solution is shown below:

$$\text{Break-even revenue} = \frac{\text{Fixed costs}}{\text{Contribution margin \%}} = \frac{\$2{,}000}{0.40} = \$5{,}000$$

Proof: $5,000 ÷ $200 = 25 units. We know the BEP in units is 25.

Using CVP to Calculate a Target Operating Income

The breakeven point (BEP) can be calculated as either the minimum sales quantity or the minimum revenue required to avoid a loss. However, the point of for-profit business is to earn a profit, not to break even. The CVP model can also be used to calculate a target operating income. Let's go back to the example of Wei Shao and Do-All Software. Wei can apply her model to determine what her quantity purchased and sold must be to make a positive operating income. Instead of setting Operating income = $0, it is set to equal a non-zero amount. The method of calculating this target quantity is identical to the method already described. Wei selects $1,500 as her target operating income.

$$\$1{,}500 = Q \times (\text{Unit sales price} - \text{Unit variable cost}) - \text{Fixed cost}$$

$$Q \times (\$200 - \$120) - \$2{,}000 = \$1{,}500$$

$$\$80 \times Q = \$2{,}000 + \$1{,}500$$

$$Q = \$3{,}500 \div \$80 \text{ per unit} = 43.75 \text{ units}$$

Alternatively, Wei knows the contribution margin per unit and can calculate the Q required to achieve a target operating income of $1,500 by starting at the second line of the solution, treating the target operating income as if it were a fixed cost. This is exactly what we have done when adding the $1,500 to the $2,000 to obtain $3,500. The $80 is the contribution margin per unit. Dividing $3,500 by the contribution margin per unit gives the identical answer of Q = 43.75 units:

$$\text{Volume of units required to be sold} = \frac{\text{Fixed costs} + \text{Target operating income}}{\text{Contribution margin per unit}}$$

$$\text{Volume of units required to be sold} = \frac{\$2{,}000 + \$1{,}500}{\$80 \text{ per unit}} = 43.75 \text{ units}$$

Proof:	Revenue, $200 per unit × 43.75 units	$8,750
	Variable costs, $120 per unit × 43.75 units	5,250

	Contribution margin, $80 per unit × 43.75 units	3,500
	Fixed costs	2,000

	Operating income	$1,500

Of course, Wei cannot sell 75% of one Do-All package. If she rounds down to Q = 43 units she will bring in only $3,440, which is less than the $3,500 she needs to cover her $2,000 fixed cost plus a target operating income of $1,500. Wei must round up to Q = 44 units to reach her target. Finally, Wei can use different information fixed cost, target operating income, and the contribution margin percentage of 40% to calculate her target revenue without first calculating her target Q. She will simply divide the sum of fixed cost plus her target operating income by the contribution margin percentage to obtain the target revenue required, as shown:

$$\text{Revenue needed to earn } \$1{,}500 = \frac{\$2{,}000 + \$1{,}500}{0.40} = \frac{\$3{,}500}{0.40} = \$8{,}750$$

Contribution Margin, Gross Margin, Operating Margin and Net Income Margin

The CVP model enables us to clearly distinguish the contribution margin, which provides information for CVP analysis. There are two formats in which costs can be classified: the contribution and the financial format. Both formats report identical costs, but the costs are classified differently. The difference between contribution and gross margin is shown in the two equations below:

$$\text{Revenue - Cost of goods sold} = \text{Gross margin}$$

$$\text{Revenue - Total variable costs} = \text{Contribution margin}$$

Gross margin is a measure of competitiveness how much a company can charge for its products over and above the cost of either purchasing (cost of sales) or producing them (cost of goods sold). The size of the gross margin depends on the successful competitive strategy of a company. The gross margin can be expressed as a total, as an amount per unit, or as a percentage (called gross margin percentage).

Operating margin has the same meaning as operating income. It is the result of deducting all business function costs from revenue. Neither interest nor tax expense is considered a business function cost. The operating margin percentage is simply the operating income divided by revenue. It does not matter what format is used to report costs because total costs are identical, the reported operating income will be identical. Net income margin is an alternative technical term for net income. The non-technical term that is readily recognized is net profit margin. The net income margin percentage is calculated by dividing net income by revenue.

Target Net Income and Income Taxes

So far we have ignored the effect of income taxes when calculating the sales volume required to achieve a target income. The after-tax profit, however, is what matters to any business. Targets are set in terms of net income. In a real situation, managers must gather information on tax. In our example we will assume a corporate tax rate of 40%. Let's return to the Do-All Software example. Wei's new problem is to calculate the required sales volume Q to earn a net income of $960, assuming an income tax rate of 40%. Using the contribution margin format:

$$\text{Target operating income} = \text{Revenue - Total variable costs - Fixed costs}$$

Assuming there is no interest expense, a 40% tax rate means the company retains 60% of its operating income. The company's net income = Operating income × (1 – Tax rate), or simply:

$$\frac{\text{Net income}}{1 - \text{Tax rate}} = \text{Operating income}$$

It is now straightforward to calculate the number of units that must be sold to achieve a target net income based on a target operating income. First, using the relationship between revenue and total costs, both variable and fixed:

$$\frac{\text{Target net income}}{1 - \text{Tax rate}} = \text{Revenue - Total variable costs - Fixed costs}$$

Substituting numbers from our Do-All Software example:

$$\frac{\$960}{1-0.40} = (\$200 \times Q) - (\$120 \times Q) - \$2,000$$

$$\$1,600 = (\$200 \times Q) - (\$120 \times Q) - \$2,000$$

$$\$80 \times Q = \$3,600$$

$$Q = \$3,600 \div \$80 \text{ per unit} = 45 \text{ units}$$

Alternatively, we can use the contribution margin and calculate Q as shown:

$$\frac{\text{Target net income}}{1-\text{Tax rate}} = \text{Target operating income}$$

$$\frac{\text{Fixed costs} + \dfrac{\text{Target net income}}{1-\text{Tax rate}}}{\text{Contribution margin per unit}} = \text{Volume of units required to be sold}$$

$$\frac{\$2,000 + \dfrac{\$960}{1-0.40}}{\$80} = \frac{\$2,000 + \$1,600}{\$80 \text{ per unit}} = 45 \text{ units} = \text{Volume of units required to be sold}$$

Proof:	Revenue, \$200 per unit × 45 units	\$9,000
	Variable costs, \$120 per unit × 45 units	5,400

	Contribution margin	3,600
	Fixed costs	2,000

	Operating income	1,600
	Income taxes, \$1,600 × 0.40	640

	Net income	\$ 960

When we needed to calculate Q to achieve a target operating income, we obtained the rounded-up value of Q = 44 units. This is not enough, however, to achieve our target net income. But focusing the analysis on target net income instead of target operating income will never change the BEP. This is because, by definition, operating income at the breakeven point is \$0, and no income taxes are paid when there is no operating income.

Break-Even Analysis

Break-even analysis is performed to determine the value of a variable of a project that makes two elements equal, e.g. sales volume that will equate revenues and costs.

Single Project

The analysis is based on the relationship:

Profit = revenue – total cost

= R – TC

At breakeven, there is no profit or loss, hence,

Revenue = total cost

or, R = TC

It is to be noted that +ve sign is used for both the revenue and the costs. If we are to use –ve sign for costs and +ve sign for revenue, then the above relationships become:

Profit = R + TC and R + TC = 0 at breakeven.

With revenue and costs given in terms of a decision variable, the solution yields the breakeven quantity for the decision variable.

- Costs which may be linear or non-linear, usually include two components:
- Fixed costs (FC): Includes costs such as buildings, insurance, fixed overhead, equipment capital recovery, etc. These costs are essentially constant for all values of the decision variable.
- Variable costs (VC): Includes costs such as direct labour, materials, contractors, marketing, advertisement, etc. These costs change linearly or non-linearly with the decision variable, e.g. production level, workforce size, etc. For the analysis to be followed here, the variation will generally be assumed to be linear. Then, total cost,

  TC = FC + VC

Revenue also changes with the decision variable. Again, for the analysis, the variation will generally be assumed to be linear. The following diagram illustrates the basics of the breakeven analysis. It can be seen that we have profit if the production level is above the breakeven quantity and loss if it is below.

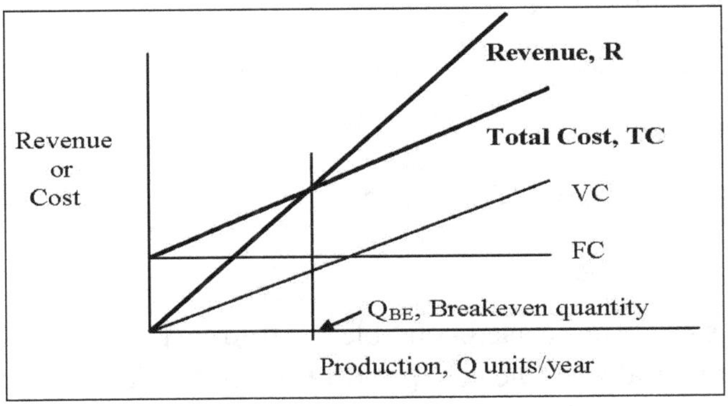

The fixed costs at Company X are $1 million annually. The main product has revenue of $8.90 per unit and $4.50 variable cost.

1. Determine the breakeven quantity per year.

2. Annual profit if 200000 units are sold.

Solution: 1. Let Q_{BE} be the breakeven quantity.

$$8.9Q_{BE} = 1{,}000{,}000 + 4.5Q_{BE}$$

$$Q_{BE} = 1{,}000{,}000/\ (8.90\text{-}4.50) = 227{,}272 \text{ units}$$

2. Profit = R – TC

$$= 8.90Q - 1{,}000{,}000 - 4.5Q$$

At 200,000 units: Profit = 8.90(200,000) – 1,000,000 - 4.50(200,000)

$$= \$\text{-}120{,}000 \text{ (loss)}$$

Example: A product currently sells for $12 per unit. The variable costs are $4 per unit, and 10,000 units are sold annually and a profit of $30,000 is realized per year. A new design will increase the variable costs by %20 and Fixed Costs by %10 but sales will increase to 12,000 units per year.

1. At what selling price do we break even?

2. If the selling price is to be kept same ($12/unit) what will the annual profit be?

Solution: Profit = revenue – costs

30000 = 10000(12) – [10000(4) + FC] FC = fixed costs

FC = 50000

1. New variable cost = $4(1.2) = $4.8 per unit.

New fixed costs = 50000(1.1) = $55000

Let x = breakeven selling price per unit, then

12000x = 55000 + 12000(4.8)

or, x = $9.38/unit

2. Profit = 12000(12) – 12000(4.8) - 55000

= $31400

Example: A defense contractor has been able to summarize its total annual fixed costs as $100,000 and the total variable cost per unit of production as $33.

1. If only 5000 units is all that is expected to sell to the government this year what should per unit selling price be to make a %25 profit this year?

2. If foreign sales of 3000 units per year is to be added to the 5000 units government contract above and a %25 profit is acceptable for this contractor again, what could be the new selling price per unit?

Solution: 1. Total costs = 100000 + 5000(33)

= 265000

% profit = 100(revenue – cost)/cost

Therefore, 25 = 100(revenue – 265000)/265000

or, revenue = 265000(1.25) = 331250

Selling price = 331250/5000

= $66.25 / unit.

2. Total cost = 100000 + 8000(33) = 364000

Revenue for 25% profit = 364000(1.25) = 455000

New selling price = 455000/8000

= $56.875 per unit.

Example: Suppose a firm is considering manufacturing a new product and the following data have been provided:

Sales price	$12.50 per unit
Equipment cost	$200 000
Overhead cost	$50 000 per year
Operating and maintenance cost	$25 per operating hour
Production time	0.1 hours per unit
Planning period	5 years
MARR	15%

Assuming a zero salvage value for all equipment at the end of five years, determine the number of unit to be produced to break even.

Let X = number of units to be provided per year to break even.

AW_C = -200000.(A/P,15%,5) – 50000 – (0.1)25X

= -109660 – 2.5X

Revenue: AW_R = 12.5X

At breakeven, 12.5X – 109660 – 2.5X = 0

X = 10966 units per year.

-ve sign for costs and +ve sign for revenue is used in the above solution.

Example: An automobile company is planning to convert a plant from manufacturing economy cars to manufacturing sports cars. The initial cost for equipment conversion will be $200 million with a 20% salvage value anytime within a 5-year period. The cost of producing a car will be $21000, and it will be sold for $33000. The production capacity for the first year will be 4000 units. At an interest rate of 12% per year, by what uniform amount will production have to increase each year in order for the company to recover its investment in 3 years?

Let x = gradient increase per year.

Total costs = -200M(A/P,12%,3)+(0.20)(200M)(A/F,12%,3)-[4000+ x(A/G,12%,3)](21,000)

Revenue = [4000 + x(A/G,12%,3)](33,000)

At breakeven, revenue + costs* = 0, then * -ve sign for costs is used.

[4000 + x(A/G,12%,3)](33,000 – 21,000) = 200M(A/P,12%,3) - (0.20)(200M)(A/F,12%,3)

[4000 + x(0.9246)](12,000) = 200M(0.41635) - 40M(0.29635)

x = 2110 cars/year increase

Example: Owners of a hotel chain are considering locating a new hotel in Karpaz. The complete cost of building a 150-room hotel (excluding furnishings) is $2million; the furnishings will cost $750 000 and will be replaced every 5 years for the same cost. Annual operating and maintenance cost for the facility is estimated to be $50 000. The average rate for a room is expected to be $15 per day. A 15-year planning period is used by the firm in evaluating new projects of this type; a terminal salvage value of 20% of the original building cost is anticipated; furnishings are estimated to have no salvage value at the end of each five-year replacement interval; land cost is not to be included. Determine the break-even value for the average number of rooms to be occupied daily based on a MARR of 10% (Assume the hotel will operate 365 days a year).

Annualizing Costs:

Building: AW_B = -2M(A/P,10%,15) = -2M(0.13147) = -262940 / yr

Furnishings: AW_F = [-750000 – 750000(P/F,10%,5) – 750000(P/F,10%,10)](A/P,10%,15)

= -197836.06 / yr

Salvage Value = (0.2)2M = 400000

AWS = 400000(A/F,10%,15) = 400000(0.03147) = 12588

Total Annual Cost, AWC = -262940 −197836 – 50000 + 12588 = -498188

Revenue = 15(365)X, where X is number of rooms occupied.

At break-even,

$$15(365)X - 498188 = 0$$

or X = 91 rooms per day on the average.

Two or More Alternatives

This is commonly applied to between alternatives that serve the same purpose. As a result, breakeven analysis is carried out between the costs of the alternatives. It involves the determination of a common variable between two or more alternatives. The procedure to follow for two alternatives is as follows:

- Define the common variable and its dimensional units.
- Use AW or PW analysis to express the total cost of each alternative as a function of the common variable. (Use AW values if lives are different).
- Equate the two relations and solve for the breakeven value of the variable.
- If the anticipated level is below the breakeven value, select the alternative with the higher variable cost (larger slope). If the level is above the breakeven point, select the alternative with the lower variable cost.

The same type of analysis can be performed for three or more alternatives. Then, compare the alternatives in pairs to find their respective breakeven points. The results are the ranges through which each alternative is more economical.

Example: A Textile company is evaluating the purchase of an automatic cloth-cutting machine. The machine will have a first cost of $22000, a life of 10 years, and a $500 salvage value. The annual maintenance cost of the machine is expected to be $2000 per year. The machine will require one operator at a total cost of $24 an hour. Approximately 1500 meters of material can be cut each hour with the machine. Alternatively, if human labor is used, five workers, each earning $10 an hour, can cut 1000 meters per hour. If the company's MARR is %8 per year, and 180,000 meters of material is to be cut every year should the company buy the automatic machine or use human labor instead? At how many meters cloth-cutting per year will the two alternatives breakeven?

Let x = meters of material to be cut.

Automatic machine:

Total annual cost, AW_A = -22000(A/P,8%,10) + 500(A/F,8%,10) – 2000 – (x/1500)(24)

= -5244.15 – x/62.5

Manual:

Total annual cost, AW_M = -(x/1000)(5)(10) = -x/20

At breakeven, $AW_A = AW_M$

-5244.15 – x/62.5 = x/20

or, x = 154240 m

Therefore, at 180000 m, select the automatic machine. (we make profit if quantity is above the breakeven).

Example: Two types of pumps are available. Pump X costs $800 and has a life of 3 years. It also requires rebuilding after 2000 operating hours at a cost of $300. Pump Y costs $1900 and is expected to last 5 years. It also requires overhaul after 8000 hours of operation at a cost of $700. If the operating cost of each pump is $1 per hour, how many hours per year must the pump be required to justify the purchase of pump Y? (Interest rate = 10% per year).

Let x = hours per year

Since lives are different, it is best to use the AW values.

Annual cost of X: AW_X = -800(A/P,10%,3) - (300/2000)x -1.0x

Annual cost of Y: AW_Y = -1,900(A/P,10%,5) - (700/8000)x - 1.0x

At breakeven, $AW_X = AW_Y$,

-800(A/P,10%,3) - (300/2000)x -1.0x = -1,900(A/P,10%,5) - (700/8000)x - 1.0x

-800(0.40211) - 0.15x - 1.0x = -1,900(0.2638) - 0.0875x - 1.0x

0.0625x = 179.532

x = 2873 hours per year

Example: Machine A has a fixed cost of $40000 per year and a variable cost of $60 per unit. Machine B has an unknown fixed cost, but with this process 200 units can be produced each month at a total variable cost of $2000. If the total costs of the two machines break even at a production rate of 2000 units per year, what is the fixed cost of machine B?

Let FCB = fixed cost for B.

Variable cost for B = 2000/200 = \$10/unit

Total costs are equal at 2000 units per year. Then,

40,000 + 60(2000 units) = FCB + 10(2000 units)

FCB = \$140,000 per year

Example: The ABC Company is faced with three proposed methods for making one of their products. Method A involves the purchase of a machine for \$5000. It will have a seven-year life, with a zero salvage value at that time. Using Method A involves additional costs of \$0.20 per unit of product produced per year. Method B involves the purchase of a machine for \$10000. It will also have a seven-year life, with \$2000 salvage value at that time. Using Method B involves additional costs of \$0.15 per unit of product produced per year. Method C involves the purchase of a machine for \$8000. It will have a \$2000 salvage value when disposed of in seven years. Additional costs of \$0.25 per unit of product per year arise when Method C is used. An 8% interest rate is used by the ABC Company in evaluating investment alternatives. For what range of annual production volume values is each method preferred?

Let X = number of units per year

$AW_A = -5000.(A/P,8\%,7) - 0.2X = -5000.(0.19207) - 0.2X$

$= -960.35 - 0.2X$

$AW_B = -10000.(A/P,8\%,7) + 2000.(A/F,8\%,7) - 0.15X = -10000.(0.19207) + 2000.(0.11207) - 0.15X$

$= -1696.56 - 0.15X$

$AW_C = -8000.(A/P,8\%,7) + 2000.(A/F,8\%,7) - 0.25X$

$= -1312.42 - 0.25X$

A vs. B: $-960.35 - 0.2X = -1696.56 - 0.15X$

$X_{AB} = 14724.2$

B vs. C: $-1696.56 - 0.15X = -1312.42 - 0.25X$

$X_{BC} = 3841.4$

A vs. C: No intersection for $X > 0$.

Example: Three types of design proposals for a commercial one-storey building is to be evaluated details given below:

	STEEL	CONCRETE	BRICK
First cost	$72/ft²	$76/ft²	$81/ft²
Annual maintenance	$14000	$9000	$6000
Annual heating cost	$3/ft²	$3.4/ft²	$3.9/ft²
SV (%of first cost)	%80	%100	%110
Life (years)	20	20	20

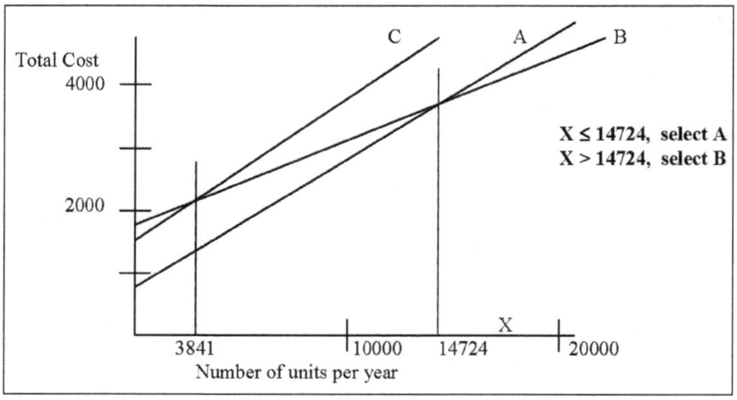

For what range of building area (ft²) which type of design is the most suitable (cheapest) to select? Carry out breakeven analysis using an interest rate of %18 per year and plot your ranges to illustrate.

Let X = area in ft²

First cost of steel = 72x and its salvage value = (0.8)72x

Using AW values:

AW_S = -(72x)(A/P,18%,20) + (0.8)(72x) – 14000 – 3x

= -13.45x + 0.393x – 14000 – 3x

= -16.057x – 14000

Similarly,

AW_C = -(76x)(A/P,18%,20) + (1.0)(76x) – 9000 – 3.4x

= -17.082x – 9000

AW_B = -(81x)(A/P,18%,20) + (1.1)(81x) – 6000 – 3.9x

= -18.423x – 6000

Breakevens:

Steel vs. Concrete: -16.057x – 14000 = -17.082x – 9000

$x = 4878\ ft^2$

Steel vs. Brick: -16.057x – 14000 = -18.423x – 6000

$x = 3381\ ft^2$

Concrete vs. Brick: -17.082x – 9000 = -18.423x – 6000

$x = 2237\ ft^2$

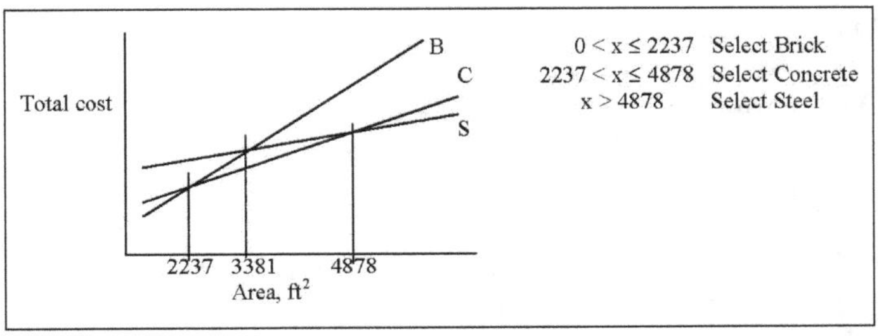

Example: Three options are considered for an engine part:

A – Complete in-house manufacturing, with initial equipment cost of $50 000, labor cost of $26 000 per year, and material cost of $10 per engine part.

B – Partial manufacture, (i.e. partially finished engine parts are purchased), with initial equipment cost of $35 000, labor cost of $10 000 per year, material cost of $3 per engine part, and an additional cost of $40 per the partially finished engine part.

C – Purchase from outside at a cost of $120 per engine part.

Any equipment purchased will have a life of 6 years. If the MARR is 10% per year, determine the number of engine parts that must be manufactured to justify:

1. Complete in-house manufacture.

2. Partial manufacture.

3. Plot the total cost lines for all three options, and state the ranges of engine parts for which each option will have the lowest cost.

Solution: Let x = number of engine parts per year.

Using AW values:

$AW_{IN} = -50000(A/P,10\%,6) - 26000 - 10x$

AW_{PM} = -35000(A/P,10%,6) – 10000 – 3x – 40x

AW_{OUT} = -120x

1. Complete in-house manufacturing vs. purchase from outside:

$AW_{IN} = AW_{OUT}$

or, -50,000(A/P,10%,6) - 26,000 - 10x = -120x

x = 341 parts per year.

2. Partial manufacture vs. purchase from outside:

$AW_{PM} = AW_{OUT}$

-35,000(A/P,10%,6) - 10,000 - 3x - 40x = -120x

x = 234 parts per year.

3. Complete in-house vs. partial manufacture

$AW_{IN} = AW_{PM}$

-50,000(A/P,10%,6) - 26,000 - 10x = -35,000(A/P,10%,6) - 10,000 - 3x - 40x

x = 589 parts per year from outside.

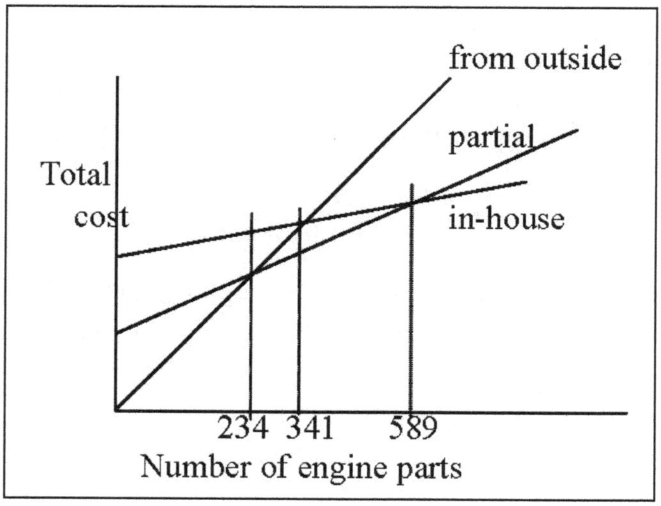

Ranges for the lowest total cost are:

0 < x ≤ 234 select purchase from outside cost in-house

234 < x ≤ 589 select partial manufacture

589 < x select in-house manufacture

Decision Regarding Sales Mix

Decision making is one of the basic functions of a manager and cost is always a relevant factor in such decision making. It is the process of evaluating two or more alternatives leading to a final choice. Managers are generally faced with various decision making problems. These include variety of questions relating to price, production method, make or buy decisions etc. Irrespective of its nature, every decision has two aspects, quantitative and qualitative. The qualitative aspects include the factors like public image, social responsibilities, employee attitude, consumer's reaction etc. Management accounting is basically concerned with the quantitative factors of decision making. It deals with the relevant information such as costs, revenues, capital invested etc. required to take a decision. Decision making is the process of selecting one out of several alternative courses of actions available and the choice is made on the basis of profitability or cost savings.

In managerial decision making only relevant information should be used by the managers in evaluating the alternative courses of actions and taking the final decisions. Relevant information implies relevant costs and relevant revenues which are useful to evaluate the alternatives. Cost is an important factor in decision making. The managers have to evaluate the cost of one option against the cost of other. However it happens that some of the costs associated with the alternative may not be relevant for the decision to be made. In order to take the sound decision, the manager must be able to understand and distinguish between the relevant and irrelevant costs. A relevant cost may be defined as cost that is the applicable to a particular decision situation and it has a bearing on which alternative is selected by the manager.

The irrelevant costs in any case must be eliminated from the decision making. Relevant costs are expected future costs that will differ between the alternatives being considered in a decision situation. Any cost that can be eliminated completely or in part, as a result of choosing one alternative over another is relevant cost. On the other hand, the cost that cannot be avoided irrespective of which alternative is chosen by the manager, is irrelevant cost. These costs have low relevance to the future actions and therefore must be ignored in the decision process. Relevant costs are future costs that are expected to occur during the period covered by the decision. Costs that are identical for all alternatives have no impact on decision and therefore must be ignored. Relevant (differential) revenue is the amount of increase or decrease in revenue expected from a particular course of action as compared with the other alternatives.

Relevant costs and relevant revenues are those current and future values that differ among the alternatives under considerations. These are not same in amount for all the alternatives under considerations. There are differences between the alternatives and the amount of such differences are called differentials. Thus relevant costs and revenues are also called differential costs and revenues. A differential analysis of relevant cost is always preferable to the complete analysis of all costs because of the following reasons:

- Differential analysis focuses only on those items that differ thus providing a clearer picture of the impact of the decision.
- A differential analysis considers fewer items making it easier and quicker.

Decision Making Process – Decision Model

The overall decision making process, also known as the decision model, involves following steps:

- Identify and define the problem.
- Identify alternatives as possible solutions to the problem.
- Collect relevant data (costs and benefits) associated with each feasible alternative.
- Identify costs and benefits (revenues) as relevant or irrelevant and eliminate irrelevant.
- Costs and benefits (revenues) from considerations.
- Identify, to the extent possible, non-financial advantages and disadvantages (also known as qualitative factors) about each feasible alternatives.
- Total the relevant costs and benefits (revenues) for each alternative.
- Select the alternative with the greatest overall benefits, i.e. make the decision.
- Implement or execute the decision.
- Evaluate the results of the decision made.
- Carry our monitoring or modification, if need be.

Precautions in Decision Making

Relevant revenues and relevant costs are important variables in the decision making process. Managers must be careful about the following four mistakes while taking a decision:

- Sunk costs: Sunk cost is the acquisition cost of an asset minus depreciation. Sunk costs are irrelevant in decision making.

- Unitized fix costs: Unitized fixed cost is the cost that is incurred jointly for all the products manufactured by a firm. Such costs are generally divided by some activity measure and assigned to individual units of the product. But in decision making analysis it is better to include fixed cost in its total amount rather than as per unit cost.
- Allocated fixed costs: It is common to allocate fixed costs across divisions, departments or product lines. It is possible that a particular product or department may appear unprofitable but actually it does make a contribution towards covering fixed costs and generating profits. Therefore before deciding to eliminate a department, it must be asked which cost will be avoided if a particular alternative is selected. A fixed cost that has been allocated to a particular department may continue even after a department has been eliminated.
- Opportunity costs: Opportunity costs are important while taking a correct decision therefore the opportunity costs must be properly identified and included in the decision making process.

Types of Managerial Decisions

Determination of Suitable Sales Mix

Any business firm which manufactures more than one product generally faces a decision problem as to in what proportion the products should be manufactured and sold i.e. what should be the composition of its sales mix. In other words, the firm has to decide as to how much quantity of which product should be manufactured and sold. The CVP analysis technique helps in determining the best sales mix. The best suitable sales mix is one which gives the maximum contribution. Here, contribution under various sales mix is computed and compared and the sales mix giving the maximum contribution is selected. Let us understand with the help of an example. The following information has been drawn from the cost records of Samar Ltd manufacturing parts P1 and P2.

	Part P1	Part P2
Direct Materials	$8000	$6000
Direct Wages (Hours)	24 Hrs.	16 Hrs.
Wage Rate	$200/Hr.	$200/Hr.
Variable overheads (150% of direct wages)		
Fixed Overheads (Total)		$7,50,000
Selling price	$25,000	$20,000

The company has an option to adopt any of the following sales mix alternatives in the budget for the next period.

1. 250 units of P1 and 250 units of P2.

2. 400 units of P2 only.

3. 400 units of P1 and 100 units of P2.

4. 150 units of P1 and 350 units of P2.

Suggest which of the above alternative sales mixes should be adopted by the company.

Solution:

Variable cost statement per unit		
	P1	P2
Direct Materials	8000	6000
Direct Wages	4800	3200
Variable overheads	7200	4800
Total Variable cost	20,000	14,000
Selling price	25,000	20,000
Contribution	5000	6000

Selection of sales mix alternatives:

1. 250 units of P1 and 250 units of P2:

Contribution of Product P1	= 12,50,000
Contribution of Product P2	= 15,00,000
Less: Fixed Overheads	= 7,50,000
Profit (contr. – FC)	= (12,50,000 + 15,00,000) – 7,50,000 = 20,00,000

2. 400 units of Product P2 only:

Contribution of Product P2	= 24,00,000
Less: Fixed Overheads	= 7,50,000
Profit (contr. – FC)	= 16,50,000

3. 400 units of P1 and 100 units of P2:

Contribution of Product P1	= 20,00,000
Contribution of Product P2	= 6,00,000
Less: Fixed Overheads	= 7,50,000
Profit (contr. – FC)	= (20,00,000 + 6,00,000) – 7,50,000 = 18,50,000

4. 150 units of P1 and 350 units of P2:

Contribution of Product P1	= 7,50,000
Contribution of Product P2	= 21,00,000
Less: Fixed Overheads	= 7,50,000
Profit (contr. – FC)	= (7,50,000 + 21,00,000) – 7,50,000 = 21,00,000

Decision: Since profits under sales mix (d) are the maximum ($ 21,00,000), therefore alternative (d) of the available sales mixes should be adopted by the firm.

Decision Regarding Discontinuation (Drop) or Addition of a Product

The decision to eliminate an unprofitable product is a special case profitability evaluation. To evaluate the financial consequences of eliminating a product, it is necessary to concentrate on the differential or incremental profit effect of the decision. An important factor in the decision to drop or add a product is whether it will decrease or increase the future income of the business. Appropriate costs and profit measures must be developed for each alternative. Care must be taken not only to consider the profitability of the product being analyzed but also to evaluate the extent to which sales of other products will be adversely affected when one product is removed. The unprofitable product may also be a complement to more profitable products, in which case some customers may buy the more profitable products because the unprofitable product is also available from the same company. If the expected sales decrease of related products is severe enough, it probably would be desirable to retain the unprofitable product. Management needs data that will permit development of warning signals for products that may be in trouble. Following are some of the warning signals of an unprofitable product:

- Increasing number of customer complaints.
- Declining sales volume.
- Decreasing market share.
- Expected future sales and market potential not favorable.
- Return on investment below a minimum acceptable level.
- Variable cost approaching or exceeding revenue.
- Variable cost consistently increasing as a percentage of sales.
- Increasing percentage of executive time required.
- Constant reduction in price to maintain the sales.
- Constantly increasing promotional budget to maintain sales.

To explain the decision regarding discontinuation of a product, let us assume that a company is considering dropping of one of its product B from its line because it is found that product B is being sold at a loss.

Income Statement				
Products	A	B	C	Total
Sales Revenue	50,000	10,000	15,000	75,000
Cost of Sales:				
Direct Material	8,000	1,000	2,000	11,000
Direct Labor	14,000	2,000	3,000	19,000
Indirect manufacturing cost (50% Labor)	7,000	1,000	1,500	9,500
	29,000	4,000	6,500	39,500
Gross Margin on Sales	21,000	3,500	8,500	35,500
Administrative Expenses	12,500	4,500	4,000	21,000
Net Income (loss)	8,500	(1,000)	4,500	14,500

Other information of income statement:

- Factory overhead costs are made up of fixed costs of $5,850 and variable costs of $ 3,900. Variable costs by products are: Product A $ 3,000, Product B $400 and Product C $500.
- Fixed costs and expenses will not be changed if product B is eliminated.
- Variable selling and administrative expenses to the extent of $11,000 can be traced to the product as follows: A, $ 7,500; B, $ 1,500; C, $2,000.
- Fixed selling and administrative expenses are $ 10,000.

Solution:

Products	A	B	C	Total
Sales Revenue	50,000	10,000	15,000	75,000
Less: Variable Product Cost:				
Direct Material	8,000	1,000	2,000	11,000
Direct Labor	14,000	2,000	3,000	19,000
Factory Overhead	3,000	400	500	3,900
Selling and Administrative expenses	7,500	1,500	2,000	11,000
	32,500	4,900	7,500	44,900
Contribution Margin	17,500	5,100	7,500	30,100
Less: Fixed Costs:				
Factory Overhead	5,850			
Selling and Administrative expenses	10,000			

Total Fixed costs	15,850
Net Profit (loss)	14,250

Product B generates a contribution of $ 5,100. If the sales of the product B were discontinued, its marginal contribution would be lost and the net income of the firm would be reduced by $5,100. That is, net income will be $9,150. In this case, it is assumed that the sales of the products A and C will not be increased after product B is dropped. Further it has been assumed that dropping product B will not change the fixed costs. If these assumptions are not true, new analysis must be made. Let us assume, for example, that after dropping product B, the sales of the product A increase by 10%. The overall total profit of the firm will not increase by this sales increase.

Sales Revenue	50,000	100%
Variable costs	32,500	65%
Marginal Contribution	17,500	35%

On additional sales of $ 5000 (10% increase) of product A, the marginal contribution would be $ 1,750 (10% of 17,500):

Sales Revenue	5,000
Variable costs (66 %)	3,250
Marginal Contribution	1,750

Decision: This marginal contribution is less than $ 5,100 now being realized on the sales of product B. It would take additional sales of product A of approximately $ 14,571 ((5000/1750)×5,100) to equal the marginal contribution of $ 5,100 now being made by product B:

Marginal Contribution of Product B / Marginal Contribution of Product A = 5,100 / 35% = $14,571.

It is possible that dropping product B may result in the reduction in some of the fixed costs. Product B now contributes $ 5,100 towards recovery of fixed costs and expenses. Only if the fixed costs and expenses can be reduced by more than this amount it will be advisable to drop product B.

Key Factor (Limiting Factor)

Key factor is that factor which is the most important one for taking decisions about profitability of a product. The extent of its influence must be assessed first so as to maximize the profits. Generally on the basis of contribution, the decision regarding product mix is taken. But actually, it is not the maximization of total contribution that matters, but the contribution in terms of key factors, that is to be compared for relative profitability. Thus it is called the limiting factor or governing factor or principal budget factor. If sales can't exceed a given quantity, sales is considered as the key factor; if production capacity is limited, contribution per unit i.e. in terms of output has to be compared. If raw materials are in short supply, contribution has to be expressed in terms of per unit of raw materials required. For example, there may be labour shortage, and in such a case contribution per labour hour is to be compared. If machine capacity is a limitation, contribution per machine hour is to be considered for appropriate decision making. Thus, profitability can be measured by: Contribution per unit / Key Factor required per unit. The concept of key factor is explained below with the help of an example.

Example: A company manufactures and sells three products: P, Q and R. All the three products are made from the same set of machines. Production is limited by machine capacity. From data given below, indicate priorities for products P, Q and R with a view to maximizing profits.

	Product P	Product Q	Product R
Raw material cost per unit	$ 225	$325	$ 425
Direct labour cost per unit	$ 50	$ 50	$ 50
Other variable cost per unit	$ 30	$ 45	$ 71
Selling price per unit	$ 500	$ 600	$ 700
Standard machine time required per unit	39 mts.	20 mts.	28 mts.

During the, year the company faces extreme shortage of raw materials. It is noted that 3 Kg, 4 Kg and 5 Kg of raw materials are required to produce one unit of P, Q and R respectively. How would product priorities change considering the key factor?

Solution:

Comparative statement of profitability			
	Product P	Product Q	Product R
Selling price per unit	$ 500	$600	$ 700
Raw materials	$ 225	$ 325	$ 425
Direct Labour	$ 50	$ 50	$ 50
Other variable costs	$ 30	$ 45	$ 71
Total variable costs	$ 305	$ 420	$ 546
Contribution per unit (Sales – variable costs)	$ 195	$ 180	$ 154
P/V Ratio	39 %	30%	22%
Contr. per minute of std machine time	5	9	5.5
Contr. per Kg of raw material	65	45	31

Decision: If the machine capacity is limited, contribution per minute of standard machine time is to be considered for correct decision making. Product Q is most profitable, Product R comes next and then Product P last. If the key factor is raw materials, contribution per Kg. of raw materials should be considered for decision making. Thus, Product P is most profitable, Product Q comes next and Product R last.

Diversification of Production

A business firm tries to go for product diversification in the following cases:

- To utilize the idle capacity efficiently.
- To maintain the interest of the consumers in the products of the enterprise.
- Sometimes it becomes compulsions because of competition.
- To capture more market share.

The new product should be introduced only if it can add to the contribution of the business firm as a whole. It is preferable to undertake the production of the new product if it is capable of contributing something towards fixed cost and profits after meeting the relevant variable cost of sales. Fixed costs are not to be considered on the premise that the new product can be manufactured in the existing resources without incurring any additional fixed costs. However, if it involves the incurrence of special or product specific costs, these should be deducted from the contribution of new product before making any decision.

Make or Buy and Replace or Retain

The make or buy decision refers to the problem encountered by an organization when deciding whether a product or service should be purchased from outside sources or manufactured internally. Theoretically, every item, which is currently purchased from an outside supplier, is always a candidate for internal manufacture and every item currently manufactured in house is a potential candidate for purchase.

The majority of the make or buy decisions are made on the basis of price. But this is only one of the criteria, which is to be evaluated in this strategic decision. Many non-cost factors encourage long term contracts with the suppliers to aid in the achievement of production and quality levels and encourage investments in appropriate resources and new ideas. This result in excellent, mutually beneficial customer-supplier relationships developed over long periods based on trust and achievement of common objectives. Most have the make or buy decisions are complex, time consuming and affect many parts of the organization. Senior management involvement is required in a number of the stages of this strategic decision. The following situations demand for the evaluation of make or buy decisions:

- When the organization introduces new products.
- The fluctuating demand for the company's products.
- When the organization carries out value analysis or cost reduction programs.

- Deteriorating quality and delivery commitment of the supplier if presently the item is bought.
- The scarcity of funds for investment in additional plant and equipment.

Factors Influencing Make or Buy Decision

- Volume of Production: The quantity or volume of production affects the make or buy decision to the greater extent. If the volume of production is high, it favors the make decision and low volume favors buy decisions.
- Cost Analysis: The cost analysis refers to the determination of costs to make an item as well as the cost to buy it. The cost to make include – the material cost, direct lab our cost, set up and tooling up costs, depreciation, administrative overheads, interest, insurance, taxes and inventory carrying costs of raw materials and work in process. The cost to make also includes the appropriate allowances, spoilage of work or scrap, and the risk associated with doing business. The cost to buy an item should include -purchase price of the item or component, transportation cost, sales tax and octopi, procurement cost, carrying cost, receiving and incoming inspection costs. The analysis of these two costs helps take decision whether to make or buy.
- Utilization of Production Capacity: The organization, which has created large production capacity, favors the decision to make.
- Integration of Production System: The vertical integration favors the make decision whereas horizontal integration favors buy decision.
- Availability of Manpower: Availability of skilled and competent manpower favors makes decision where as scarce manpower prefers buy decision.
- Secrecy or Protection of Patent Right: This condition favors the make decision.
- Fixed Cost: A lower fixed cost favors the decision to make and higher fixed cost the make decision.
- Availability of competent suppliers or vendors.
- Quality and reliability of vendors.

Functional Aspects of Make or Buy Decision

Make or buy decision should be viewed with both long term and short term perspectives in mind. Some of the effects are tangible and others are intangible. These are classified as follows:

- Financial Aspects: The make decision is always demands an investment in plant, machineries and equipment. The investments can be categorized in to fixed cost and variable cost. The buy decision is associated with only variable cost. Expressing all factors in to money terms carries out a thorough and comparative analysis. Then the decision is to be taken based on which one is more economical, to make or to buy.

- Technological Aspects: The make or buy decision is influenced by:
  - The access to the latest technology to the organization.
  - Feasibility and terms and conditions of technology transfer.
  - Outdating of technology.
  - Product life cycle.
- Marketing Aspects: The marketing aspects have the influence on make or buy decision. When there is a fierce competition, an organization tries to enhance the quality and cut down the costs. The make decision assures the quality and reliability of the parts. Under the situation of increasing market share and a good future sales potential company can have an additional investment potential and hence can opt for make decision. When there is a doubt about the market potential, the company should opt for buy decision. The large organizations pay greater attention to quality which favors the make decision to maintain quality and reliability of items.
- Purchasing Aspects: The decision is influenced by:
  - The availability of items or components in sufficient quantities.
  - The delivery commitments must be reliably met.
  - The acceptable quality and price level of the product.
  - Economy in transportation from the source to the organization.
  - Competence and reliability of vendors.
- Strategic Aspects: Any decision that is to be taken including make or buy decision should be taken with due consideration to overall objective of the organization. Due importance should be given to the economy, secrecy and flexibility in taking decision regarding make or buy.
- Intangible Aspects: Intangible aspects like environmental factors, labour union acceptance, goodwill, support to ancillarisation and growth of SSI units, technical assistance to vendors also influences the make or buy decision.

Economic and Non-Economic Factors Influencing Make or Buy Decisions

Decisions regarding whether to make or buy the components involve both economic and non-economic factors. Economically, an item or component is a candidate for in house production, if the company has sufficient capacity and if the components value is high enough to cover the variable costs of production and make some contribution towards the fixed cost. Low volumes favor buying, which incurs very little or no fixed costs. Figure shows the relationship between cost factors. The non-economic factors are:

- Availability of infrastructure and skilled personnel.
- Desire for alternate sources of supply.
- Employee preferences and stability concerns.
- Need to maintain trade secrets.
- Desire to expand in to new product line.
- Forward or backward integration.
- Long lasting and mutually rewarding relationships with vendors.

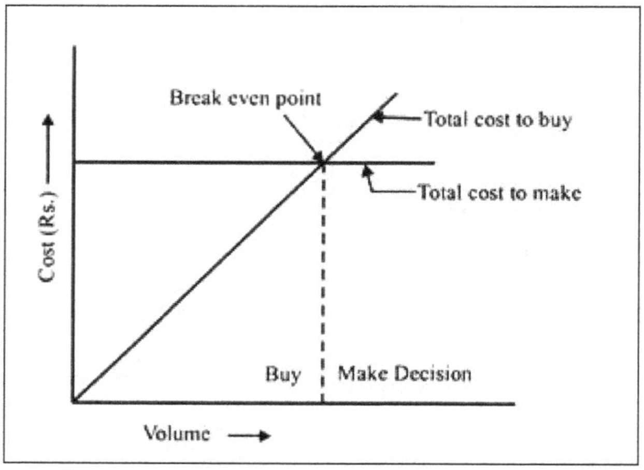

Relationship between Cost to Make and Cost to Buy.

Example: Demand for the component is at the rate of 6000 per year and this demand is going to continue for next three years. The company has two options. It can get the component manufactured from outside or it can manufacture in house. It costs the company $ 2.8 per unit to buy the component. The in house manufacture will incur a fixed cost to the extent of $ 10,000 and variable cost of $ 1.5 per unit. Give the decision rule for make or buy.

Solution: Let x represent the number of units. The total cost incurred in buying the component is,

Total cost(Y) =2.8 x

Total cost incurred in making the component in house,

Total cost (Y) = 10,000 + 1.5 x

At BEP, both alternatives result in equal total cost. At BEP,

$$2.8x = 10{,}000 + 1.5x$$
$$1.3x = 10{,}000$$
$$x = 7692.3 \text{ say } 7693$$

The decision rules are:

- If the quantity is 7693, both make and buy are equally economical (Results in same costs).
- Quantity less than 7693, it is economical to buy.
- Quantity more than 7693, it is economical to manufacture.

Example: The ABC Company is investigating the decision whether to make or buy a plastic packaging, which is currently being purchased at $ 7 each. The demand estimate is shown below:

Demand (Units)	20,000	30,000	40,000	50,000	60,000
Chance (%)	10	30	40	15	5

The decision to manufacture in house costs the company an annual fixed cost of $ 80,000 towards renovation and conditioning. Variable costs are estimated at $ 5 per unit Give your decision whether to make or buy. At what quantity it is profitable to produce rather than buy.

Solution: The expected demand (or volume) is determined treating the percentage chance as a probability:

Demand (D)	Probability (P)	D.P (D)
20,000	0.10	2,000
30,000	0.30	9,000
40,000	0.40	16,000
50,000	0.15	7,500
60,000	0.05	3,000
	Total	37,500

1. The Expected Cost to Produce:

TC = Fixed cost + Variable cost ´Quantity

=80,000 + 5 x 37,500

= 2,67,500

Expected cost to buy:

TC=7´37,500=2,62,500

The decision is economical to continue to buy.

2. Break Even Point: BEP is the volume of production where the total costs to make is equal to the total costs to buy.

$$\text{Total cost to make} = \text{Total cost to buy}$$
$$\therefore \quad 80{,}000 + 5x = 7x$$
$$\therefore \quad x = 40{,}000$$

It is economical to produce, if the quantity is > 40,000 units.

Example: An item, which is required by the company, can be manufactured on any of the three following machines and also it can be purchased at a price of $1.2 per component. Suggest the best option if the requirement is 2,000 units and give the decision rules.

Machine	Fixed Cost ($)	Variable Cost ($/unit)
M1	9,000	0.75
M2	3,500	0.50
M3	92,500	0.05

Solution: Let x be the quantity required. The cost equations for 4 options are:

Buy $TC_B = 1.2\ x$

M1 $TC_{M1} = 9{,}000 + 0.75\ x$

M2 $TC_{M2} = 3{,}500 + 0.50\ x$

M3 $TC_{M3} = 92{,}000 + 0.05\ x$

The relationship between cost and volume is established. The total costs for all the four alternatives are determined at various quantities (volume). The costs are tabulated below:

Alternative	Buy	Machines		
Volume (x)	(TC_B)	TCM_1	TCM_2	TCM_3

10,000	12,000	16,500	40,000	97,000
20,000	24,000	24,000	45,000	93,000
50,000	60,000	46,500	60,000	94,500
60,000	72,000	53,000	65,000	95,000
80,000	96,000	69,000	75,000	96,000
1,00,000	1,20,000	84,000	85,000	97,000
1,10,000	1,32,000	91,000	90,000	97,500
1,20,000	1,44,000	99,000	95,000	98,000
1,30,000	1,56,000	1,06,500	1,00,000	98,500
1,50,000	1,80,000	1,21,000	1,10,000	99,500

Plot the cost and quantity on a graph:

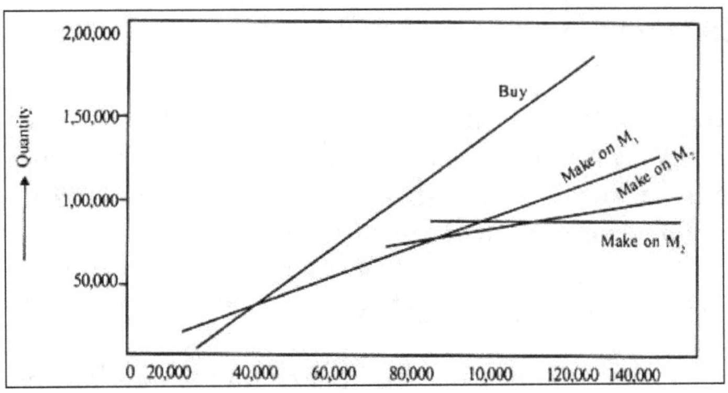

The requirement is to the extent of 1, 20,000. The best option is to make on M_2, which results in lowest cost.

References

- Horngren, multi-product-showcase: pearsoncanada.ca, Retrieved 19, January 2020
- Breakeven-Analysis: iamrcoe.com, Retrieved 30, April 2020
- Make-or-buy-decisions-of-a-product-introduction-factors-and-functional-aspects, production-management-57483: yourarticlelibrary.com, Retrieved 18, August 2020

5

Statement Analysis and Reporting

The process which is involved in the analysis of the financial statements of a company for the purpose of decision making is known as statement analysis. It comprises ratio analysis, horizontal and vertical analysis, and cash flow analysis. This chapter has been carefully written to provide an easy understanding of these facets of statement analysis.

Ratio Analysis

The accounting ratios indicate a quantitative relationship which is used for analysis and decision-making. It provides basis for inter-firm as well as intra-firm comparisons. Besides, in order to make the ratios effective, they are compared with ratios of base period or with standards or with the industry average ratios.

Classification of Accounting Ratios

Accounting ratios may be classified in a number of ways to suit any particular purpose. Different kinds of ratios are selected for different types of situations. The most widely used classifications are:

- Classification According to Sources: Accounting ratios can be further classified into following three groups:
    - Balance Sheet Ratios: These ratios are also known as financial ratios. These ratios deal with relationship between two items or group of items which are both available in Balance sheet. Examples of these ratios are: Current ratio, Liquid ratio, Debt-Equity ratio, Capital bearing ratio, Proprietary ratio, etc.
    - Profit and Loss Account Ratios: These ratios deal with the relationship between two items or group of items which are usually taken out from the profit and loss account. Examples of these ratios are: Gross profit ratio, Net profit ratio, Operating ratio, Operating profit ratio, Interest coverage ratio etc.
    - Inter-statement Ratios or Combined Ratios: These ratios deal with the relationship between items, one of which is drawn from profit and loss account and other is from balance sheet. Examples of these ratios are: Stock turnover

ratio, Debtors turnover ratio, Creditors turnover ratio, Assets turnover ratio. Return on capital employed, etc.

- Classification According to Nature: Under this classification, ratios are grouped as:
    - Liquidity Ratios: The terms liquidity and short-term solvency are synonymously used. The liquidity ratios indicate the liquidity position of the enterprise. These ratios analyse the ability of the firm to meet its current liabilities out of current assets. Liquid ratios are of help in ascertaining the effectiveness of the working capital management. Examples of these ratios are: Current ratio, Quick ratio, Inventory turnover ratio, Debtors turnover ratio, Creditors turnover ratio etc.
    - Leverage Ratios: It refers to those financial ratios which measure the long-term solvency and capital structure of the firm. They show the mix of funds provided by the owners and lenders and also the risk involved in debt financing. Examples of these ratios are: Debt-Equity ratio, Capital gearing ratio, Fixed assets to Net worth ratio, Interest coverage ratio etc.
    - Turnover or Activity Ratios: These ratios measure the efficiency with which the funds have been employed in the business. They indicate frequency of sales with respect to its assets. These are computed with reference to sales or cost of goods sold and expressed in terms of times or rates. Examples of these ratios are: Stock Turnover ratio, Debtors Turnover ratio, Creditors Turnover ratio, Fixed Assets Turnover ratio, etc.
    - Profitability Ratios: Profitability is an indication of the efficiency with which the operations of the business are carried on. Profitability ratios show the effect of business transactions on the profits. A lower profitability ratio may arise due to lack of control over business expenses. Examples of these ratios are: Gross profit ratio, Net profit ratio, Operating ratio, Operating profit ratio, Return in capital employed, etc.

Analysis of Liquidity or Liquid Ratios

These ratios play a vital role in the analysis of short-term financial position of a business. Banks and other short-term loan creditors are generally interested in such an analysis. Shareholders, debenture holders and other long term creditors can use these ratios to assess the ability of the firm to pay dividend and interest charges. In short, these ratios indicate the capacity or ability of the firm to meet the maturing or current liabilities, the efficiency of the management in utilizing the working capital and the progress attained in current financial position. Some of these ratios are:

- Current Ratio or Working Capital Ratio.

- Liquid Ratio or Add-test Ratio or Quick Ratio.
- Absolute Liquidity Ratio.
- Working Capital Turnover Ratio.

Current Ratio or Working Capital Ratio

Current ratio may be defined as the ratio of current assets and current liabilities and is obtained by dividing current assets by current liabilities. It is also known as working capital ratio. Working capital is defined as excess of current assets over current liabilities. This ratio is the indicator of short-term liquidity position of a firm. The term liquidity means the ability of the firm to meet its short-term maturing obligations. Thus, if current assets amount to $ 2,00,000 and current liabilities $ 1,00,000, then,

$$\text{Current Ratio} = \frac{\text{Current Assets}}{\text{Current Liabilities}} = \frac{\$2,00,000}{\$1,00,000} = 2:1$$

Current assets mean cash or those assets convertible or expected to be converted into cash within a year. It includes: Cash in hand and at bank, Marketable securities or readily realisable investments, Bills receivables, Book debts (excluding bad debts and provision), Inventories and Pre-paid expenses. Current liabilities mean those liabilities which are to be paid within a year. It includes Sundry creditors, Bills payable, Short-term loans, Bank-overdraft, Cash credit, Outstanding expenses, Provision for taxation, Proposed dividend, Unclaimed dividend, etc.

Significance and Interpretation of Current Ratio or Working Capital Ratio

Current ratio measures short-term solvency or liquidity position of the firm. It indicates the availability of current assets to meet its current liabilities. A relatively high current ratio is considered as an indication that the company is in a position to pay its current liabilities out of current assets and its liquidity position is good. But, at the same time, a higher current ratio would mean that the company may have an excessive investment in current assets that does not produce a significant return.

If the balance sheet is window-dressed i.e., current assets are made to appear stronger than what really is, then this ratio will not be an ideal indicator of liquidity. On the other hand, a low current ratio is considered as an indication of difficult liquid position. It indicates that the company will face difficulty in meeting its maturing liabilities.

An increase in the proportion of inventory and a decrease in the proportion of cash in the current assets make the position less liquid. This ratio has a particular significance to short-term creditors. Higher the ratio, greater is the margin of safety to creditors. As a convention, current ratio 2:1 is taken as standard which means that for every \$ 1 of current liabilities, current assets of the value of \$ 2 are available for payment. The logic is that if the current assets are reduced to half i.e., \$ 1 instead of \$ 2, then also the creditors will be able to get their payments in full. But such a generalisation is not always true. The standard ratio will vary from industry to industry and season to season.

However, this ratio fails to indicate the liquidity of individual components of current assets. For example, if current assets of a firm include huge amount of old and doubtful debts and obsolete inventory, its debt paying capacity is deteriorated. Hence, current ratio should not always be used as the sole index of short-term solvency. The size and nature of business and quality of current assets are also material consideration in determining liquidity. Therefore, current ratio should be considered in conjunction with liquid ratio to ascertain the true liquidity position of the business.

Liquid Ratio or Add-Test Ratio or Quick Ratio

Current ratio is a crude test of liquidity. For better analysis of liquidity the current ratio is modified. The modified version is called 'Liquid ratio' or 'Quick ratio'. Thus current ratio is a liberal test of liquidity while quick ratio is a conservative test of liquidity. Quick ratio or liquid ratio is the ratio between quick or liquid assets and quick or liquid liabilities. It shows the availability of funds for meeting the immediate liabilities. This ratio is obtained by dividing liquid assets by liquid liabilities. If the liquid assets amount to \$ 1,00,000 and liquid liabilities \$ 1,00,000, then,

$$\text{Liquid Ratio} = \frac{\text{Liquid Assets}}{\text{Liquid Liabilities}} = \frac{\$1,00,000}{\$1,00,000} = 1:1$$

$$\text{Liquid Assets} = \text{Current Assets} - (\text{Inventory} + \text{Prepaid Expenses})$$

$$\text{Liquid Liabilities} = \text{Current Liabilities} - \text{Bank Overdraft}$$

$$\text{Liquid Ratio} = \frac{\text{Current Assets} - (\text{Inventory} + \text{Prepaid Expenses})}{\text{Current Liabilities} - \text{Bank Overdraft}}$$

Liquid assets mean those assets which are immediately convertible into cash without much loss. It includes cash, debtors-less bad debts, short-term bills receivable and temporary investments held in lieu of cash. Inventories and pre-paid expenses are excluded from liquid assets. Inventories are not included in quick assets as it takes long time for its conversion into cash.

Similarly, pre-paid expenses are excluded from quick assets since no cash will be realized from it. Liquid liabilities mean those liabilities which are payable within a short period of time. Normally, bank overdraft and cash credit facility are excluded from quick liabilities as they are used as permanent mode of financing by the firm. If bank overdraft is payable on demand, it is to be included in quick liabilities.

Significance and Interpretation of Liquid Ratio or Add-Test Ratio or Quick Ratio

This ratio is an important indicator of financial health of a firm. As per convention, normal quick ratio should be 1: 1. It implies that every rupee of quick liabilities should be backed by quick assets of equal value. If the ratio is less than this, it means that arrangement from outside sources of funds will have to be made for meeting some portion of the immediately maturing liabilities. This is not a desirable situation and it should be avoided.

However, liquidity position of an organisation is largely effected by the composition of debtors figure. If huge amount of old and doubtful debts are included in the figure of debtors, then, obviously, the conclusions from the ratio will be invalid. The ratio used in combination with current ratio can be a very good test of liquidity. If the current ratio is 2:1 and quick ratio is nearly 1:1, the liquidity position may be considered to be satisfactory. If the current ratio is higher than 2: 1 but quick ratio is less than 1: 1, it indicates excessive inventory. Like current ratio, quick ratio also should not be followed blindly. Its interpretation will depend upon size, nature of business and velocity of the turnover of stock etc.

Absolute Liquidity Ratio

Absolute liquidity is represented by cash and near cash items. Hence, in computation of this ratio, only absolute liquid assets are compared with liquid liabilities. The absolute liquid assets are cash in hand, cash at Bank and marketable securities. It is calculated as follows:

$$\text{Absolute Liquid Ratio} = \frac{\text{Cash} + \text{Bank} + \text{Marketable Securities}}{\text{Liquid Liabilities}}$$

Significance and Interpretation of Absolute Liquidity Ratio

This ratio measures the instant capacity of the firm to meet its quick liabilities. Debtors are excluded from the list of liquid assets in order to obtain absolute liquid assets since there are some doubts relating to their liquidity. However this ratio is not widely used in practice.

Working Capital Turnover Ratio

This ratio indicates that whether or not working capital (i.e., excess of current assets over current liabilities) has been effectively used in making sales. It is calculated as:

$$\text{Working Capital Turnover Ratio} = \frac{\text{Net Sales}}{\text{Net Working Capital}}$$

Significance and Interpretation of Working Capital Turnover Ratio

This ratio makes it clear whether the business is being carried on with small or large amount of working capital in relation to sales. A low working capital turnover ratio may reflect an inadequacy of net working capital as a result of low turnovers of inventory or receivables. On the other hand, a high turnover ratio may be due to high turnover of inventory or receivables. This ratio takes a number of forms in the analysis. Some of them are as follows:

- Inventory Turnover Ratio.
- Debtors Turnover Ratio.
- Creditors Turnover Ratio.

Inventory Turnover Ratio

It is also known as Stock Turnover Ratio. Normally, it establishes a relationship between cost of goods sold during a period and average inventory held in that period. This ratio indicates whether investment in inventory is within proper limit or not.

It is an index of liquidity of a firm showing the rate at which inventories are converted into sales and then into cash. This ratio helps the financial manager to evaluate the inventory policy. This ratio is obtained by dividing cost of goods sold by average inventory or by dividing net sales by average inventory. Thus:

$$\text{Inventory Turnover Ratio} = \text{Cost of goods sold} / \text{Average inventory}$$

$$\text{Cost of goods sold} = \text{Opening stock} + \text{Purchases} - \text{Closing stock}$$

$$\text{or Cost of goods sold} = \text{Sales} - \text{Gross profit.}$$

$$\text{Average Inventory} = 1/2(\text{Opening stock} + \text{Closing stock})$$

When number of days in a year (i.e., 365 days) are divided by the inventory turnover ratio, we get the average inventory holding period:

$$\text{Average Inventory holding period} = \frac{365 \text{ days}}{\text{Inventory Turnover}}$$

$$= \frac{365 \text{ days} \times \text{Average Inventory}}{\text{Cost of goods sold}}$$

If the average inventory holding period is expressed in month, 365 days will be replaced by 12 months in the numerator. Sometime inventory turnover ratio is computed with reference to sales instead of cost of goods sold. However, the use of the first formula is more logical as, in that case, both the numerator and denominator are expressed at cost.

Significance and Interpretation of Inventory Turnover Ratio

Inventory turnover ratio indicates the efficiency of inventory management. It shows how fast inventory is used/sold. It is an effective tool to measure the liquidity of inventory and thereby to avoid any danger of over-stocking. A high inventory turnover ratio indicates brisk sales which is good from liquidity point of view. A low ratio indicates that inventories are not used/sold and lying in the warehouse for a long time. It may reflect dull business, over-investment in inventory, accumulation of huge amount of slow-moving and obsolete stock, etc.

A high level of obsolete stock means blockage of capital. This will cause high interest and other inventory carrying cost. The ultimate impact is impairment of profitability. It is also warned that a high inventory turnover ratio should also be carefully analysed. A high turnover ratio might be achieved by slashing the selling price which reduces profit. A too high inventory turnover may also be a result of low inventory level. There may be many out-of-stock situations. Thus high turnover ratio should also be investigated further.

So inventory turnover ratio should not be too high or too low. It should be kept in mind that stock turnover ratio is greatly influenced by nature of business. For example, stock turnover ratio in food and vegetables will be much higher than the engineering industry.

Debtors Turnover Ratio

When a firm sells goods on credit and the realisation of credit sales is delayed, the receivable or book debt is created. Cash is received from these receivables or debtors afterwards. The speed or velocity at which these receivables are being converted into cash affects the liquidity of the firm. This ratio indicates the efficiency of the credit and collection policies of the firm. It is computed as:

$$\text{Debtors Turnover Ratio} = \frac{\text{Credit Sales}}{\text{Average Receivables}}$$

When the number of days in a year (i.e., 365 days) are divided by the debtors turnover ratio we get the average collection period i.e., the period during which fund remains blocked in the hands of customer.

$$\text{Average Collection Period} = \frac{365\text{ days}}{\text{Debtors Turnover Ratio}}$$

$$= \frac{365\text{ days} \times \text{Average Receivables}}{\text{Credit Sales}}$$

If the average collection period is to be expressed in month, 365 days will be replaced by 12 months in the numerator. Receivables consist of sundry debtors and bills receivable. Average receivable may be the average of opening receivables and closing receivables.

Significance and Interpretation Debtors Turnover Ratio

The velocity or turnover of debtors gives an indication of the efficiency with which the debtors or receivables are being managed. The higher the ratio or, in other words, shorter the average collection period, better will be quality of debtors. It implies prompt payment by debtors. Average collection period is the determinant of the age of the debtors. It depends upon credit policy and collection policy and sales volume. This ratio offers an indication of the degree to which the credit policy of the firm is being in-forced. A shorter average collection period indicates better liquidity position as the firm which realizes debts in time will be able to make prompt payment to suppliers, employees etc.

On the other hand, if the debtors turnover ratio is low, it will mean longer average collection period. Longer collection period implies a too liberal and inefficient credit collection performance. Apart from weakening the liquidity of the firm, if may result in bad debt which will erode the profitability. But a low collection period or a high debtors turnover ratio may not necessarily be favourable. It may be the result of a very conservative credit policy of the firm.

Conservative credit policy ensures good quality of debtors but it may affect sales volume and profit adversely In order to judge the efficiency of credit policy of the firm, debtors turnover ratio or average collection period should be compared with industry average.

Creditors Turnover Ratio

This ratio also measures the liquidity of the firm. It indicates whether the firm is making payment to the trade creditors in time or not. In other words, this ratio shows what period will be required to pay the suppliers in respect of credit purchases. This ratio is calculated by dividing the credit purchase with the figure of average accounts payable. Accounts payable include both sundry creditors and bills payable. It is calculated as:

$$\text{Creditors Turnover Ratio} = \frac{\text{Credit Purchases}}{\text{Average Accounts Payable}}$$

Average payment period is obtained by dividing the number of days in a year (365 days) by the creditors turnover ratio:

$$\text{Average Payment Period} = \frac{365 \text{ days}}{\text{Creditors Turnover Ratio}}$$

$$= \frac{\text{Average Accounts Payable}}{\text{Credit Purchases}} \times 365 \text{ days}$$

If the average payment period is expressed in month, 365 days will be replaced by 12 months in the numerator.

Significance and Interpretation of Creditors Turnover Ratio

The ratio indicates the number of days the firm usually takes on an average to pay its creditors. A higher creditors turnover ratio or lower creditors payment period signifies that the creditors are being paid promptly, thus enhancing the credit-worthiness of the firm. But the firm has to invest more in working capital. A low creditors turnover ratio is apparently favourable as, in that case the firm enjoys a lengthy credit period. Therefore, the firm has to invest less in working capital. But it will diminish the credit-worthiness of the firm. So the creditors turnover ratio should be neither too high nor too low.

Solvency or Long-Term Financial Position Ratios

Solvency generally refers to the capacity or ability of the firm to meet its short-term and long-term obligations. The capacity to pay-off the current debts of a firm is represented by the liquidity ratios. Liquidity ratios which indicate the short-term financial position of the firm have been already explained. Now, under this heading, only the long-term solvency ratios are dealt with. Generally, shareholders, debenture holders and other long-term creditors like banks, financial institutions etc. are interested in these ratios. These ratios are also used to analyse the capital structure i.e., the mix of funds provided by owners and outsiders. Some selected ratios are discussed:

- Debt-Equity Ratio.
- Capital Gearing Ratio.
- Proprietary Ratio.
- Fixed Assets to Proprietors' Fund.
- Interest Coverage Ratio.

Debt-Equity Ratio

This ratio shows the relationship between debt capital and equity or shareholders fund in the capital structure of the firm. It is determined to measure the firm's obligations to creditors in relation to funds invested by the owners. Generally it is calculated as:

$$\text{Debt-Equity Ratio} = \frac{\text{Long-term Debt}}{\text{Shareholder's Fund}}$$

$$\text{Shareholder's Fund} = \text{Equity Share Capital} + \text{Pref. Share Capital} + \text{Reserves \& Surplus} - \text{Fictitious Assets}$$

or

$$\text{Debt-Equity Ratio} = \frac{\text{Long-term Debt} + \text{Short-term Debt}}{\text{Shareholder's Fund}}$$

or

$$\text{Debt-Equity Ratio} = \frac{\text{Long-term Debt} + \text{Short-term Debt} + \text{Pref. Share Capital}}{\text{Shareholder's Fund}}$$

There is some controversy whether current liabilities should be included in debt or not. Argument forwarded for inclusion of current liabilities is that they are part of a company's total obligation and, like other sources of funds such as equity, long-term debts they are also not cost-free. Similarly, the modern approach is to include Redeemable Preference Shares in debt and Irredeemable Preference Shares in equity.

Significance and Interpretation of Debt-Equity Ratio

Debt-Equity ratio indicates the respective claim of creditors and owners in the assets of the firm. It shows the extent to which debt financing has been used in the business. A higher debt-equity ratio indicates higher proportion of debt content in the capital structure of the firm. There is possibility of increasing the rate of return or EPS to equity shareholders so long as the cost of debt is lower than the rate of return on investment. But financing from debt increases the financial risk of shareholders.

Normally, cost of debt capital is much cheaper than the cost of equity since the interest on debt is tax-deductible. For this reason, under favourable conditions (i.e., when sales are rising), a high debt-equity ratio may be adopted to take advantage of cheaper debt capital. On the other hand, a low debt-equity ratio indicates lesser claims of creditors or outside suppliers of capital and a higher margin of safety for them. Under unfavorable conditions (i.e., when sales are falling), it is desirable to use a low debt-equity ratio. A debt-equity ratio of 2:1 is the norm accepted by financial institutions for financing firms in the private sector, whereas, for public sector enterprises, a 1: 1 ratio is expected to be maintained.

Capital Gearing Ratio

The capital gearing ratio is used to analyse the capital structure of a firm. The term capital gearing refers to the proportion between the fixed interest or dividend bearing funds and non-fixed interest or dividend bearing funds. The fixed interest bearing funds are raised through debentures and long-term loans. Fixed dividend bearing funds are raised through issue of preference shares. The non-fixed interest or dividend bearing funds are provided by equity shareholders whose interest is represented by equity share capital and reserve and surplus. Thus, the proportion of debentures and preference share capital to net-worth or equity shareholders fund is referred to as gearing ratio. It is calculated as:

$$\text{Capital Gearing Ratio} = \frac{\text{Pref. Share Capital} + \text{Debentures} + \text{Long - term Debt}}{\text{Equity Shareholder's Fund}}$$

Equity Shareholders Fund = Equity Share Capital + Reserve & Surplus – Fictitious Assets.

Significance and Interpretation of Capital Gearing Ratio

If the fixed interest or dividend bearing funds are more than equity shareholders fund or net worth, the capital structure is said to be highly geared. In other words, the gearing is in inverse ratio to the equity capital i.e., low equity based firms are highly geared, high equity based firms are low geared. The study of this ratio indicates whether the firm is trading on equity or not. If the firm is trading on equity or is a highly geared firm, the return in equity shareholders will be high. But the firm has a high degree of financial risk. It has to redeem the debt capital as per stipulated schedule.

It has to pay interest on debt at fixed rate even if there is no profit, and pay fixed rate of dividend on preference share capital only in the year in which the company earns profit. So, a too high gearing ratio is not preferable from the solvency point of view. However, in favourable conditions (when sales are rising) when the rate of return on investment is higher than rate of interest on debt or rate of dividend on preference shares, a high gearing ratio will enhance the return to equity shareholders. Again, in unfavorable conditions (i.e., when sales are falling) if rate of return on investment is very low, a high gearing ratio becomes disastrous to equity shareholders. So gearing ratio should be carefully planned so that equity shareholders' interest is not impaired.

Proprietary Ratio

This ratio establishes the relationship between total assets and shareholders' fund. The purpose of the ratio is to indicate the percentage of owner's fund invested in fixed assets. It is calculated by dividing proprietary fund by total assets:

$$\text{Proprietary Ratio} = \frac{\text{Proprietary Fund}}{\text{Total Assets}}$$

Proprietary Fund = Equity Share Capital + Pref. Share Capital + Reserve & Surplus – Fictitious Assets

Total assets do not include fictitious assets.

Significance and Interpretation of Proprietary Ratio

This ratio is a test of long-term financial position of the firm. It indicates how much of the total assets have been procured with shareholders fund. Higher the ratio, lower is the dependence on external fund and hence, greater is the solvency of the firm.

Fixed Assets to Proprietors' Fund

This ratio establishes the relationship between fixed assets and shareholders fund. It is calculated as:

$$\text{Fixed Assets - Proprietary Ratio} = \frac{\text{Fixed Assets}}{\text{Proprietary Fund}}$$

Significance and Interpretation of Fixed Assets to Proprietors' Fund

The ratio indicates the extent of proprietors fund invested in acquisition of fixed assets. If it is less than 1, it will mean that a part of proprietor's fund is investment in financing working capital of the firm. For example, if the ratio is 0.75:1, it will mean that 75% of the proprietor's fund is investment in fixed assets and 25% is invested in working capital. If the ratio is more than 1, it will mean that creditors have been used to acquire a part of fixed assets. If short-term funds are used in the purchase of fixed assets, it will adversely affect the liquidity position, as it will not be possible to liquidate fixed assets for paying short-term liabilities. Thus, a fundamental principle of sound financing policy is that all fixed assets should be financed out of long-term funds. Short-term funds should be utilised only for working capital requirement of the firm.

Interest Coverage Ratio

This ratio relates to the fixed interest charges to the income earned by the company. It is an important test of solvency for the company. All long-term creditors are interested to know the company's ability to meet its current interest charges. The ratio between fixed interest charges and earnings before interest and taxes (EBIT) is a rough indication of the company's ability to pay fixed interest charges out of profit. Thus,

$$\text{Interest Coverage Ratio} = \frac{\text{Net Profit interest and taxes}}{\text{Fixed interest charges}}$$

Significance and Interpretation of Interest Coverage Ratio

This ratio gives an idea of the number of times that fixed interest charges are covered by earnings. It is an index of the financial strength of an enterprise and indicates the margin of safety of the long-term creditors. If the ratio is 5 times, it will mean that the company is able to pay interest five times out of its earning. A high ratio assures the lender regular and periodical interest income. However, a too high interest coverage ratio may be the result of using a very small amount of debt in the capital structure. In this case, the firm cannot avail the full benefit of trading on equity. Again, a too low interest coverage ratio may be the result of using excessive amount of debt capital than warranted by the profitability of the firm. So, an immediate action may be taken to redeem a portion of debt to improve profitability.

Analysis of Profitability

Profitability indicates the efficiency or effectiveness with which the operations of the business is carried on. Poor operational performance may result in poor sales and, therefore, low profit. Low profitability may be due to lack of control over expenses. Profitability is the main base for liquidity as well as solvency. Creditors, banks and financial institutions are interested in profitability ratios as they indicate liquidity or the capacity of the business to meet interest obligations. A company with sufficient profits will enhance the long-term solvency position of the business. Equity shareholders are interested in profitability ratios since they indicate the growth as well as rate of return on their investment. The major types of profitability ratios are:

- Gross Profit Ratio.
- Net Profit Ratio.
- Operating Ratio.
- Operating Profit Ratio.
- Return on Capital Employed (ROCE).
- Return on Equity Capital.

Gross Profit Ratio

This is the ratio of gross profit to net sales and is expressed in percentage. Thus:

$$\text{Gross Profit Ratio} = \frac{\text{Gross Profit}}{\text{Net Sales}} \times 100$$

Significance and Interpretation of Gross Profit Ratio

The ratio throws light on the degree of managerial efficiency in production and sales. It indicates the ability of the firm to widen the gap between sales and cost of sales. This ratio may be high due to higher selling prices in relation to costs or lower costs in relation to selling price or increased sales volume of the higher profit margin items. A low gross profit ratio should be carefully investigated. The gross profit ratio may be low due to:

- Failure to control cost and to take the benefits of large scale economies.
- Excessive investment in plant and machinery.
- Cut-throat competition.

Net Profit Ratio

This is the ratio of net profit after taxes to net sales. Net profit, is the balance of profit and loss account which is arrived at after considering all non-operating incomes such as interest on investment, dividend received etc. and operating expenses such as office and administrative expenses, selling and distribution expenses and non-operating expenses like loss on sale of fixed assets, provision for contingent liability, etc. Thus:

$$\text{Net Profit Ratio} = \frac{\text{Net Profit}}{\text{Net Sales}} \times 100$$

Significance and Interpretation of Net Profit Ratio

This ratio is used to measure the overall profitability and is useful to owners. This ratio indicates how much of sales is left after meeting all expense. For examples, if the ratio is 10%, it will mean that 10 paise per rupee of sale belongs to the owners as their reward for taking risk in investment. So, higher this ratio, more is the return to shareholders.

Operating Ratio

This is the ratio of cost of goods sold plus operating expenses to net sales of the firm. This is closely related to the ratio of operating profit to net sales:

$$\text{Operating Ratio} = \frac{\text{Operating Cost}}{\text{Net Sales}} \times 100$$

Operating cost consists of cost of goods sold, office and administrative expenses and selling and distribution expenses. Financial charges such as interest, provision for taxation and loss on sale of investments etc. are excluded from operating expenses.

Significance and Interpretation of Operating Ratio

This ratio indicates the operational efficiency with which the business is being carried on. It reveals the percentage of net sales that is absorbed by cost of goods sold and operating expenses. Hence, the lower the operating cost, the higher will be operating profit. On the other hand, a higher operating ratio leaves a lesser margin for meeting non-operating expenses, creation of reserves and payment of interest and dividend.

Operating Profit Ratio

This is the ratio of operating profit and net sales and is expressed in percentage.

$$\text{Operating Profit Ratio} = \frac{\text{Operating Profit}}{\text{Net Sales}} \times 100$$

Operating Profit = Net Profit + Non-operating Expenses – Non-operating Income = Sales – (Cost of goods sold t Office & Adm. Expenses + Selling & Dist. Expenses).

Significance and Interpretation of Operating Profit Ratio

This ratio can also be computed by subtracting the operating ratio from 100. For example, if the operating ratio is 85% then the operating profit ratio would be 15% (i.e., 100 – 85). The implication of operating ratio and operating profit ratio is the same. This ratio indicates the extent of sales revenue available for interest, tax and dividend payments etc.

Return on Capital Employed (ROCE)

The main objective of making investment in any business is to earn adequate return on capital invested. Hence, the return on capital employed is used as a measure of success of a business in achieving this objective. Otherwise known as return on investment, this is the barrometer of overall performance of the firm. It is calculated as:

Capital employed may be either gross capital employed or net capital employed:

$$\text{Gross Capital Employed} = \text{Total Assets} - \text{Fictitious Assets}$$
$$= \text{Fixed Assets} + \text{Current Assets}$$

$$\text{Net Capital Employed} = \text{Total Assets} - \text{Current Liabilities}$$

$$= \text{Fixed Assets} + \text{Current Assets} - \text{Current Liabilities}$$

$$\text{Alternatively,} = \text{Fixed Assets} + \text{Working Capital}$$

$$\text{Net Capital Employed} = \text{Share Capital} + \text{Reserve \& Surplus} - \text{Fictitious Assets}$$
$$+ \text{Long - term Loans} + \text{Short - term Loans}$$

Significance and Interpretation of Return on Capital Employed (ROCE)

Return on capital employed is considered to be the best measure of profitability in order to assess the overall performance of the business. A comparison of the ratio with similar firms, with the industry average and over time would provide sufficient insight into how efficiently the long-term funds of owners and creditors are being used. The higher the ratio, the more efficient use of the capital employed. So, determining a minimum rate of return on investment is very essential part of management planning and control. The investments which generate rates lower than the minimum rate of return are rejected. However, it is very difficult to set a standard rate of return on capital employed as number of factors such as nature of business, risk involved, inflation, changes in economic conditions etc. may influence such a rate.

Return on Equity Capital

This ratio relates to the net profits finally available to equity shareholders to the amount of capital invested by them. It is obtained by dividing the profits available to equity shareholders by the equity shareholders fund.

$$\text{Return on Equity Capital} = \frac{\text{Net Profit - Tax and Pref.Dividend}}{\text{Equity Shareholders Fund}} \times 100$$

$$\text{Earning per Equity Share} = \frac{\text{Net Profit - Tax and Pref.Dividend}}{\text{No. of Equity Shares}}$$

Significance and Interpretation of Return on Equity Capital

The ratio indicates how efficiently the equity shareholders fund is being managed in the firm. Return on equity share capital or EPS helps to determine the market price of equity of the company. Therefore, this ratio is of special interest to the existing as well as prospective equity shareholders.

Activity Ratios or Turnover Ratios

These ratios are used to evaluate the efficiency with which the firm uses its assets. They indicate the frequency of sales with respect to its assets. These are computed with reference to sales or cost of goods sold and expressed in terms of times or rates. Some activity ratios are:

- Capital Turnover Ratio.
- Fixed Assets Turnover Ratio.

Capital Turnover Ratio

It is the ratio of sales to capital employed. Thus,

$$\text{Capital Turnover Ratio} = \frac{\text{Sales}}{\text{Capital Employed}}$$

$$\text{Alternatively, Capital Turnover Ratio} = \frac{\text{Cost of goods sold}}{\text{Capital Employed}}$$

Significance and Interpretation of Capital Turnover Ratio

It indicates the firm's ability to generate sales per rupee of long-term investment. The greater the ratio, the more efficient is the utilisation of long-term creditors and owners fund.

Fixed Assets Turnover Ratio

This is the ratio of net sales to net fixed assets. Thus,

$$\text{Fixed Assets Turnover Ratio} = \frac{\text{Net Sales}}{\text{Net Fixed Assets}}$$

Significance and Interpretation of Fixed Assets Turnover Ratio

It is a measure of efficiency of utilisation of fixed assets. The ratio is calculated in determining to what extent the investment in fixed assets has been achieving its objective of generating sales. The higher the ratio, the more efficient is the utilisation of fixed assets in generating sales.

Horizontal and Vertical Analysis

Today's economy is undergoing constant and significant change thanks to digital disruption, complex globe-spanning phenomena like climate change and the COVID-19 pandemic, and the ever-expanding impact (and importance) of Big Data. To compete effectively and strategically, it's important for businesses of all sizes to make use of the tools at their disposal. Both horizontal and vertical analysis each have a role to play in a company's financial management, business process management, and overall strategic and competitive planning.

Horizontal Analysis

Also known as trend analysis, this method is used to analyze financial trends that occur across multiple accounting periods over time usually by the quarter or year. It's often used when analyzing the income statement, balance sheet, and cash flow statement. Generally speaking, the greatest utility of horizontal analysis lies in mining insights gleaned from comparing changes to specific line items over time, identifying and targeting both opportunities and potential disasters and reacting accordingly. You can use horizontal analysis to examine (for example) your company's profit margins over time, and create strategic spend projections to match projected revenue growth or hedge against seasonality or increased cost of materials. You can examine the data from horizontal analysis in a number of ways, depending on your goals. Three of the most common ways include:

- Direct Comparison, which is a straightforward comparison of two periods to one another in the original format (e.g., dollar amounts). So if revenue for Q1 of 2019 was $4,700,000 and Q2 revenue was $3,200,000, the difference of $1,500,000 is where you would start looking for answers (e.g., does the business have a strong seasonal component, have costs risen or sales fallen due to disruptions, etc.)
- Variance, which is useful in establishing positive or negative changes between periods based on comparison to the average of the squared difference from the mean for the total time measured. Let's say you're analyzing revenue for a three-year period.
    - 2017 revenue was $4,500,000.
    - 2018 revenue was $5,300,000.
    - 2019 revenue was $6,000,000.

The mean of these three values is $5,266,700. After squaring the differences and adding them up, then dividing by the total number of items, we find that the variance is $5,633,400. Taking the square root of that, we get the standard deviation, which is $750,600. The average growth over the period measured is $750,600 each year. This method is particularly useful for both internal analysis to identify areas of growth and external analysis by investors or lenders who want to see demonstrable growth before committing their resources to your business.

- Percentage, which provides the option for greater granularity within horizontal analysis. Using this approach, the first value measured is considered the "base period" value, and all other values are compared against it, line by line.
    - 2017 Revenue (Base Value): $4,500,000.
    - 2018 Revenue: $5,300,000.
    - 2019 Revenue: $6,000,000.

By calculating the difference and converting to percentages, we can quickly create a thumbnail snapshot of revenue growth or contraction.

$5,300,000 – $4,500,000 = $800,000

$800,000 ÷ $4,500,000 × 100 = 17.8% revenue growth from 2017 to 2018.

Using the same approach, we can do the same for 2019:

$6,000,000 – $4,500,000 = $1,500,000

$1,500,000 ÷ $4,500,000 × 100 = 33.33% revenue growth from 2017 to 2019.

Horizontal analysis can be very useful in answering common questions whose answers are critical to strategic planning and effective use of working capital, including:

- Is net income growing or shrinking?
- Has the cost of goods sold (COGS) risen or fallen?
- How much has revenue grown compared to last quarter? Last year?
- Which areas of our business have changed the most in the past quarter/year/etc.?
- Is our company managing liquidity well enough to cover our outstanding debts?

The more periods you have to compare, the more robust your data set will be, and the more useful the insights gathered. In order to be accurate and effective, horizontal analysis must be performed on complete and accurate data from reliable sources. A consistent, centralized, and optimized data management environment goes a long way toward ensuring the insights and opportunities you gather from horizontal analysis are legitimate and useful.

Implementing an eProcurement solution can help you centralize and organize all your financial information, eliminate common roadblocks to data transparency (including rogue spend and invoice fraud), and ensure all your stakeholders are connected and collaborating using complete, accurate, and secure data in real time.

Vertical Analysis

Like horizontal analysis, vertical analysis is used to mine useful insights from your financial statements. It can be applied to the same documents, but is exclusively percentile-based and travels (as the name implies) vertically within each period across periods, rather than horizontally across periods. So, for example, when analyzing an income statement, the first line item, sales, will be established as the base value (100%), and all other account balances below it will be expressed as a percentage of that number. Let's review a very simple example of vertical analysis:

XYZ Incorporated Vertical Analysis			
	2017	2018	2019
Sales	$25,000,000	$27,500,000	$35,000,000
COGS	$12,500,000	$14,000,000	$19,000,000
Gross Profit	$12,500,000	$13,500,000	$16,000,000
Salaries	$4,500,000	$4,800,000	$6,000,000
Marketing	$1,100,000	$1,100,000	$1,900,000
Rent	$2,000,000	$2,000,000	$2,000,000
Utilities	$300,000	$300,000	$300,000
Misc. Expenses	$500,000	$750,000	$680,000
Total Expenses	$8,400,000	$8,950,000	$10,880,000
Net Income	$4,100,000	$4,550,000	$5,120,000

If we convert these values to percentages, our new chart looks like this:

XYZ Incorporated Vertical Analysis			
	2017	2018	2019
Sales	100 %	100 %	100 %
COGS	50 %	51 %	54 %
Gross Profit	50 %	49 %	46 %
Salaries	18 %	17.5 %	17.2 %
Marketing	4.4 %	4 %	5.5 %

Rent	8 %	7.3 %	5.8 %
Utilities	1.2 %	1 %	0.9 %
Misc. Expenses	2 %	2.7 %	1.9 %
Total Expenses	33.6 %	32.6 %	31.3 %
Net Income	16.4 %	16.4 %	14.7 %

Based on this financial statement analysis, it's clear that while the company's gross profits are growing, and total gross sales are increasing over previous years, they're being hampered by concurrent increases elsewhere, including cost of goods sold. The result? A shrinking profit margin that might spell trouble ahead.

Clearly, further investigation is required. This could take the form of a deep dive into internal processes to identify pain points and bottlenecks that are hampering efficiency (and increasing costs), or supply chain management to look for opportunities to source essential raw materials at better pricing or terms. In fact, this single vertical analysis could be the starting point for a much larger analysis of internal workflows (e.g., the procure-to-pay (P2P) process) to implement system-wide changes that will increase profits and value while slashing both hard and soft costs.

Another similarity to horizontal analysis is vertical analysis' utility during external as well as internal analysis. Two companies with vastly different financial profiles (e.g., a $10 million company and a $10 billion dollar international corporation) can still be meaningfully compared by investors and lenders by using the base year system and rendering their financial performance as percentage changes against a base figure. One major difference between horizontal and vertical analysis is the depth of their utility with regard to answering "why" as well as "how." Vertical analysis excels at providing useful snapshots of trends within financial statements, but does not provide easy answers for why those trends are occurring. Further analysis via horizontal analysis will likely be required to unlock those insights, and make use of them in a strategic way.

Cash Flow Analysis

The statement of cash flow shows how a company spends its money (cash outflows) and from where a company receives its money (cash inflows). The cash flow statement includes all cash inflows a company receives from its ongoing operations and external investment sources, as well as all cash outflows that pay for business activities and investments during a given quarter. These include cash flows from operating activities (CFO), but also cash flows from financing (CFO) and investing (CFI) activities.

There are two forms of accounting that determine how cash moves within a company's financial statements. They are accrual accounting and cash accounting. Accrual accounting is used by most public companies and is the accounting method where revenue is reported as income when it's earned rather than when the company receives payment. Expenses are reported when incurred, even though no cash payments have been made. For example, if a company records a sale, the revenue is recognized on the income statement, but the company may not receive cash until a later date. From an accounting standpoint, the company would be earning a profit on the income statement and be paying income taxes on it.

However, no cash would have been exchanged. Also, the transaction would likely be an outflow of cash initially, since it costs money for the company to buy inventory and manufacture the product to be sold. It's common for businesses to extend terms of 30, 60, or even 90 days for a customer to pay the invoice. The sale would be an accounts receivable with no impact on cash until collected. Cash accounting is an accounting method in which payment receipts are recorded during the period they are received, and expenses are recorded in the period in which they are paid. In other words, revenues and expenses are recorded when cash is received and paid, respectively.

A company's profit is shown as net income on the income statement. Net income is the bottom line for the company. However, because of accrual accounting, net income doesn't necessarily mean that all receivables were collected from their customers. From an accounting standpoint, the company might be profitable, but if the receivables become past due or uncollected, the company could run into financial problems. Even profitable companies can fail to adequately manage their cash flow, which is why a cash flow statement is a critical tool for analysts and investors.

Cash Flow Statement

A cash flow statement has three distinct sections, each of which relates to a particular component operations, investing, and financing of a company's business activities.

- Cash Flow from Operations: This section reports the amount of cash from the income statement that was originally reported on an accrual basis. A few of the items included in this section are accounts receivables, accounts payables, and income taxes payable. If a client pays a receivable, it would be recorded as cash from operations. Changes in current assets or current liabilities (items due in one year or less) are recorded as cash flow from operations.
- Cash Flow from Investing: This section records the cash flow from sales and purchases of long-term investments like fixed assets that include property, plant, and equipment. Items included in this section are purchases of vehicles, furniture, buildings, or land. Typically, investing transactions generate cash outflows, such as capital expenditures for plant, property and equipment, business acquisitions, and the purchase of investment securities. Cash inflows come from the sale of assets, businesses, and securities. Investors typically monitor capital expenditures used for the maintenance of, and additions to, a company's

physical assets to support the company's operation and competitiveness. In short, investors can see how a company is investing in itself.

- Cash Flow from Financing: Debt and equity transactions are reported in this section. Any cash flows that include payment of dividends, the repurchase or sale of stocks, and bonds would be considered cash flow from financing activities. Cash received from taking out a loan or cash used to pay down long-term debt would be recorded in this section. For investors who prefer dividend-paying companies, this section is important since it shows cash dividends paid since cash, not net income, is used to pay dividends to shareholders.

A company's cash flow can be defined as the number that appears in the cash flow statement as net cash provided by operating activities, or "net operating cash flow." However, there is no universally accepted definition. For instance, many financial professionals consider a company's cash flow to be the sum of its net income, depreciation, and amortization (non-cash charges in the income statement). While often coming close to net operating cash flow, the shortcut can be inaccurate, and investors should stick with using the net operating cash flow figure. While cash flow analysis can include several ratios, the following indicators provide a starting point for an investor to measure the investment quality of a company's cash flow.

Operating Cash Flow/Net Sales

This ratio, which is expressed as a percentage of a company's net operating cash flow to its net sales, or revenue (from the income statement), tells us how many dollars of cash are generated for every dollar of sales. There is no exact percentage to look for, but the higher the percentage, the better. Industry and company ratios will vary widely. Investors should track this indicator's performance historically to detect significant variances from the company's average cash flow/sales relationship along with how the company's ratio compares to its peers. It is also essential to monitor how cash flow increases as sales increase since it's important that they move at a similar rate over time.

Free Cash Flow

Free cash flow (FCF) is often defined as the net operating cash flow minus capital expenditures. Free cash flow is an important measurement since it shows how efficient a company is at generating cash. Investors use free cash flow to measure whether a company might have enough cash, after funding operations and capital expenditures, to pay investors through dividends and share buybacks. To calculate FCF from the cash flow statement, find the item cash flow from operations, also referred to as "operating cash" or "net cash from operating activities" and subtract capital expenditures required for current operations from it.

You can go one step further by expanding what's included in the free cash flow number. For example, in addition to capital expenditures, you could also include dividends for the amount to be subtracted from net operating cash flow to arrive at a more comprehensive free cash flow figure. This figure could then be compared to sales. As a practical matter, if a company has a history of dividend payments, it cannot easily suspend or eliminate them without causing shareholders some real pain. Even dividend payout reductions, while less injurious, are problematic for many shareholders. For some industries, investors consider dividend payments to be necessary cash outlays similar to capital expenditures. It's important to monitor free cash flow over multiple periods and compare the figures to companies within the same industry. If free cash flow is positive, it should indicate the company can meet its obligations, including funding its operating activities and paying dividends.

Comprehensive Free Cash Flow Coverage

You can calculate a comprehensive free cash flow ratio by dividing the free cash flow by net operating cash flow to get a percentage ratio. Again, the higher the percentage, the better.

Contemporary Issues in Management Accounting

Balanced Scorecard

A balanced scorecard is a strategic planning framework that companies use to assign priority to their products, projects, and services; communicate about their targets or goals; and plan their routine activities. The scorecard enables companies to monitor and measure the success of their strategies to determine how well they have performed.

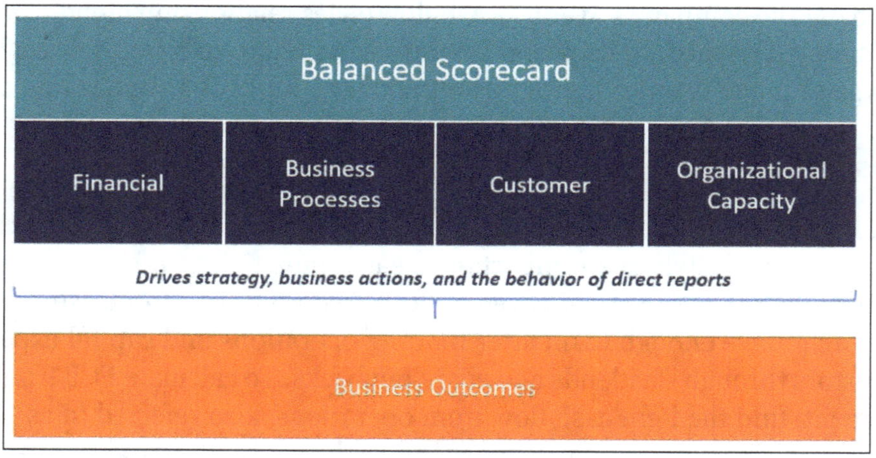

The balanced scorecard acts as a structured report that measures the performance of company management. The management team can be evaluated against Key Performance Indicators (KPIs) to show their contributions to the strategy and attainment of the targets set forth. Success is measured against the specified goals or targets to determine the rate at which the business is growing and how it compares to its competitors. Other personnel in the organizational hierarchy can depend on the balanced scorecard to show their contribution to the growth of the business, or their suitability for job promotions and salary reviews. The key features of a balanced scorecard include a focus on a strategic topic relevant to the organization, and the use of both financial and non-financial data to create strategies.

Four Perspectives of the Balanced Scorecard

The following are the key areas that a balanced scorecard focuses on:

- Financial perspective: Under the financial perspective, the goal of a company is to ensure that it earns a return on the investments made and manages key risks involved in running the business. The goals can be achieved by satisfying the needs of all players involved with the business, such as the shareholders, customers, and suppliers. The shareholders are an integral part of the business since they are the providers of capital; they should be happy when the company achieves financial success. They want to be sure that the company is continually generating revenues and that the organization meets goals such as improving profitability and developing new revenue sources. Steps taken to achieve such goals may include introducing new products and services, improving the company's value proposition, and cutting down on the costs of doing business.
- Customer perspective: The customer perspective monitors how the entity is providing value to its customers and determines the level of customer satisfaction with the company's products or services. Customer satisfaction is an indicator of the company's success. How well a company treats its customers can obviously affect its profitability. The balanced scorecard considers the company's reputation versus its competitors. How do customers see your company vis-à-vis your competitors? It enables the organization to step out of its comfort zone to view itself from the customer's point of view rather than just from an internal perspective. Some of the strategies that a company can focus on to improve its reputation among customers include improving product quality, enhancing the customer shopping experience, and adjusting the prices of its main products and services.
- Internal business processes perspective: A business' internal processes determine how well the entity runs. A balanced scorecard puts into perspective the measures and objectives that can help the business run more effectively. Also, the scorecard helps evaluate the company's products or services and determine whether they conform to the standards that customers desire. A key part of this perspective is aiming to answer the question, "What are we good at?" The answer to that question can help the company formulate marketing strategies

and pursue innovations that lead to the creation of new and improved ways of meeting the needs of customers.

- Organizational capacity perspective: Organizational capacity is important in optimizing goals and objectives with favorable results. The personnel in the organization's departments are required to demonstrate high performance in terms of leadership, the entity's culture, application of knowledge, and skill sets. Proper infrastructure is required for the organization to deliver according to the expectations of management. For example, the organization should use the latest technology to automate activities and ensure a smooth flow of activities.

Target Costing

Target costing is a system under which a company plans in advance for the price points, product costs, and margins that it wants to achieve for a new product. Target costing is not just a method of costing, but rather a management technique wherein prices are determined by market conditions, taking into account several factors, such as homogeneous products, level of competition, no/low switching costs for the end customer, etc. When these factors come into the picture, management wants to control the costs, as they have little or no control over the selling price. "A market-based cost that is calculated using sales price necessary to capture a predetermined market share is known as Target Cost." In competitive industries, a unit selling price is set independent of initial cost of the product. If target cost is lower than the initial forecast of product cost, the manufacture/producer drives the unit cost to come down over a definite period, so that it should compete. Target cost is found by deducting desired profit from predetermined sales price. Hence,

Target Costing = Selling Price – Desired Profit

Here, sales price is one which is appropriate for a targeted market share. Desired profit is the contribution that the product is expected to make towards the enterprise's business sustaining costs. The residual is target cost. Thus, target costing takes full advantage of the equation Profit = Sales – Costs.

Example: ABC Inc. is a big FMCG player that operates in a very competitive market. It sells packaged food to end customers. ABC can only charge $20 per unit. If the company's intended profit margin is 10% on the selling price, calculate the target cost per unit.

Solution:

Target Profit Margin = 10% of 20 = $2 per unit

Target Cost = Selling Price – Profit Margin ($20 – $2)

Target Cost = $18 per unit

Features of Target Costing

The main features of target costing are as follows:

- The price of the product is determined by market conditions. The company is a price taker rather than a price maker.
- The minimum required profit margin is already included in the target selling price.
- It is part of management's strategy to focus on cost reduction and effective cost management.
- Product design, specifications, and customer expectations are already built-in while formulating the total selling price.
- The difference between the current cost and the target cost is the "cost reduction," which management wants to achieve.
- A team is formed to integrate activities such as designing, purchasing, manufacturing, marketing, etc., to find and achieve the target cost.

Objectives of Target Costing

The fundamental objective of target costing is to enable management to use proactive cost planning, cost management and cost reduction practices whereby, costs are planned and managed out of a product and business, early in the design and development cycle, rather to a during the later stages of product development and production. Broadly speaking, a target costing system has three objectives:

- To lower the costs of new products so that the required profit level can be ensured.
- The new products meet the levels of quality, delivery timing and price required by the market.
- To motivate all company employees to achieve the target profit during new product development by making target costing a companywide profit management activity.

Process of Target Costing

Target Costing applies to new products and succeeding generations of a product. It begins with understanding the market thoroughly and an intention to satisfy customer needs, concerning product quality, features, timeline and price. The process of target costing is depicted in the following diagram:

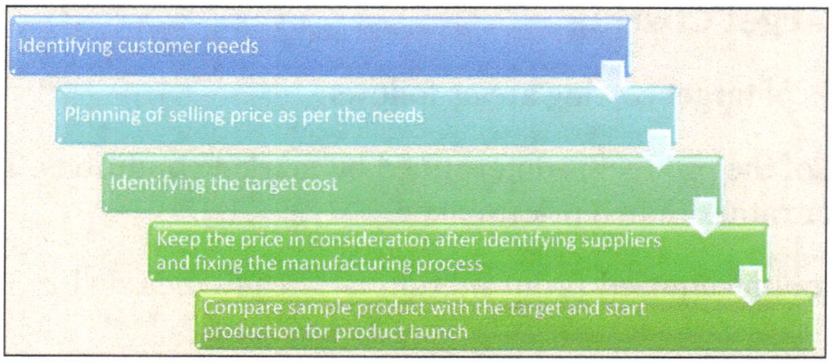

Advantages of Target Costing

The major advantages/benefits of target costing are as follows:

- It shows management's commitment to process improvements and product innovation to gain competitive advantages.
- The product is created from the expectation of the customer and, hence, cost is also based on similar lines. Thus, the customer feels more value is delivered.
- With the passage of time, the company's operations improve drastically, creating economies of scale.
- The company's approach to designing and manufacturing products becomes market driven.
- New market opportunities can be converted into real savings to achieve the best value for money rather than to simply realize the lowest cost.

Key Principles of Target Costing

Target costing involves seven key principles listed as follows:

- Price-Led Costing: Target costing sets the target cost by first determining the price at which a product can be sold in the marketplace. Subtracting the target profit margin from this target price yields the target cost, that is, the cost at which the product must be manufactured. Notice that in a target costing approach, the price is set first, and then the target product cost is determined. This is opposite from the order in which the product cost and selling price are determined under traditional cost-plus pricing.
- Focus on the Customer: To be successful at target costing, management must listen to the company's customers. What products do they want? What features are important? How much are they willing to pay for a certain level of product quality? Management needs to aggressively seek customer feedback, and then products must be designed to satisfy customer demand and be sold at a price they are willing to pay. In short, the target costing approach is market driven.

- Focus on Product Design: Design engineering is a key element in target costing. Engineers must design a product from the ground up so that it can be produced at its target cost. This design activity includes specifying the raw materials and components to be used as well as the labour, machinery, and other elements of the production process. In short, a product must be designed for manufacturability.
- Focus on Process Design: Every aspect of the production process must be examined to make sure that the product is produced as efficiently as possible. The use of touch labour, technology, global sourcing in procurement and every aspect of the production process must be designed with the product's target cost in mind.
- Cross-Functional Teams: Manufacturing a product at or below its target cost requires the involvement of people from many different functions in an organisation: market research, sales, design engineering, procurement, production engineering, production scheduling, material handling and cost management. Individuals from all these diverse areas of expertise can make key contributions to the target costing process. Moreover, a cross-functional team is not a set of specialists who contribute their expertise and then leave; they are responsible for the entire product.
- Life-Cycle Costs: In specifying a product's target cost, analysts must be careful to incorporate all of the product's life-cycle costs. These include the costs of product planning and concept design, preliminary design, detailed design and testing, production, distribution and customer service. Traditional cost-accounting systems have tended to focus only on the production phase and have not paid enough attention to the product's other life-cycle costs.
- Value-Chain Orientation: Sometimes the projected cost of a new product is above the target cost. Then efforts are made to eliminate non-value-added costs to bring the projected cost down. In some cases, a close look at the company's entire value chain can help managers identify opportunities for cost reduction.

Cost-Based Pricing vs. Target Pricing Method

A clear picture regarding process of both the methods can be understood by following diagram.

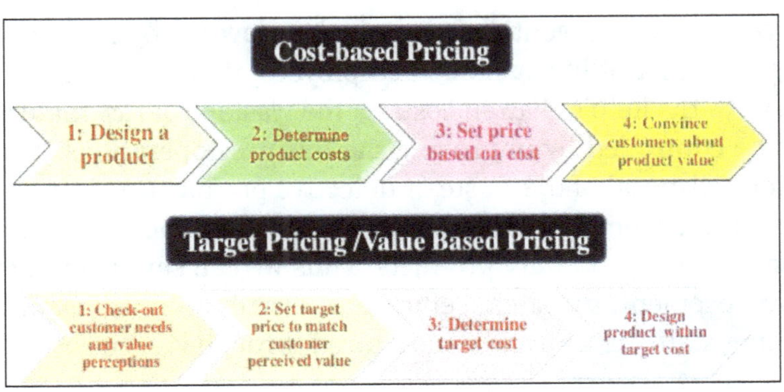

The basic difference between Target Costing and cost based pricing or traditional costing are as follows:

Target Costing	Traditional Costing
• Competitive market considerations drive cost planning. • Price determines costs. • Design is focus for reducing cost. • Customer input guides cost reduction. • Cross-functional teams manage costs. • Suppliers are involved during product design. • Minimizes cost of ownership to customers. • Involves the whole value chain in cost planning.	• Market considerations not part of cost planning. • Costs determine price. • Inefficiency is focus for reducing cost. • Cost reduction is not customer driven. • Cost Accountants are responsible. • Suppliers are involved only after product design. • Minimizes initial price paid by customers. • Little or no involvement of value chain in cost planning.

Kaizen Costing

Kaizen costing is a technique of controlling the cost incurred over unproductive activities and resources which does not add any value to the organization. In simple words, it is a practical approach to solving cost-related problems to improve the overall efficiency of the organization. Kaizen costing is implemented in business organizations to manage different types of costs in a business:

The cost of the supply chain, including administration, order procurement, inventory and transportation costs can be controlled through kaizen costing. It regulates all the cost incurred in the production of goods or services, including the cost of machinery, tools, labour, raw material and other equipment. Cost of acquiring a patent, license, registration fees, hiring of chartered accountant and all other legal formalities require kaizen costing. At the same time, it is also applicable at the time of redesigning of any product which involves cost on research, analysis, hiring of expert personnel, etc.

Human resource is another essential arena which is covered by this technique. It functions to manage the cost of hiring skilled employees, their training and development and retention. With the help of kaizen costing, the wastage of raw material and time of the labour can be controlled by improving the business operations. The organization also incurs cost on disposal of the waste or defective products. Kaizen costing provides a solution through reusability of the waste and improving the production efficiency to reduce the manufacturing of faulty products. Thus we can say that the cost of product promotion, advertisement, dispatch, selling and distribution, transportation, recruitment of marketing staff, etc. can all be monitored through kaizen costing.

Types of Kaizen Costing

Kaizen costing can be on a mass level for any fixed asset or the whole organization. Or it can be product-based, i.e., transforming the product or its process of manufacturing.

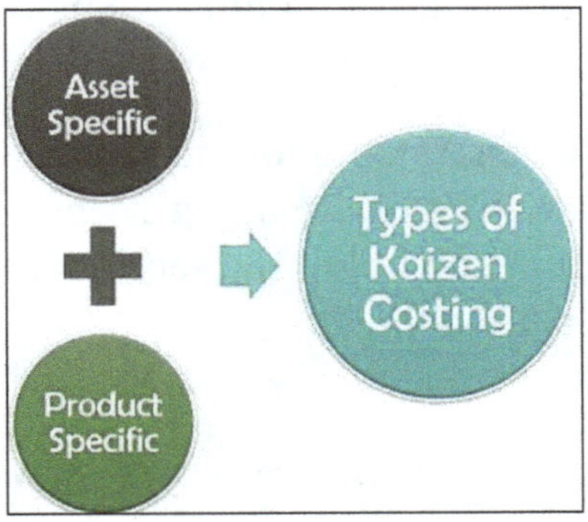

- Asset Specific: The asset and organization-specific kaizen costing focuses on the need for a particular deal or the business unit.
- Product Specific: The activity which is project or product-oriented, aiming at value analysis is termed as product-specific kaizen costing.

5S in Kaizen Costing

Workplace improvement, especially in the production or manufacturing unit, is not possible without the application of 5S kaizen technique. It involves the following five steps:

- Sort (Seiri): The first step in the 5S approach is categorizing the items based on their necessity. The unnecessary items should be labelled red and needs to be moved out of the organization. These items can be sold to the staff or as scrap else can be dumped by the organization.
- Straighten (Seiton): Now, the organization is left with essential items. These have to be arranged in an orderly manner for simplifying the operations. This step improves the visibility, availability and accessibility of all the tools and items.

- Shine (Seiso): Shine here refers to maintaining cleanliness in the workplace. It creates a positive work environment for the employees.
- Standardize (Seiketsu): One of the most vital tasks is to establish standards for cleanliness, usability and maintaining the placement of items in day to day business operations.
- Sustain (Shitsuke): The final step is to communicate and educate the employees about the changes made. Thus, developing a sense of self-control and discipline among them to maintain and follow the set standards.

Kaizen Costing Process

Now that we know about the kaizen costing, you must be wondering how is kaizen costing applied in real life?

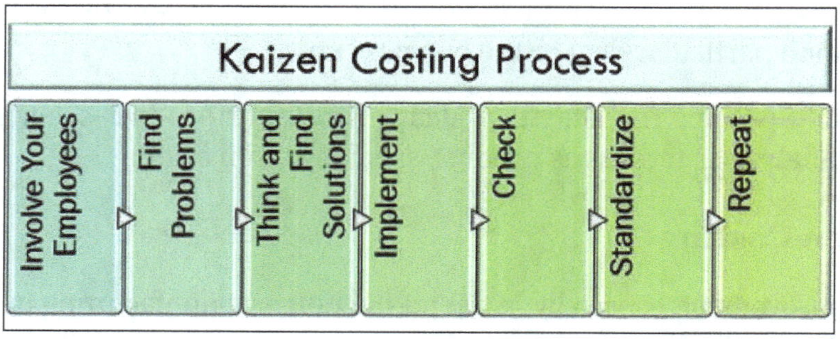

- Involve Your Employees: The involvement of employees plays a vital role in implementing any change. The participation of employees and their feedback helps in generating ideas and information. It also eliminates the resistance to change from their side.
- Find Problems: The organization together with its employees of all the departments (such as customer support, finance, human resource, production, design, etc.), needs to find out the various problems in the organization with the help of techniques like 360-degree feedback.
- Think and Find Solutions: The next step is solving the identified problems. This step needs a lot of brainstorming and tactical approach; therefore, managers form a team of ingenious employees to find out a practical solution to each question.
- Implement: Implementing any change involves cost and risk simultaneously. Therefore to be on a safer side, the new idea must be testified on a small part of the organization.
- Check: The managers need to look after the proper implementation of the kaizen costing. That is, a new idea should not just remain in words; instead, it should be practically applied to the business process.

- Standardize: After being satisfied with the results, the organization needs to set this change as a standard procedure for all the departments and across the whole organization.
- Repeat: A standardized procedure becomes the organizational culture when continuously practised over a period.

Advantages of Kaizen Costing

When we talk about the benefits of kaizen costing, the first thing that clicks in our mind is that it improves business efficiency by reducing the various types of cost involved in running an organization. The various advantages of kaizen costing are as follows:

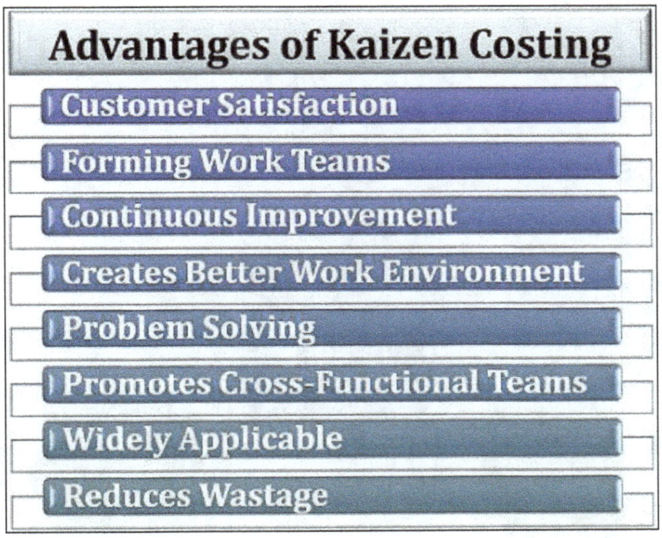

- Customer Satisfaction: The kaizen costing is a customer-oriented technique which focuses on providing better service to the consumers.
- Forming Work Teams: Every employee involved in the implementation of the kaizen practice needs to perform in a work team with a common aim of improvement.
- Continuous Improvement: Kaizen costing is a technique which emphasizes on improvement and betterment of the product, process, project and the organization.
- Creates Better Work Environment: It also promotes a positive work environment for the employees and the management. Like, sharing canteen and the dress code, is a part of work culture in many organizations.
- Problem Solving: One of the crucial functions of kaizen costing is to solve the identified problem to achieve perfection in business operations.
- Promotes Cross-Functional Teams: The teams so formed include employees

with different skills and knowledge; thus, this technique encourages the formation of a cross-functional team.

- Widely Applicable: Kaizen costing is universally applicable to all kinds of organizations, whether it is service industry or manufacturing industry.

- Reduces Wastage: Due to better time management and material management in kaizen costing technique, the wastage of time and resources can be avoided.

Drawbacks of Kaizen Costing

Kaizen costing is a positive change process though there are some severe disadvantages of it which makes it a risky affair. Following are some of these:

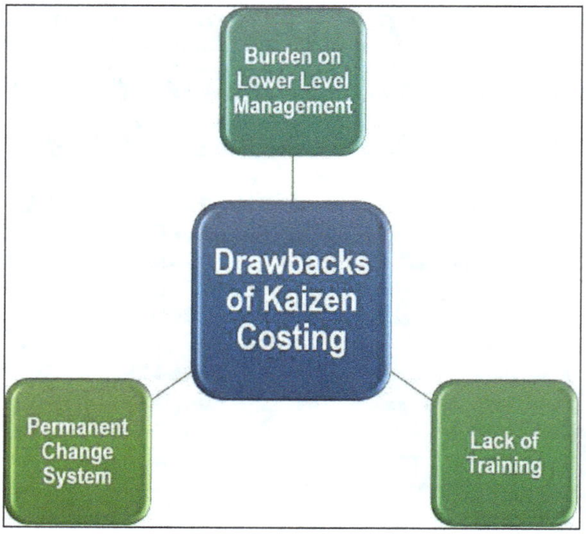

- The burden on Lower Level Management: It becomes confusing and tedious for the bottom level management to adopt the change in process or product so implemented through kaizen costing.

- Lack of Training: Kaizen costing requires a lot of expertise and training, and if not implemented strategically, it may even lead to adverse effects.

- Permanent Change System: The change so implemented through kaizen costing is irreversible, and it requires a lot of efforts and cost in withdrawing such decisions.

Example, Nestle is one of the most renowned Foods and Beverage Company producing a wide range of products including baby food, dairy products, medical food, tea and coffee, snacks, confectionery, ice-creams, mineral water and many more. The company used the kaizen costing technique for attaining lean production, and the approach was stated as Nestle Continuous Excellence (NCE). In this process, Nestle addressed its problem of wastage and time consumed in the production to improve the efficiency of the company. Less wastage means incurring a low cost, better profit margin, high output and proper utilization of resources. Nestle was able to reduce wastage in the production of FMCG and also successfully decreased the time consumed in the manufacturing of the products.

Life Cycle Costing

Life cycle costing is a system that tracks and accumulates the actual costs and revenues attributable to cost object from its invention to its abandonment. Life cycle costing involves tracing cost and revenues on a product by product base over several calendar periods. The Life Cycle Cost (LCC) of an asset is defined as: "The total cost throughout its life including planning, design, acquisition and support costs and any other costs directly attributable to owning or using the asset".

Life Cycle Cost (LCC) of an item represents the total cost of its ownership, and includes all the cots that will be incurred during the life of the item to acquire it, operate it, support it and finally dispose it. Life Cycle Costing adds all the costs over their life period and enables an evaluation on a common basis for the specified period (usually discounted costs are used). This enables decisions on acquisition, maintenance, refurbishment or disposal to be made in the light of full cost implications. In essence, Life Cycle Costing is a means of estimating all the costs involved in procuring, operating, maintaining and ultimately disposing a product throughout its life.

Life cycle costing is different from traditional cost accounting system which reports cost object profitability on a calendar basis (i.e. monthly, quarterly and annually) whereas life cycle costing involves tracing costs and revenues of a cost object (i.e. product, project etc.) over several calendar periods (i.e. projected life of the cost object). Thus, product life cycle costing is an approach used to provide a long-term picture of product line profitability, feedback on the effectiveness of the life cycle planning and cost data to clarify the economic impact on alternative chosen in the design, engineering phase etc. It is also considered as a way to enhance the control of manufacturing costs. It is important to track and measure costs during each stage of a product's life cycle.

Characteristics of Life Cycle Costing

- Product life cycle costing involves tracing of costs and revenues of a product over several calendar periods throughout its life cycle.
- Product life cycle costing traces research and design and development costs and total magnitude of these costs for each individual product and compared with product revenue.
- Each phase of the product life-cycle poses different threats and opportunities that may require different strategic actions.

- Product life cycle may be extended by finding new uses or users or by increasing the consumption of the present users.

Stages of Product Life Cycle Costing

Following are the main stages of Product Life Cycle:

- Market Research: It will establish what product the customer wants, how much he is prepared to pay for it and how much he will buy.
- Specification: It will give details such as required life, maximum permissible maintenance costs, manufacturing costs, required delivery date, expected performance of the product.
- Design: Proper drawings and process schedules are to be defined.
- Prototype Manufacture: From the drawings a small quantity of the product will be manufactured. These prototypes will be used to develop the product.
- Development: Testing and changing to meet requirements after the initial run. This period of testing and changing is development. When a product is made for the first time, it rarely meets the requirements of the specification and changes have to be made until it meets the requirements.
- Tooling: Tooling up for production can mean building a production line; building jigs, buying the necessary tools and equipment's requiring a very large initial investment.
- Manufacture: The manufacture of a product involves the purchase of raw materials and components, the use of labour and manufacturing expenses to make the product.
- Selling.
- Distribution.
- Product support.
- Decommissioning: When a manufacturing product comes to an end, the plant used to build the product must be sold or scrapped.

Benefits of Product Life Cycle Costing

Following are the main benefits of product life cycle costing:

- It results in earlier action to generate revenue or lower costs than otherwise might be considered. There are a number of factors that need to be managed in order to maximize return in a product.

- Better decision should follow from a more accurate and realistic assessment of revenues and costs within a particular life cycle stage.
- It can promote long term rewarding in contrast to short term rewarding.
- It provides an overall framework for considering total incremental costs over the entire span of a product.

Life Cycle Costing Process

Life cycle costing is a three-staged process. The first stage is life cost planning stage which includes planning LCC Analysis, Selecting and Developing LCC Model, applying LCC Model and finally recording and reviewing the LCC Results. The Second Stage is Life Cost Analysis Preparation Stage followed by third stage Implementation and Monitoring Life Cost Analysis. The three stages are:

Stage 1 : LCC Planning.
Stage 2 : Life Cost Analysis Preparation.
Stage 3 : Implementing and Monitoring Life Cost Analysis.

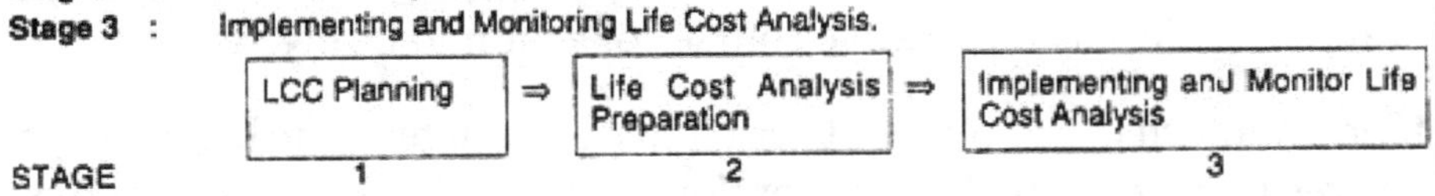

LCC Analysis is a multi-disciplinary activity. An analyst, involved in life cycle costing, should be fully familiar with unique cost elements involved in the life cycle of asset, sources of cost data to be collected and financial principles to be applied. He should also have clear understanding of methods of assessing the uncertainties associated with cost estimation. Number of iteration may be required to perform to finally achieve the result. All these iterations should be documented in detail to facilitate the interpretations of final result.

Stage 1: LCC Analysis Planning:

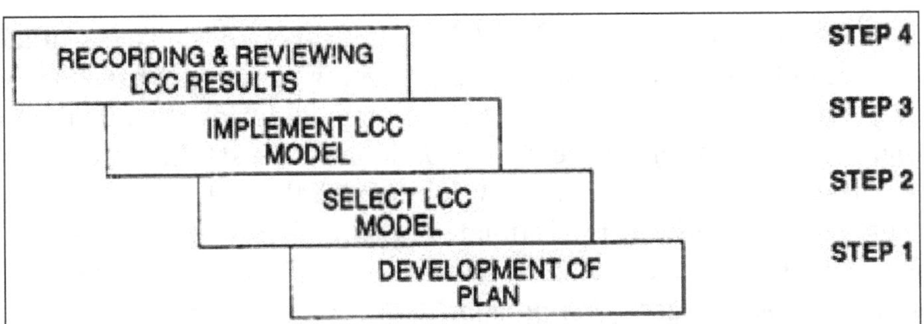

LCC Analysis Planning

The Life Cycle Costing process begins with development of a plan, which addresses the purpose, and scope of the analysis. The plan should:

- Define the analysis objectives in terms of outputs required to assist a management decision.

Typical objectives are:

- Determination of the LCC for an asset in order to assist planning, contracting, budgeting or similar needs.
- Evaluation of the impact of alternative courses of action on the LCC of an asset (such as design approaches, asset acquisition, support policies or alternative technologies).
- Identification of cost elements which act as cost drives for the LCC of an asset in order to focus design, development, acquisition or asset support efforts.

- Make the detailed schedule with regard to planning of time period for each phase, the operating, technical and maintenance support required for the asset.
- Identify any underlying conditions, assumptions, limitations and constraints (such as minimum asset performance, availability requirements or maximum capital cost limitations) that might restrict the range of acceptable options to be evaluated. Identify alternative courses of action to be evaluated.
- Identify alternative courses of action to be evaluated. The list of proposed alternatives may be refined as new options are identified or as existing options are found to violate the problem constraints.
- Provide an estimate of resources required and a reporting schedule for the analysis to ensure that the LCC results will be available to support the decision-making process for which they are required.

Next step in LCC Analysis planning is the selection or development of an LCC model that will satisfy the objectives of the analysis. LCC Model is basically an accounting structure which enables the estimation of an asset components cost.

Stage 2: Life Cost Analysis Preparation: The Life Cost Analysis is essentially a tool, which can be used to control and manage the ongoing costs of an asset or part thereof. It is based on the LCC Model developed and applied during the Life Cost Planning phase with one important difference: it uses data on real costs. The preparation of the Life Cost Analysis involves review and development of the LCC Model as a "real-time" or actual cost control mechanism. Estimates of capital costs will be replaced by the actual prices paid. Changes may also be required to the cost breakdown structure and cost elements to reflect the asset components to be monitored and the level of detail required. Targets are set for the operating costs and their frequency of occurrence based initially on the estimates used in the Life Cost Planning phase. However, these targets may change with time as more accurate data is obtained, from the actual asset operating costs or from the operating cost of similar other asset.

Stage 3: Implementing and Monitoring: Implementation of the Life Cost Analysis involves the continuous monitoring of the actual performance of an asset during its operation and maintenance to identify areas in which cost savings may be made and to provide feedback for future life cost planning activities. For example, it may be better to replace an expensive building component with a more efficient solution prior to the end of its useful life than to continue with a poor initial decision.

Reporting to Management

A Report is a document comprising information organized in a descriptive, graphic, or tabular form, prepared on ad hoc, periodic, regular, or as per the requirement. Reports may refer to specific periods, procedures, occurrences, or subjects, and may be communicated or obtainable in the oral or written form. Business managers often need to write reports to inform senior management and other departments about various business conditions. Business reports can include sales, financial, production, logistics and marketing research reports. The key to writing an actual business report is creating a logical flow to it. Business reports must also be written in layman's terms so less technical individuals can understand them. There are numerous key elements common to most business reports.

Elements of Business Report

- Objectives: Business report should include key objectives of the topic for which it is being written. For example, a marketing research report outlines key findings of a customer satisfaction study.
- Summary of Findings: Summary of findings may include quarterly financial results, charts and graphs in relation to the findings.
- Conclusion and Recommendations: The last two parts of the report should include a conclusion and recommendations section and these sections can also be merged conclusion can be written in paragraph form & Recommendations can be written in bullet points on the very last page of the report.
- Executive Summary: The executive summary section is given at the front of the report after the cover page. Executive summary must be a brief, one-page synopsis of all key results of the project or study.

To conclude, written reports are forms which extant focused outstanding content to a precise audience. Reports are used to display the end result of an experiment, or investigation. The audience may be public or private, an individual or the public in general. Reports are used in government, corporate, education, and other fields. Reports use structures such as graphics, images, voice, or specialized vocabulary in order to persuade that specific audience to undertake an action. One of the most communal set-ups for presenting reports is IMRAD: Introduction, Methods, Results and Discussion. Reporting is an important part of the aim to improved business intelligence and knowledge management. With the affected expansion of information technology, and the want for increased competitiveness in corporate world, there has been an increase in the use of calculating power to produce incorporated reports which join different opinions of the enterprise in one place. This reporting process contains enquiring data sources with different reasonable models to produce a human understandable report.

Cost Presentation and Management Information System

Cost Presentation

Cost accounting is a process of collecting, analyzing, summarizing and assessing various alternative courses of action. Its goal is to guide the management on the most proper course of action based on the cost efficiency and capability through carefully generated Reports. Cost accounting offers the comprehensive cost information that management needs to control present operations and plan for the future. Since managers make decisions only for their own organization, there is no need for the information to be comparable to similar information from other organizations. Instead, information must be relevant for a particular environment. Cost accounting facts and findings usually used in financial accounting information, but its main purpose is for use by managers to assist to make the Reports & based on such reports, making decisions.

The accounting systems help in the preparation of financial reports intermittently, the cost accounting systems and reports are not based on the rules and standards like the Generally Accepted Accounting Principles. Hence, there is wide variety in the cost accounting systems of the diverse companies and at times even in different parts of the same company. Costs are presented in a manner that the manager may deem fit or is the requirement of the hour. Advantages of Cost Presentation are:

- A good Cost presentation System helps in recognizes the unprofitable activities, losses or inefficiencies in any form.
- The application of cost reduction procedures, operations research procedures and value analysis procedure helps in attaining the objective of economy in concern's operations.
- Cost presentation is useful for identifying the exact causes for decrease or increase in the, profit/loss of the business.
- It also helps in recognizing the unsuccessful products or product lines so that these may be substitute measures may be taken.
- It provides information and data, in the form of Reports, to the management, to

serve as guides in making decisions involving financial considerations.

- It serves as a guide to test the adequacy of selling prices. The price determined may be useful for preparing estimates or filling tenders.
- The use of cost accounting technique viz., variance analysis, points out the deviations from the pre-determined level and thus demands suitable action to eliminate such deviations in future.
- Cost comparison helps in cost control. Such a comparison may be prepared from period to period by using the facts in respect of the same unit of firms or of several units in an industry by engaging the uniform costing and inter-firm comparison methods. Comparison may be complete in respect of costs of jobs, process or cost centers.
- The cost of idle capacity can be easily worked out, when a concern is not working to full capacity.
- The use of Marginal Costing technique may help the administrators in taking short term decisions.

Cost presentation is an absolute necessity for good cost control.

Management Information System (MIS)

The term Management Information System (MIS) information system, Enterprise Resource Planning (ERP), and information technology management are often used interchangeably. Information systems and MIS are broader categories that include ERP. Management information systems produce fixed, regularly scheduled reports based on data extracted and summarized, to middle and operational level managers to identify and inform structured and semi-structured decision problems. A management information system (MIS) provides information that organizations require to manage themselves efficiently and effectively. Management information systems are typical computer systems used for managing. These are distinct from other information systems because they are used to analyze and facilitate strategic and operational activities. An MIS provides three types of information to managers:

- Detailed information which confirms activities.
- Summary which puts information in an easy-to-read form.
- Exception, which deals with all information outside the normal scope of activities.

Modem businesses have been leveraging management information systems (MIS) to manage order, organize and manipulate the gigabytes and masses of information generated for various purposes MIS helps businesses optimize business process, address information needs of employees and various stakeholders and take informed strategic decisions. However, budget allocation and monitoring issues can affect the efficacy of MIS. It has its advantages and disadvantages depending on organizational deployment and usage.

Advantages of MIS

- Companies are able to highlight their strengths and weaknesses due to the existence of revenue reports, employees' enactment record etc.
- The identification of these aspects can help the company develop their business processes and procedures.
- MIS acts as a communication and planning tool.
- The availability of consumer data and feedback can provide the assistance the company to align their business processes according to the requirements of the customers.
- The effective management of consumer data can help the corporation to execute direct marketing and promotion undertakings.
- MISs can help a company gain a economical advantage.
- MIS have changed the dynamics of running businesses proficiently.
- Decentralization is one of the major advantages; it allows monitoring of operations at low levels and frees up resources for departmental managers to devote time to strategic activities.
- Coordination of specialized projects and undertakings is much improved and decision makers in the association are aware of issues and problems in all departments.
- Another advantage of MIS is that it reducing the information overload, which can be relatively common with conventional businesses in the modern era.
- It enables the management to achieve Better Planning and Control.
- MIS has to be designed and managed in such way that it aggregates information, monitors the company's activities and operations and enhances communication and cooperation among employees.
- MIS Aids better Decision Making. Top management and board members can take planned decisions, plan future development and business expansion activities based on the data and information generated by MIS.

Disadvantages of MIS

- Distribution of budgets for MIS upgrading, alterations and other revisions can be quite difficult at times.
- If budgets are not allocated uniformly or as per instant requirements, key functions might get affected and benefits of MIS might not be realized consistently.
- Integration issues can affect the quality of output and vital business intelligence reports.
- Since MIS is a critical component of an organization's risk management strategy and allied systems, constant monitoring is necessary to ensure its effectiveness.

Objectives of MIS

- The key objective of MIS is the efficient processing of company information.
- To produce meaningful reports to enable managers to make sound business decisions.
- To produce MIS reports in a format that makes corporate data meaningful for managers and provides a solid foundation on which they can base their routine operational and functional decisions.
- To gather, store and analyze corporate data.

Apart from Top Level Managers, Middle managers are the main users of MIS within an organization as they are the key decision-makers at an operational and functional level. Though lower level managers also generate MIS and also use MIS generated at other levels for making decisions at their level.

Principles of Reporting, Need and Significance of Reporting

Principles of Reporting

On one hand, a good Report is dependent on the validity and substance of cost data; on the other hand, it is equally important for the user of the MIS to have the wisdom to understand the report. A good level of understanding of report ensures competent decisions. Therefore it is very necessary for the person making an MIS to follow certain fundamental principles of presentation & preparation of cost information. Principles of sound reporting are:

- Principle as to form: Different forms of presentation must be designed for different items which are to be reported. A report must clearly state the title suggesting the subject matter for which it has been prepared and presented. The title must be kept brief and if need be, sub-titles should be used. If abbreviations are used, the same must be elaborated within the body of the report.

- Principle as to timing: It is based on the premise" delayed information is dead information". Since reports are used as a controlling device, they must be made available to those for whom they are meant, in time. A big time gap between the occurrence of an event and its reporting would definitely defeat the very purpose of a report. The time frame devised for MIS must be rigidly followed. For example, MIS is based on daily, weekly, fortnightly, monthly, quarterly, bi-annual and annual basis. It must be generated on these parameters regularly.

- Principle as to accuracy: Effort must be made to use and provide accurate information. The maker and user of MIS must keep in mind the fact that report depends on Data and an inaccurate data would lead to an unreliable Report. Report rests on the premise of "garbage in, garbage out policy". Therefore it is necessary to ensure use of accurate & correct data.

- Principle as to content: The content of the report must be concrete, yet simple and understandable to all. Use of technical jargons should be avoided so that a non-technical person may also be able to comprehend the contents of the Report. Where ever possible, the bulk data should be graphically represented because "what one thousand words cannot say, a figure can".

- Principle of comparative statements: It is desirable to make comparative statements using past data or targets to be achieved so that the spirit of the Report becomes clear.

- Principle as to cost-benefit: A cost-benefit analysis must be carried out with respect to expenditure relating to MIS and the benefits derived from the system as such.

- Principle as to Transparency: Full disclosure of the processes, procedures, and assumption in report preparation are essential to its credibility so that it becomes fully transparent.

- Principle as to Inclusiveness: The reporting organization should systematically engage all its stakeholders such as shareholders, creditors, bankers etc. to help focus and continually enhance the quality of its reports.

- Principle as to Audit ability: Reported data and facts should be recorded, compiled, analyzed and revealed in a way that would enable internal auditors or external assurance providers to attest to its reliability.

- Principle as to Completeness: All information that is material to users for assessing the reporting organization's economic, environmental and social performance should appear in the report in a manner consistent with the declared boundaries, scope and time period.

- Principle as to Relevance: Relevance is the degree of importance assigned to a particular aspect, indicator, or piece of information, and represents the threshold at which information becomes significant enough to be reported on.
- Principle of Neutrality: Reports should avoid bias in assortment and presentation of information and should endeavor to provide a balanced account of the reporting organization's performance Attempts are being made to present the information in a neutral fashion.
- Principle of Comparability: The reporting organization should maintain consistency in the boundary and scope of its reports, disclose any changes, and restate previously reported information for making logical comparisons.

Need for Reporting

- Reporting is needed because it influences behaviour of personnel and management & provides the framework within which more long-term decisions can be made, unlocking financial capital for investment as well as providing a more holistic picture of how value is created over time. In short, reporting contributes towards a more financially stable and sustainable corporate world.
- It promotes a more cohesive and efficient approach to corporate reporting and aims to improve the quality of information available to providers of financial capital to enable a more efficient and productive allocation of capital.
- Reporting is needed by everyone including business and investors. Businesses need a reporting environment that is conducive to understanding and articulating their strategy, which helps to drive performance internally and attract financial capital for investment. Investors need to understand how the strategy being pursued creates a value over time.
- Reporting makes the connections clearer between the organizations' strategy, governance, performance and prospects, therefore the investors are able to assess more effectively the combined impact of diverse factors.
- The disclosure of key risks and opportunities in report stated as management views enables investors to assess the short, medium and long term impact leading to better long-term investment returns.

Benefits of Reporting

Reporting can bring companies recognizable business benefits. Through communication on its most significant sustainability issues, a company's report becomes a dependable source of information for its investors. By evidently describing its major challenges, reporting reinforces investor's engagement and symbolizes the company's values in action.

- Reporting simplifies managerial decision making.
- It accelerates the response-to-audit requests.
- It results in enhanced business value because investor confidence grows in response to evidence that the company is managing important risks and positioning itself to take advantage of emerging opportunities.
- Good reporting results in better operations as employees develop a better understanding of a company's sustainability values, and production indicators provide understanding to support continuous improvement.
- Reporting enhances trust and credibility because customers, suppliers and the wider society understand the company's brand, operations and products through the company's various reports.
- Reporting gives consolidated, factual and an up-to-date information about a particular matter or subject.
- Information in the report is well organized and can be used for future forecasting and decision making.
- A reporting of facts acts as an effective means of communication within the organization. It provides feedback to employees. It is prepared for the information and guidance of others connected with the matter or problem.
- Reporting provide reliable data which can be used in the planning and decision making process. It acts as a treasure company of consistent information for long term planning and decision making.
- Reports offer information, which may not be recognized previously. New business opportunities are visible through unknown information available in the reports.
- Reports are available to managers and departments for internal use. They are broadly used by the divisions for guidance. Report offer a feedback to employees and are beneficial for their self-improvement.
- Certain reporting involve to employees is useful while organizing personnel policies such as advancement policy, training policy and welfare services to employees.
- Approximately company reports are prepared every year for the assistance of shareholders. Annual report such as, it is prepared and sent to all

shareholders before the AGM. It gives information about the progress of the company.

- Annual report and annual accounts are sent to the Registrar every year for information. Such reports enable the government to keep supervision on the companies.
- Reporting is useful to managers while dealing with current problems faced by the company. They provide guidance while dealing with complicated problems.
- Company reports relate to internal working of the company and are extremely useful to directors in decision making and policy framing. Reports give reliable, updated and useful information in a compact form.

Types of Reports and Modes of Reporting

Levels of Reporting depend upon the various levels of Management. The term "Levels of Management' refers to the various layers of managerial positions in an organization. The number of levels in management would increase when the size of the business and work force increases and vice versa. Reporting is done by all the three levels of management. The level of management determines a chain of command, the amount of authority & status enjoyed by any managerial position. The levels of management can be divided in 3 major categories:

- Top level/Administrative level.
- Middle level/executing level.
- Lower level/Supervisory/Operative/First-line managers.

Managers at all these levels perform various distinct functions. For example, the Top Level of Management, Which comprises of board of directors, chief executive or managing director, is the ultimate & final source of authority and it manages objectives, goals and policies for an organization. It dedicates its time on decision-making, planning and coordinating functions. The role of the top management can be compiled as:

- Top management frames the goals, objectives and broad policies of the organization.
- It gives directions, instructions for preparation of department budgets, procedures, policies, schedules etc.
- Top level management makes strategic plans & policies for the enterprise.

- It is responsible for appointing executives for middle level, such as departmental managers.
- This level of management controls & coordinates the activities of all the departments.
- It is also responsible for maintaining a contact with the outside world.
- It acts as a guide and furnishes direction to the whole organization.
- The top management is accountable to the shareholders for the performance of the enterprise.

The Middle Level of Management is made up of, the branch managers and departmental managers. Such managers are responsible to the top management for the effective functioning of their department. They are more concerned with the organizational and directional functions. Its role can be identified & summarized as:

- It executes the plans of the organization in accordance with the policies, programmes and directions of the top level management.
- It crafts plan for the sub-units of the organization.
- It participates in employment & training of lower level management.
- It interprets and explains policies of top level management & transmits the same to lower level.
- Middle level is also responsible for coordinating the activities amongst the division or departments.
- It also sends significant reports and other relevant data to higher levels of management.
- This level evaluates performance of the employees working at lower levels.
- It is also holds responsibility for inspiring & motivating lower level managers towards better performance.

Lower Level of Management

Lower level management is also known as supervisory or operative level of management. It consists of supervisors, foreman, section officers, superintendent etc. "Supervisory management refers to those executives whose work has to be largely with personal oversight and direction of operative employees". The main activities include:

- Job assignment and allocation of tasks to various workers.

- The middle level guides and instructs workers for performing day to day activities.
- It is accountable for both qualitative as well as quantitative aspect of production.
- This level is also entrusted with the responsibility of maintaining good relation & congenial working environment in the organization.
- It communicates problems of workers, suggestions, and recommendatory, appeals etc. to the top level executives and convey the plans and strategies of the higher level to the workers.
- It helps to redress the grievances of the workers. It supervises & guides the subordinates.
- This level is responsible for providing training to the workers.
- It arranges necessary materials, machines, tools etc. for getting the things done & completing tasks.
- It prepares periodical reports about the performance of the workers.
- It ensures discipline in the enterprise.
- It motivates workers.
- This level is the image builder of the enterprise because it is in direct contact with the workers.

Reporting Role

Reporting roles refer to those roles in which a manager obtains and transmits information. These roles have changed dramatically over a period of time, as technology has immensely improved. The manager evaluates the performance of others and takes corrective measures and steps to improve that performance. He also watches for changes in the environment and changes that take place within the company which may affect the performance of individuals, groups and organizations. Monitoring is a phenomenon that occurs at all levels of management. Although managers working at higher levels of the organization mostly, diagnose external opportunities or threats as compared to the other people working at lower levels. The role of disseminator requires that managers inform employees of changes that affect them and the organization. They also communicate the company's mission, vision and purpose. Managers at each level, disseminates information to those who are working below them, and information of this nature travels from the top level down to the middle and lower level in the form of a report.

Types of Reporting

Reporting is done by all the three levels of management. As per requirement, they generate different types of reports. Different types of reports used in business are:

- Informational reports: These reports focus on presenting facts about certain given activity in detail without any note or suggestions. Whatever is gathered is reported without giving any personal views or adding bias & suggestions. Examples of some of these reports that can be cited are: Report on sales & production Report on selling & advertising efficiency Plant utilization report Project evaluation report Inventory report.

- Analytical reports: These reports contain facts along with analytical explanations given by the person making the report. Such reports engulfs the incorporation of facts, data collected, relevant information, classified and tabulated data and also explanatory note followed by the conclusions arrived at or interpretations followed by recommendations & suggestions. To provide an example, we can consider a Labor turnover report on actual and budgeted profit Production & productivity report.

- Research reports: These reports are based on some research work conducted by either an individual or a group of individuals on a given problem. Research division submits the report; completely detailing its findings and offering suggestions, engulfing the conclusions arrived at. For example, Price variance report.

- Statutory reports: These reports are to be presented according to the requirements of a particular law or in compliance of the statutory requirement. Prescribed format needs to be followed while preparing these reports. For example Director's report Auditor's report.

- Non statutory reports: These reports are not in the nature of legal requirements. These reports are required to be prepared and submitted:

    - For the administrative and other conveniences.

    - For taking decision in a matter.

    - For policy formulations.

    - For making projections etc.

- Routine reports: As the name suggest these reports are prepared and submitted periodically i.e. at the fixed interval of time, engulfing matters required by the organization so as to help the management of the organization to take decisions in the matters relating to day to day affairs. The chief objectives of these reports are to furnish the management with the details of what is happening in the organization. Routine reports are generally brief. They only give the facts. These reports do not engulf comments or explanations. Generally guidance and forms are prescribed for preparation and submission of such reports.

- Special report: Such reports are required to be prepared and submitted on matters which are of special nature.
- Detail report: The reason for the preparation of such report might be a grave concern thereby requiring detailed explanation such an incident might be an accident a death of the foreman occurred in a factory. The factory manager may ask for a detail report from the head foreman. These reports contain not only facts and details but they may also contain suggestions, comments and explanations as well.

Report Presentation

Modes of Presentation of Report

Reporting is a very significant aspect of communication within the organization. Different type of reports are generated & presented every day. There are basically three modes of presentation of a report:

- Narrative/written report: Formal & statutory reports are always in a written form. These reports have a format and time frame within which it is required to be submitted. As these reports are long due to facts/figures/data etc.it takes time to review the report and arrive at a decision.
- PPT or graphic mode consisting of charts, diagrams, pictures etc. power point presentations are very popular, as they make an impact with facts & figures presented in condensed form. These are simple to comprehend & they make decision making easy.
- Oral communication of reports: This is usually done by way of a presentation during a meeting or in a group of members. Organizations, today, prefer, this mode of report presentation.

Format of a Good Report

- Cover Letter: Generally, cover letter is the first component of a formal report. Similarly to a semi-formal report, this transmittal letter "transmits" the report to the intended reader. The letter contains the summary or the main aspects of the report, as well as any other detail about completing and sending the report that is relevant to the receiver. This letter is generally attached to the report with a paper clip. The need to attach this letter is to let the receiver know:
    - As to why the report was written.
    - Who commissioned the report.

- When it was demanded.
- Also how much time was allotted for completion of the report?

The formal report usually has a cover. The quality of the cover letter can have a significant impact on the receiver. Many report writers, therefore, follow the AIDA technique of writing. This technique involves, A- Attract attention, I- Kindle interest, D- Create desire, A- Urge action.

- Title Page: The title page generally has four main pieces of information:
    - The title of the report.
    - The name of the person or organization who would receive the report.
    - The person(s) or organization that authored the report.
    - The date on which the report was submitted.
- Table of Contents: The Table of Contents is an accurate and comprehensive table of the information located in the report with a corresponding page reference so as to easily locate each section. The contents are generally arranged to the left of the page, with subsections indented and identified by section numbers. Each item in the contents should have a corresponding page number that indicates where the section begins only.
- Executive Summary: The Summary or Executive Summary is separated from the main body of the report and placed as far forward in the report as possible. Generally it is located after the Table of Contents, but it could appear beforehand in some reports. It provides the main elements of the report, in a nut shell. This enables the reader to know about the basic contents of the report, at a glance.
- Body of the report.
- Introduction: Introduction is written in simple language which can be easily understood. Care should be taken to make the purpose of the report evident in this section. The introduction demonstrates the very spirit of the report.
- Conclusions: It is actually the most important component of the report as it contains the outcomes of the findings after the data has been put to various statistical tests. The conclusions should be in simple language and must be corroborated by facts.
- Recommendations: Based on the conclusions, the presenter of the report must state recommendations or suggestions to the receiver of the report. These must also be written in simple English & should not contain any ambiguity.

- Appendices: This section of the report contains all attachments which have been referred to, while arriving at conclusions. For example, balance sheets, profit & loss account, questionnaire etc.

References

- Foundations-of-Management-Accounting: microbuspub.com, Retrieved 29, June 2020
- Responsibility-accounting: wallstreetmojo.com, Retrieved 02, April 2020

Permissions

All chapters in this book are published with permission under the Creative Commons Attribution Share Alike License or equivalent. Every chapter published in this book has been scrutinized by our experts. Their significance has been extensively debated. The topics covered herein carry significant information for a comprehensive understanding. They may even be implemented as practical applications or may be referred to as a beginning point for further studies.

We would like to thank the editorial team for lending their expertise to make the book truly unique. They have played a crucial role in the development of this book. Without their invaluable contributions this book wouldn't have been possible. They have made vital efforts to compile up to date information on the varied aspects of this subject to make this book a valuable addition to the collection of many professionals and students.

This book was conceptualized with the vision of imparting up-to-date and integrated information in this field. To ensure the same, a matchless editorial board was set up. Every individual on the board went through rigorous rounds of assessment to prove their worth. After which they invested a large part of their time researching and compiling the most relevant data for our readers.

The editorial board has been involved in producing this book since its inception. They have spent rigorous hours researching and exploring the diverse topics which have resulted in the successful publishing of this book. They have passed on their knowledge of decades through this book. To expedite this challenging task, the publisher supported the team at every step. A small team of assistant editors was also appointed to further simplify the editing procedure and attain best results for the readers.

Apart from the editorial board, the designing team has also invested a significant amount of their time in understanding the subject and creating the most relevant covers. They scrutinized every image to scout for the most suitable representation of the subject and create an appropriate cover for the book.

The publishing team has been an ardent support to the editorial, designing and production team. Their endless efforts to recruit the best for this project, has resulted in the accomplishment of this book. They are a veteran in the field of academics and their pool of knowledge is as vast as their experience in printing. Their expertise and guidance has proved useful at every step. Their uncompromising quality standards have made this book an exceptional effort. Their encouragement from time to time has been an inspiration for everyone.

The publisher and the editorial board hope that this book will prove to be a valuable piece of knowledge for students, practitioners and scholars across the globe.

Index

www.ingramcontent.com/pod-product-compliance
Lightning Source LLC
LaVergne TN
LVHW080620210926
848485LV00003B/190